RIVERS OF LONDON

ACTION AT A DISTANCE

TITAN®
COMICS

RIVERS OF LONDON: ACTION AT A DISTANCE
ISBN: 9781785865466

TITAN COMICS

EDITOR KIRSTEN MURRAY

Managing Editor Martin Eden
Production Assistant Rhiannon Roy
Production Controller Peter James
Senior Production Controller Jackie Flook
Art Director Oz Browne
Sales & Circulation Manager Steve Tothill
Commercial Manager Michelle Fairlamb
Head of Rights Jenny Boyce
Publishing Director Darryl Tothill
Operations Director Leigh Baulch
Executive Director Vivian Cheung
Publisher Nick Landau

Published by Titan Comics
A division of Titan Publishing Group, Ltd.
144 Southwark St.
London
SE1 0UP

Rivers of London logo designed by Patrick Knowles
Front cover illustration by Alex Ronald
Back cover illustration by Anna Dittmann

A CIP catalogue record for this title is available from the British Library.

First edition: November 2019
10 9 8 7 6 5 4 3 2 1

Printed in China.
Titan Comics.

For rights information contact jenny.boyce@titanemail.com

WWW.TITAN-COMICS.COM

Become a fan on Facebook.com/comicstitan

Follow us on Twitter @ComicsTitan

RIVERS OF LONDON

ACTION AT A DISTANCE

CREATED BY
BEN AARONOVITCH

WRITTEN BY
ANDREW CARTMEL

ART BY
BRIAN WILLIAMSON

COLORS BY
STEFANI RENNE

LETTERING BY
ROB STEEN

Titan® COMICS

THE STORY SO FAR...

When PC Peter Grant began working for London's Metropolitan Police Force, he was worried boredom would be his biggest concern and paperwork his greatest enemy. But following an interview with a witness to a crime – who just so happened to be a ghost – Peter quickly finds himself being pulled into London's weird, supernatural underbelly.

Based in the middle of an inconspicuous row of Georgian terraced houses in Russell Square is the Met's Special Assessment Unit, known as the Folly, headed up by Detective Chief Inspector Thomas Nightingale. The last officially registered wizard in England, Nightingale takes Peter under his wing.

Trainee wizard and full-time cop, Peter finds himself becoming deeply entangled in the magical world, known as the demi-monde. He works on rather unusual crimes, finding himself coming face to face with the gods and goddesses of London's rivers, possessed cars, fiendish fae, and devious magic-wielding villains.

Despite their close master and apprentice relationship, Nightingale has always been very guarded about his past. One of the most powerful magicians in Europe, Peter has remained curious to find out more. Diving into the Folly's library, chock-full of filing cabinets packed with casefiles documenting the magical division's history, Peter is about to uncover some of his mentor's elusive past...

RIVERS OF LONDON

READER'S GUIDE

The *Rivers of London* comics and graphic novels are an essential part of the saga. Though they each stand alone, together they add a fascinating depth to the wider world of Peter Grant and the Folly!

BEN AARONOVITCH
CARTMEL • WILLIAMSON • RENNE
RIVERS OF LONDON
ACTION AT A DISTANCE

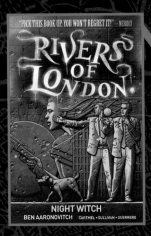

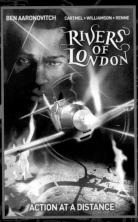

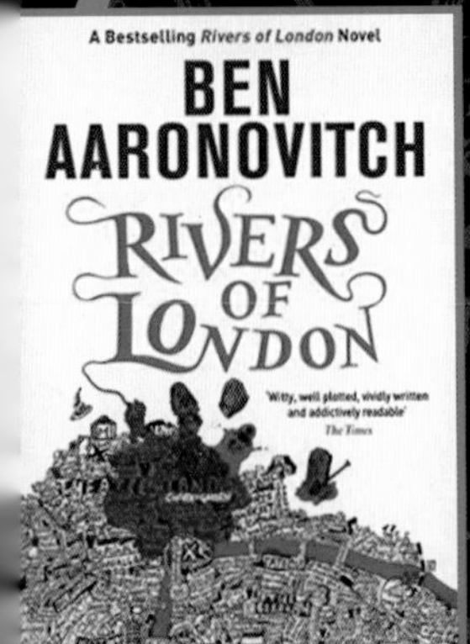

ACTION AT A DISTANCE
Graphic Novel 7

BEN AARONOVITCH
The *Sunday Times* bestselling series
WHISPERS UNDER GROUND
If you've been on the Underground you know what horrors await . . .

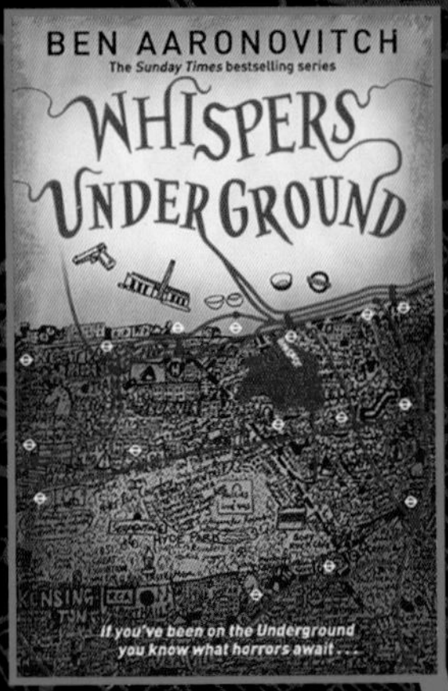

WHISPERS UNDER GROUND
Novel 3

"PICK THIS BOOK UP, YOU WON'T REGRET IT!" – NERDLY
RIVERS OF LONDON
NIGHT WITCH
BEN AARONOVITCH
CARTMEL • SULLIVAN • GUERRERO

NIGHT WITCH
Graphic Novel 2

A Bestselling *Rivers of London* Novel
BEN AARONOVITCH
RIVERS OF LONDON
'Witty, well plotted, vividly written and addictively readable'
The Times

RIVERS OF LONDON
Novel 1

BEN AARONOVITCH
MOON OVER SOHO
'What would happen if Harry Potter grew up and joined the Fuzz' Diana Gabaldon, Sunday Times Number One bestselling author

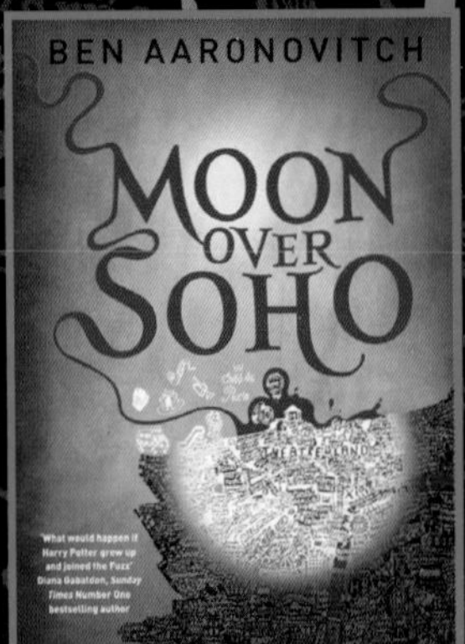

MOON OVER SOHO
Novel 2

BEN AARONOVITCH
The *Sunday Times* Bestselling Peter Grant series
BROKEN HOMES
Stuff gets serious South of the River . . .

BROKEN HOMES
Novel 4

"A PERFECT BLEND OF *CSI* AND *HARRY POTTER*." – io9
RIVERS OF LONDON
BODY WORK
BEN AARONOVITCH • CARTMEL • SULLIVAN • GUERRERO

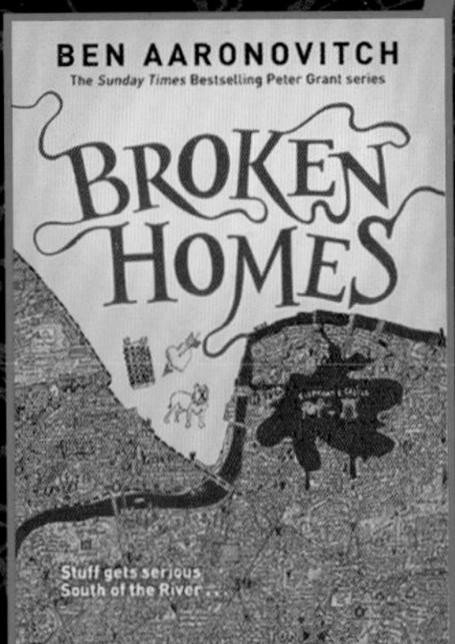

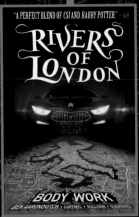

BODY WORK
Graphic Novel 1

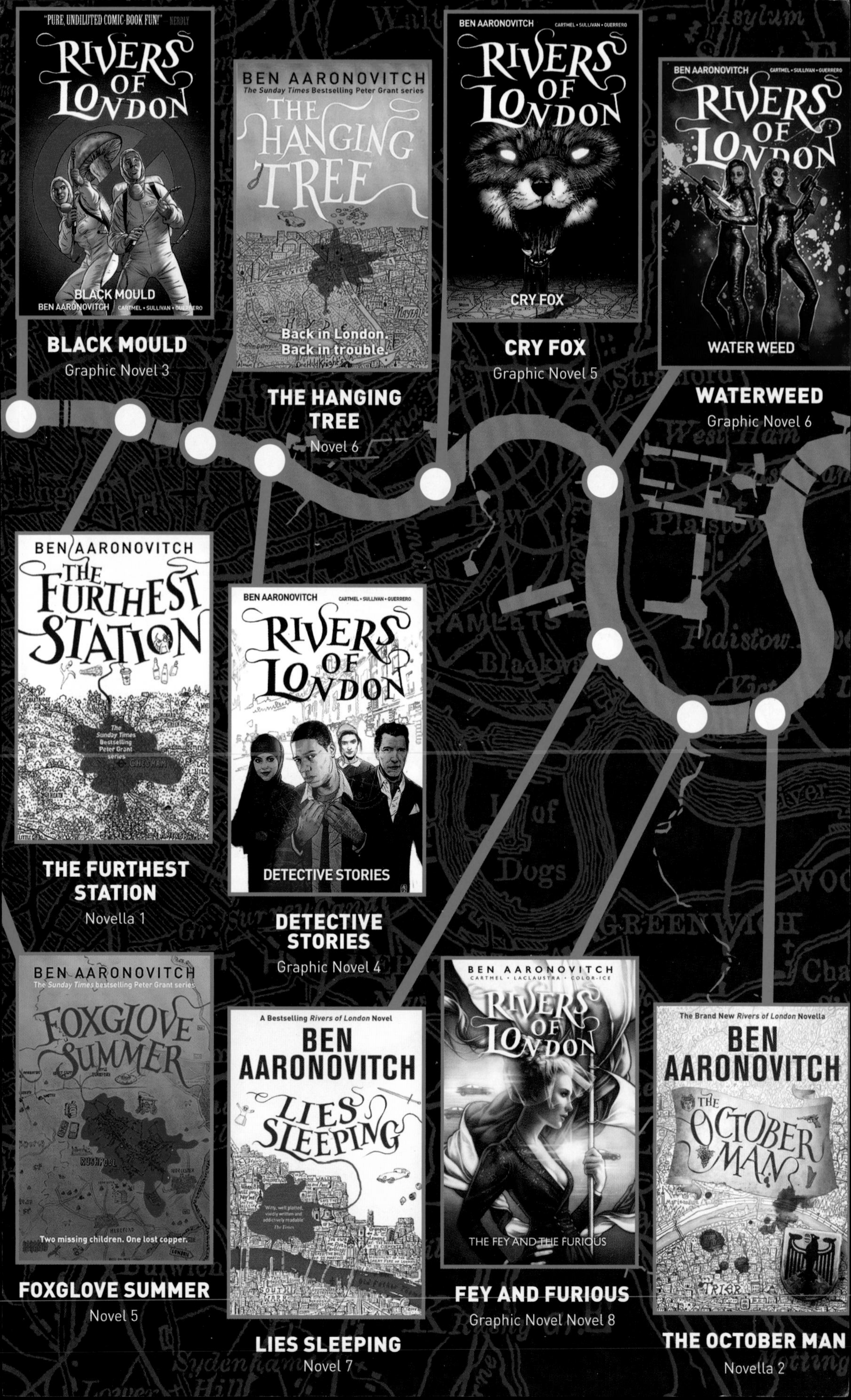
"PURE, UNDILUTED COMIC-BOOK FUN!" —NERDLY
RIVERS OF LONDON
BLACK MOULD
BEN AARONOVITCH CARTMEL • SULLIVAN • GUERRERO
BLACK MOULD
Graphic Novel 3
BEN AARONOVITCH
The Sunday Times Bestselling Peter Grant series
THE HANGING TREE
Back in London. Back in trouble.
THE HANGING TREE
Novel 6
BEN AARONOVITCH CARTMEL • SULLIVAN • GUERRERO
RIVERS OF LONDON
CRY FOX
CRY FOX
Graphic Novel 5
BEN AARONOVITCH CARTMEL • SULLIVAN • GUERRERO
RIVERS OF LONDON
WATER WEED
WATERWEED
Graphic Novel 6
BEN AARONOVITCH
THE FURTHEST STATION
The Sunday Times Bestselling Peter Grant series
THE FURTHEST STATION
Novella 1
BEN AARONOVITCH CARTMEL • SULLIVAN • GUERRERO
RIVERS OF LONDON
DETECTIVE STORIES
DETECTIVE STORIES
Graphic Novel 4
BEN AARONOVITCH
The Sunday Times bestselling Peter Grant series
FOXGLOVE SUMMER
Two missing children. One lost copper.
FOXGLOVE SUMMER
Novel 5
A Bestselling Rivers of London Novel
BEN AARONOVITCH
LIES SLEEPING
'Witty, well plotted, vividly written and addictively readable' The Times
LIES SLEEPING
Novel 7
BEN AARONOVITCH
CARTMEL • LACLAUSTRA • COLOR-ICE
RIVERS OF LONDON
THE FEY AND THE FURIOUS
FEY AND FURIOUS
Graphic Novel Novel 8
The Brand New Rivers of London Novella
BEN AARONOVITCH
THE OCTOBER MAN
THE OCTOBER MAN
Novella 2

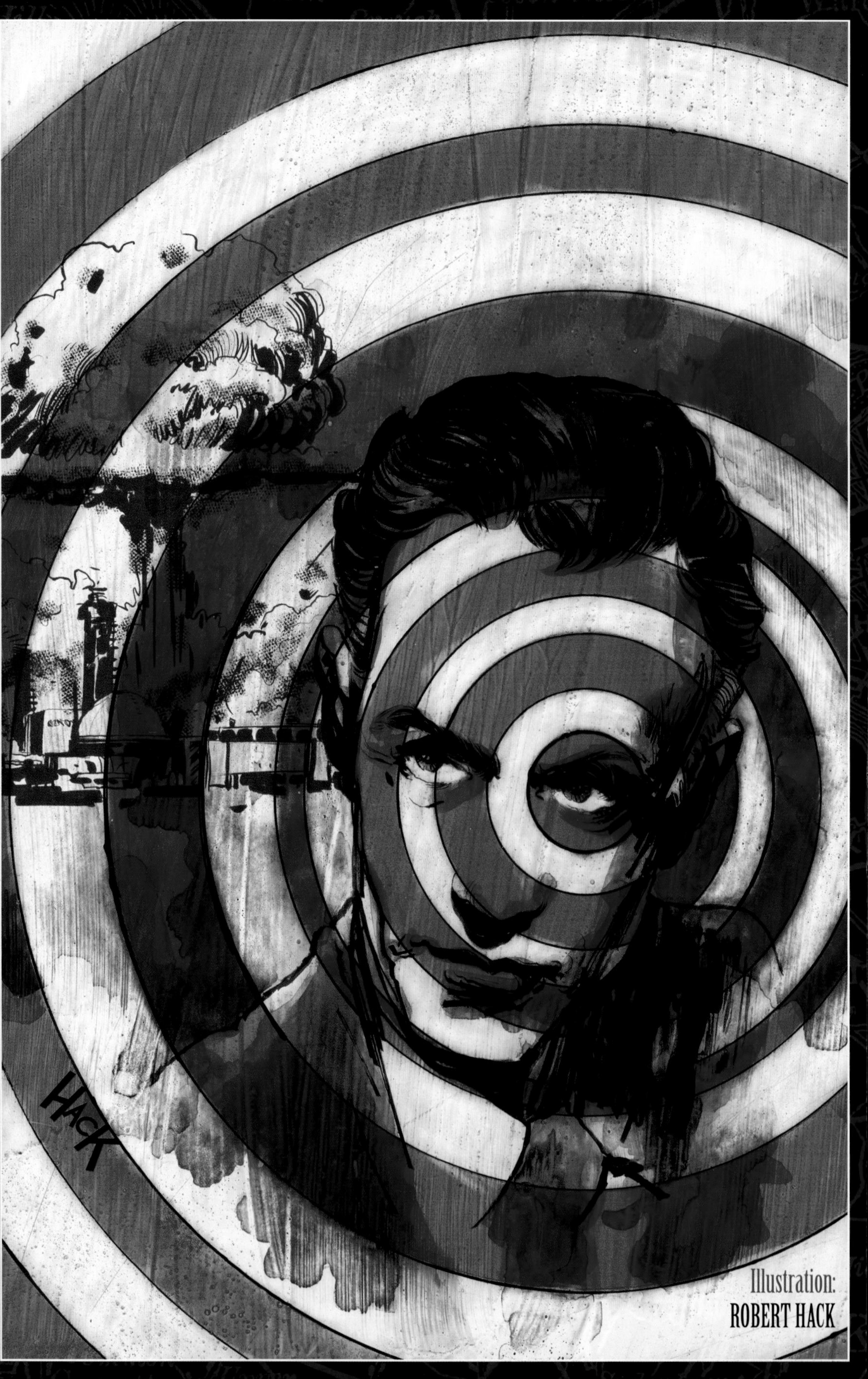
HACK

Illustration:
ROBERT HACK

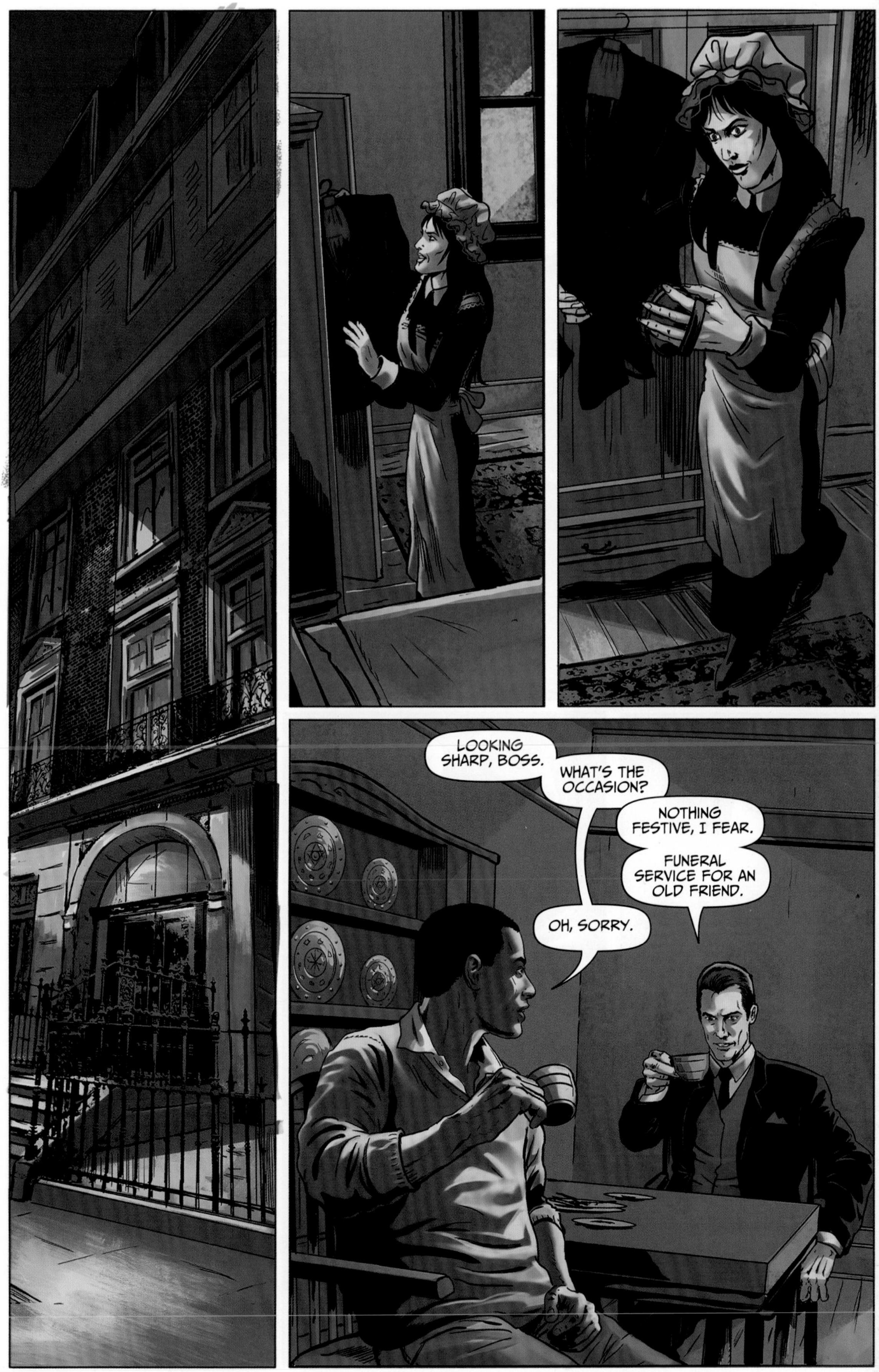
LOOKING SHARP, BOSS.
WHAT'S THE OCCASION?
NOTHING FESTIVE, I FEAR.
FUNERAL SERVICE FOR AN OLD FRIEND.
OH, SORRY.

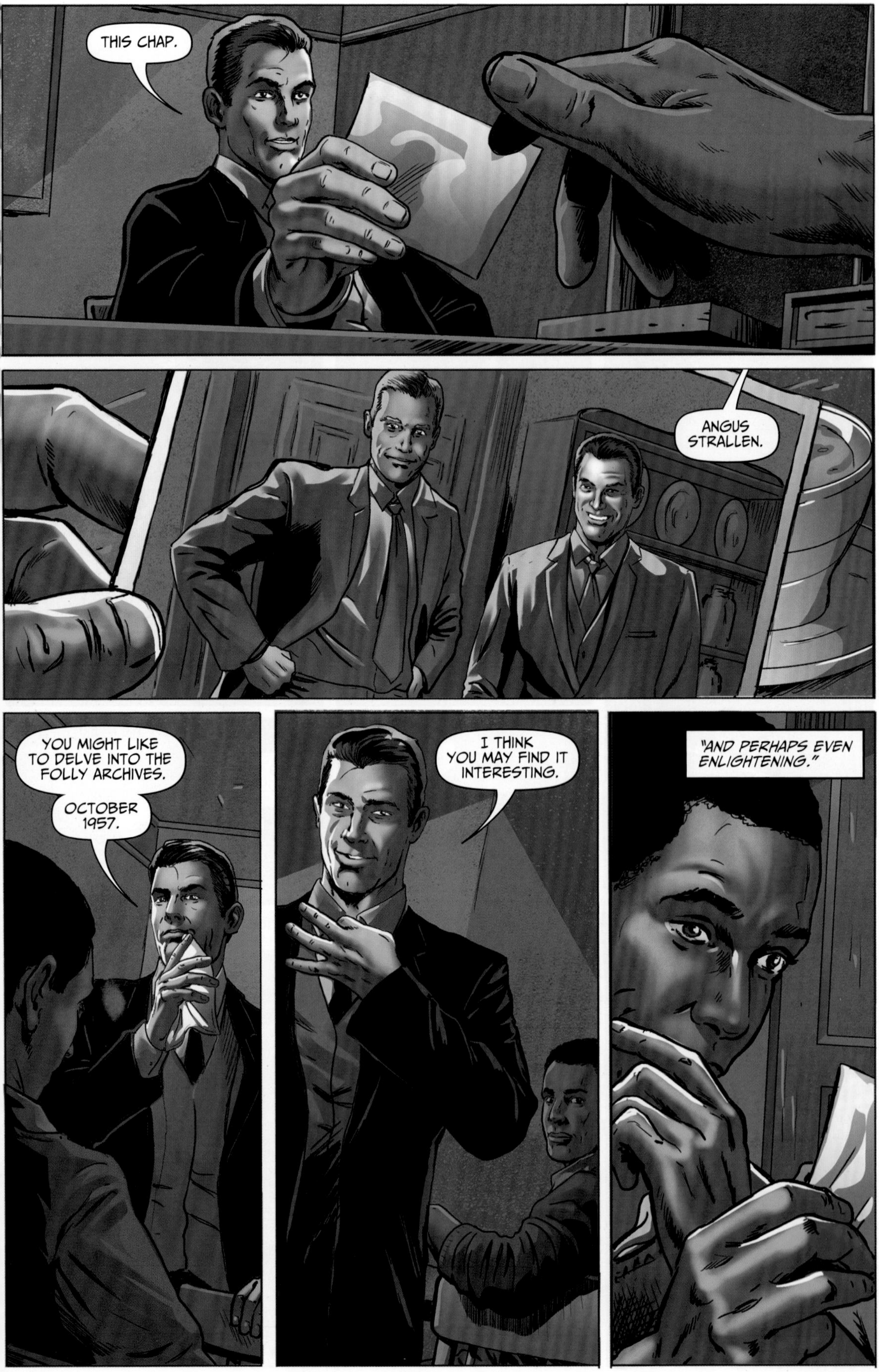

THIS CHAP.
ANGUS STRALLEN.
YOU MIGHT LIKE TO DELVE INTO THE FOLLY ARCHIVES.
OCTOBER 1957.
I THINK YOU MAY FIND IT INTERESTING.
"AND PERHAPS EVEN ENLIGHTENING."

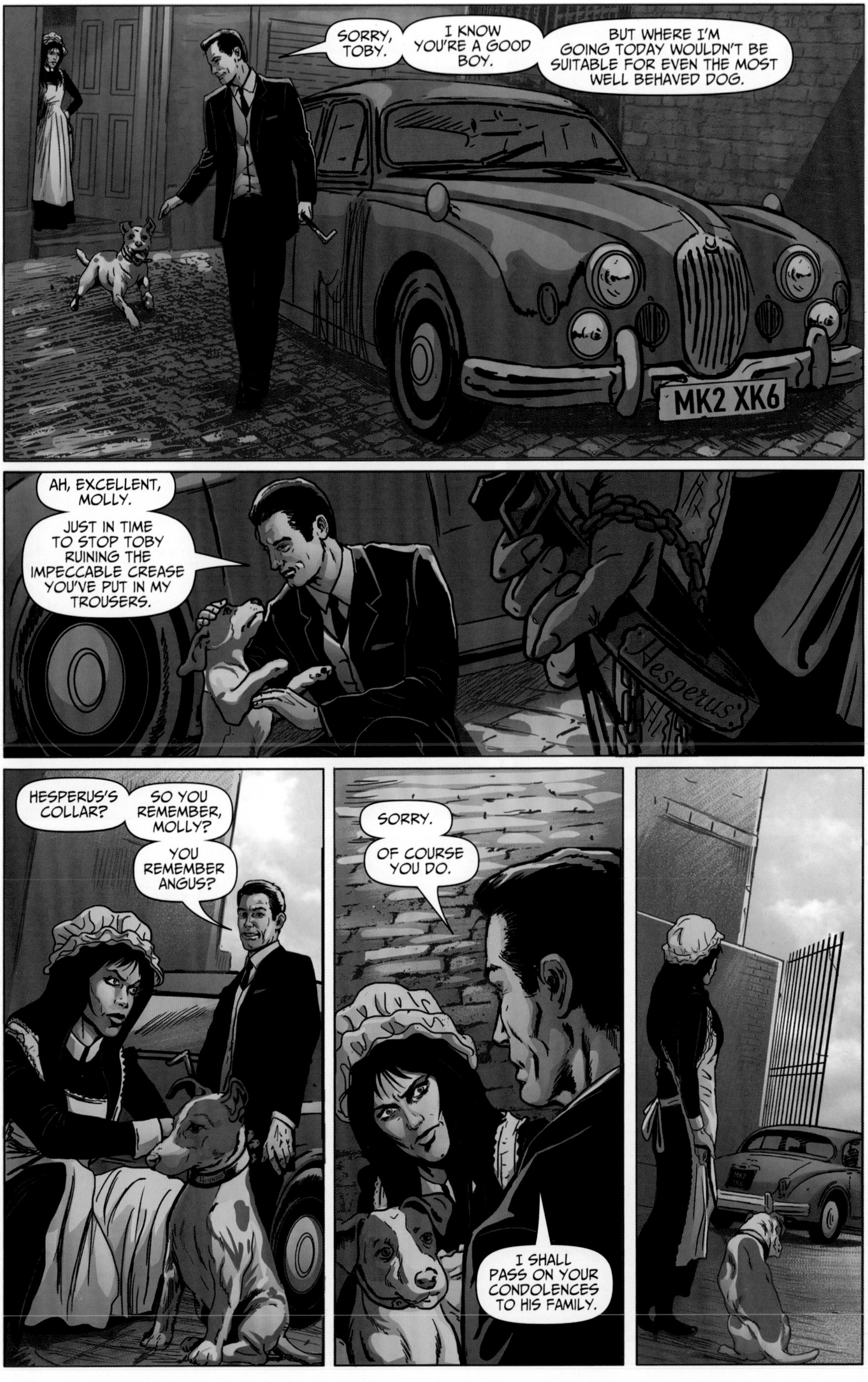
SORRY, TOBY.
I KNOW YOU'RE A GOOD BOY.
BUT WHERE I'M GOING TODAY WOULDN'T BE SUITABLE FOR EVEN THE MOST WELL BEHAVED DOG.
MK2 XK6
AH, EXCELLENT, MOLLY.
JUST IN TIME TO STOP TOBY RUINING THE IMPECCABLE CREASE YOU'VE PUT IN MY TROUSERS.
Hesperus
HESPERUS'S COLLAR?
SO YOU REMEMBER, MOLLY?
YOU REMEMBER ANGUS?
SORRY.
OF COURSE YOU DO.
I SHALL PASS ON YOUR CONDOLENCES TO HIS FAMILY.

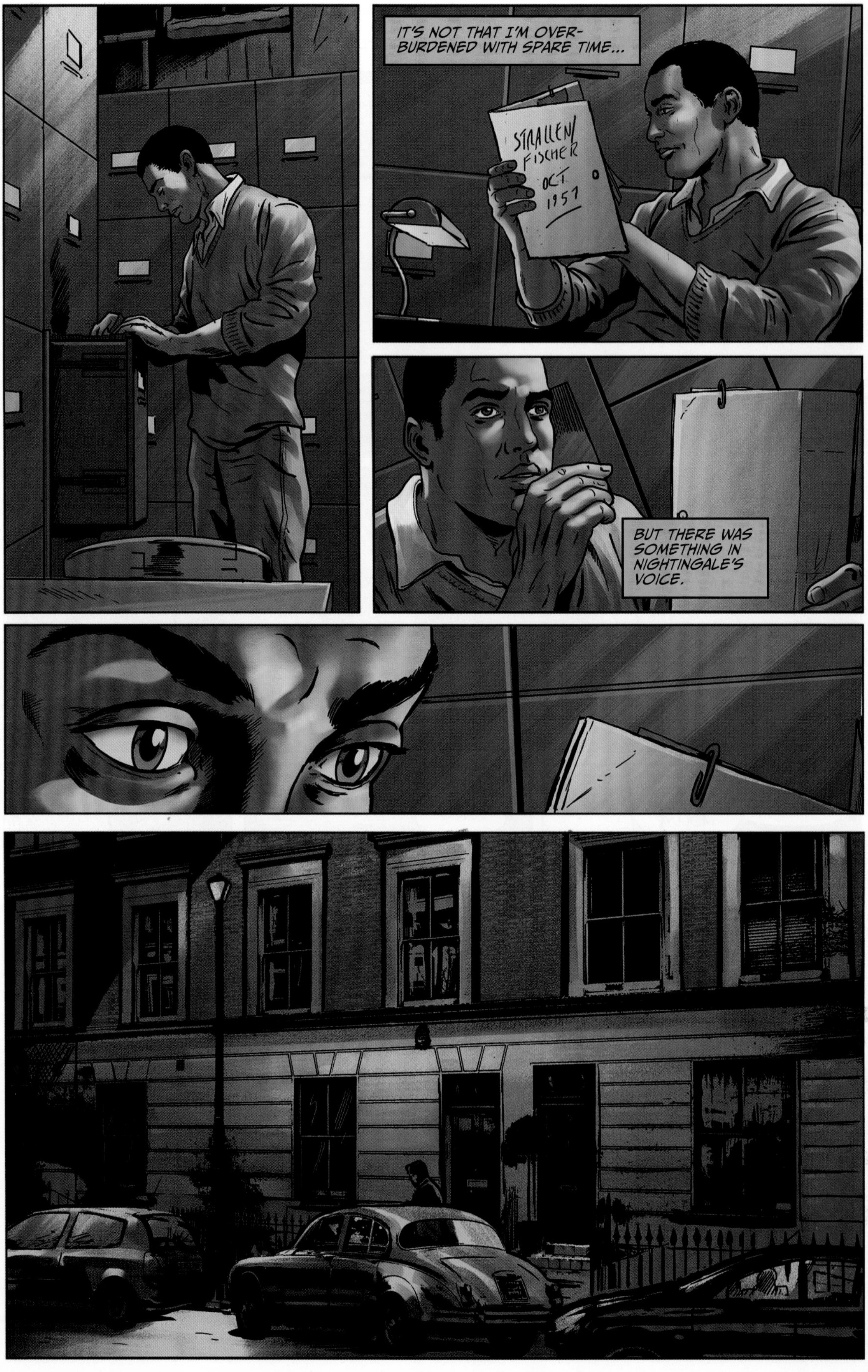
IT'S NOT THAT I'M OVER-BURDENED WITH SPARE TIME...
STRALLEN/ FISCHER OCT. 1957
BUT THERE WAS SOMETHING IN NIGHTINGALE'S VOICE.

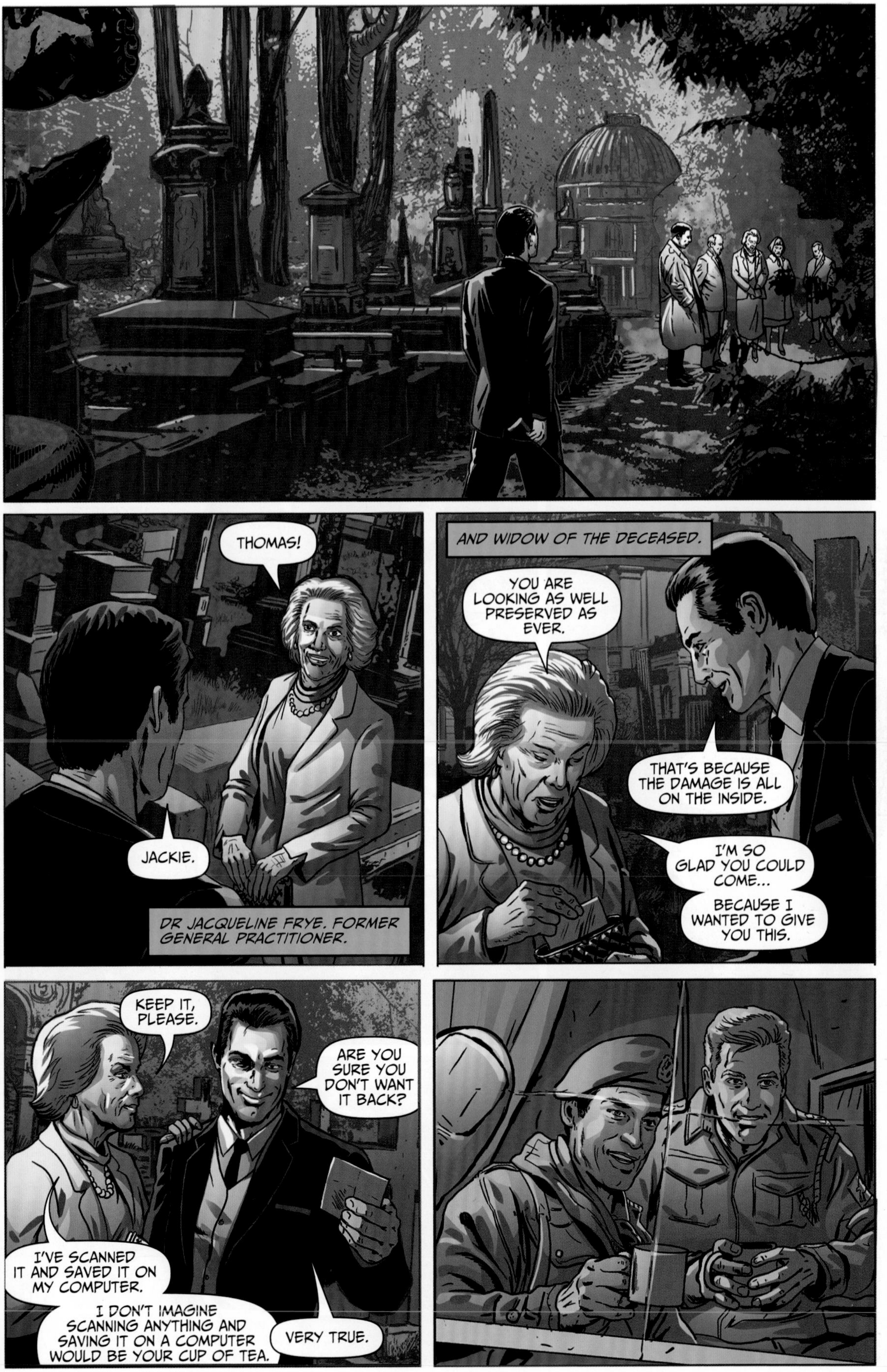
THOMAS!
JACKIE.
DR JACQUELINE FRYE. FORMER GENERAL PRACTITIONER.
AND WIDOW OF THE DECEASED.
YOU ARE LOOKING AS WELL PRESERVED AS EVER.
THAT'S BECAUSE THE DAMAGE IS ALL ON THE INSIDE.
I'M SO GLAD YOU COULD COME...
BECAUSE I WANTED TO GIVE YOU THIS.
KEEP IT, PLEASE.
ARE YOU SURE YOU DON'T WANT IT BACK?
I'VE SCANNED IT AND SAVED IT ON MY COMPUTER.
I DON'T IMAGINE SCANNING ANYTHING AND SAVING IT ON A COMPUTER WOULD BE YOUR CUP OF TEA.
VERY TRUE.

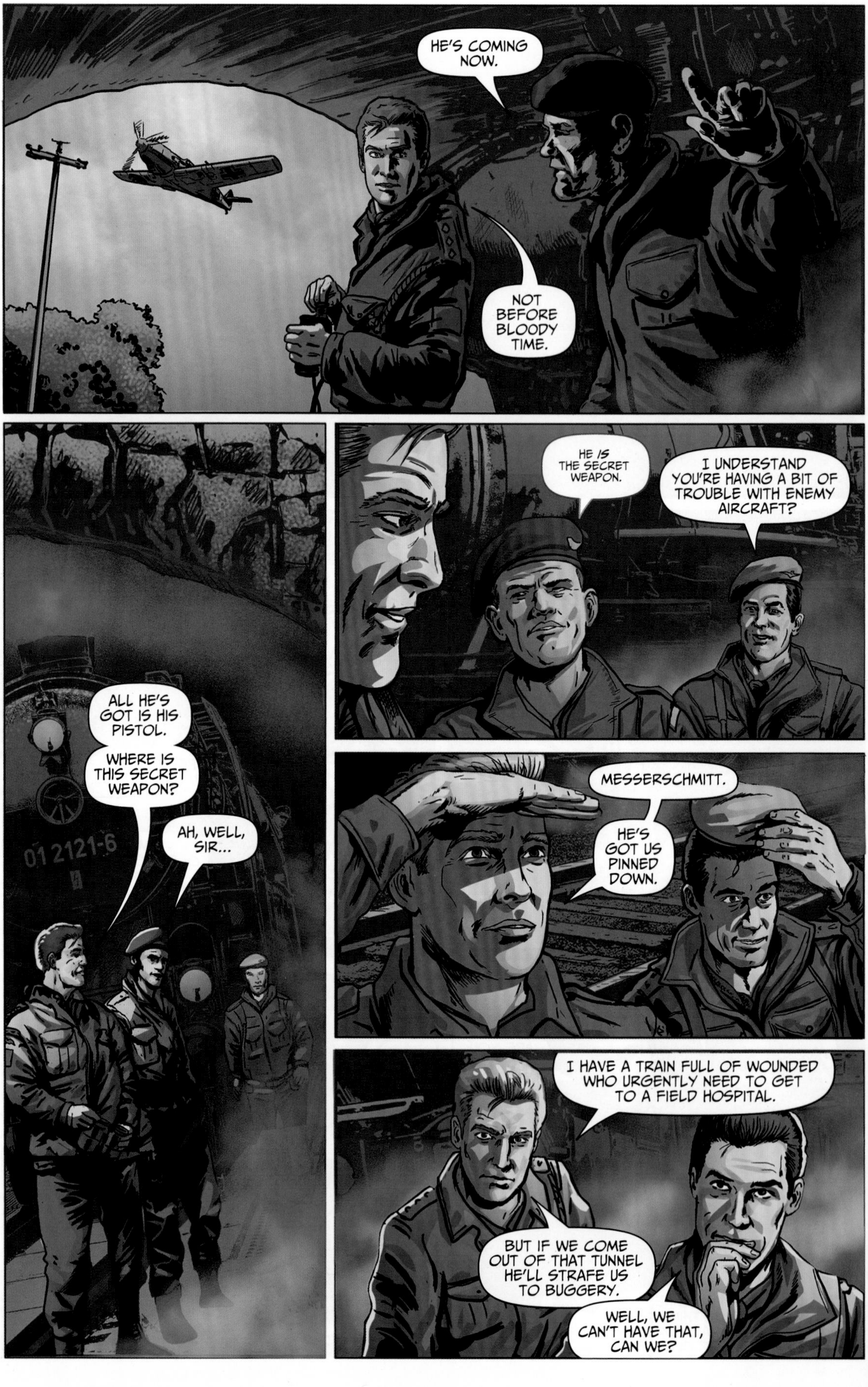
HE'S COMING NOW.
NOT BEFORE BLOODY TIME.
ALL HE'S GOT IS HIS PISTOL.
WHERE IS THIS SECRET WEAPON?
AH, WELL, SIR...
HE IS THE SECRET WEAPON.
I UNDERSTAND YOU'RE HAVING A BIT OF TROUBLE WITH ENEMY AIRCRAFT?
MESSERSCHMITT.
HE'S GOT US PINNED DOWN.
I HAVE A TRAIN FULL OF WOUNDED WHO URGENTLY NEED TO GET TO A FIELD HOSPITAL.
BUT IF WE COME OUT OF THAT TUNNEL HE'LL STRAFE US TO BUGGERY.
WELL, WE CAN'T HAVE THAT, CAN WE?

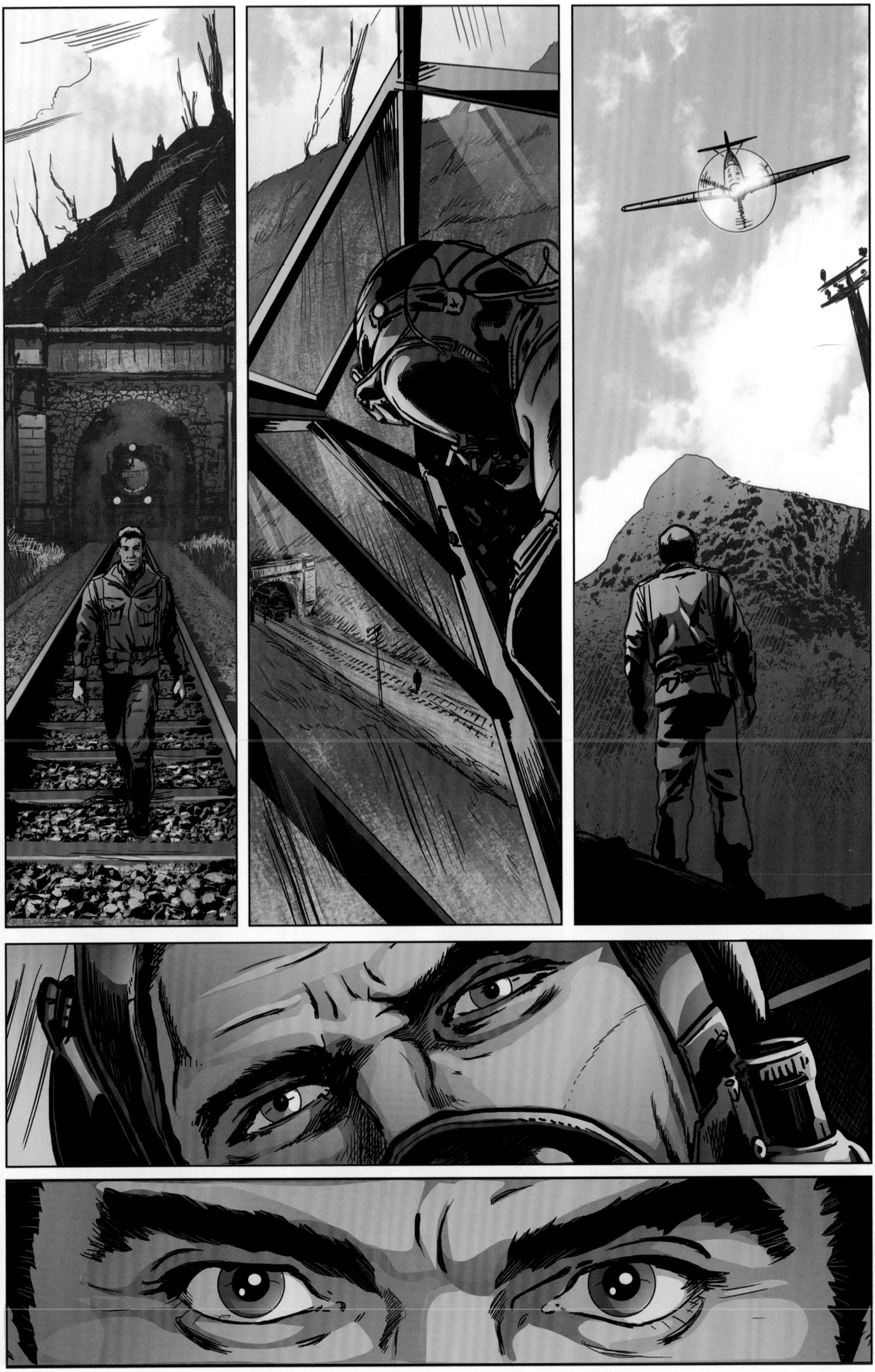

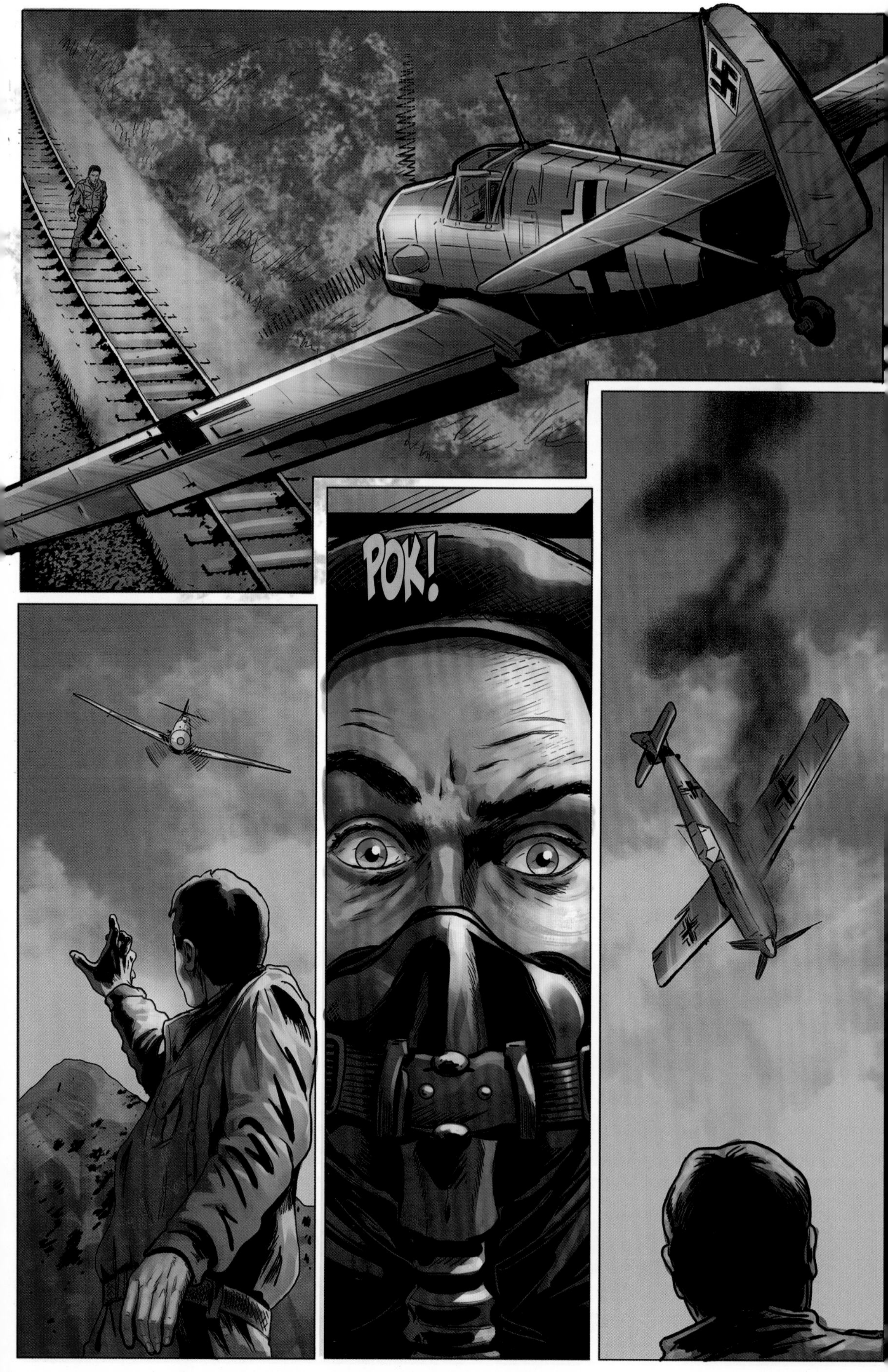
POK!

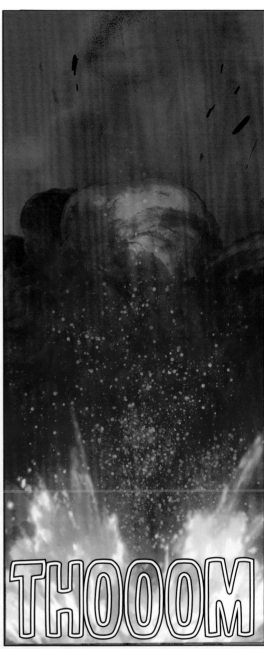

THOOOM

SEEMS THE FELLOW DEVELOPED ENGINE FAILURE.

WHAT A LUCKY COINCIDENCE.

LUCKY COINCIDENCE MY ARSE.

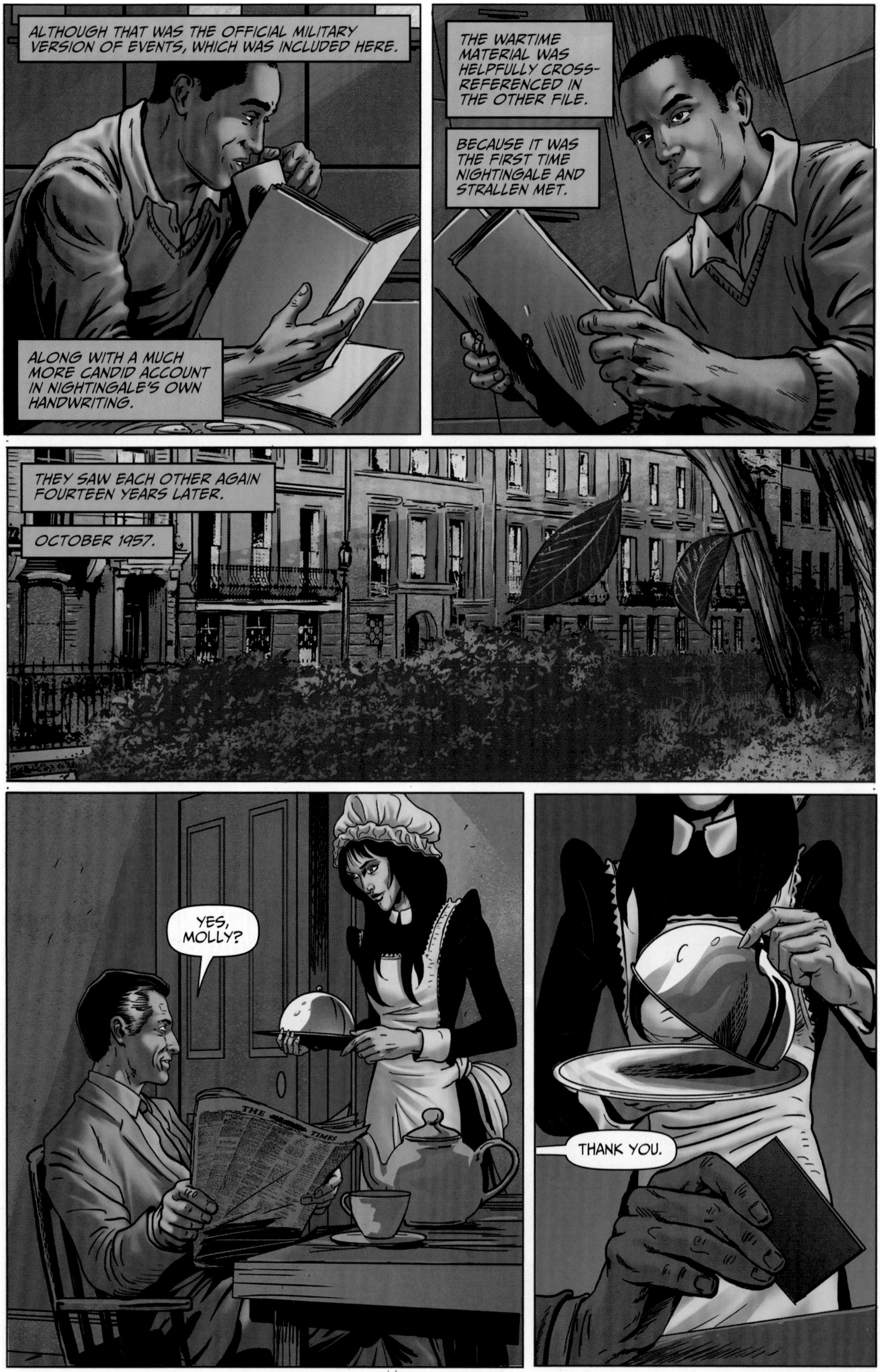
ALTHOUGH THAT WAS THE OFFICIAL MILITARY VERSION OF EVENTS, WHICH WAS INCLUDED HERE.
ALONG WITH A MUCH MORE CANDID ACCOUNT IN NIGHTINGALE'S OWN HANDWRITING.
THE WARTIME MATERIAL WAS HELPFULLY CROSS-REFERENCED IN THE OTHER FILE.
BECAUSE IT WAS THE FIRST TIME NIGHTINGALE AND STRALLEN MET.
THEY SAW EACH OTHER AGAIN FOURTEEN YEARS LATER.
OCTOBER 1957.
YES, MOLLY?
THANK YOU.

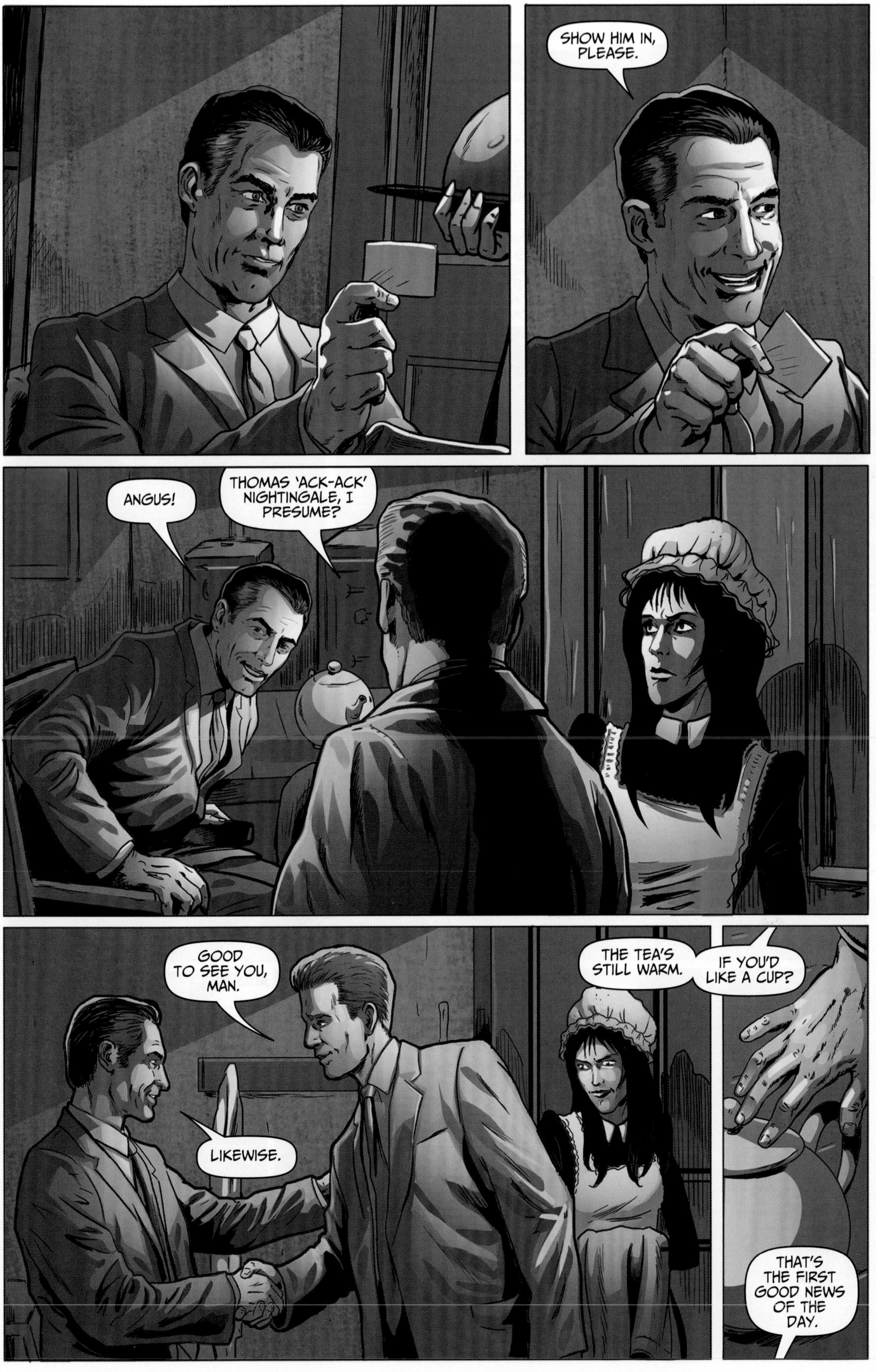
SHOW HIM IN, PLEASE.
ANGUS!
THOMAS 'ACK-ACK' NIGHTINGALE, I PRESUME?
GOOD TO SEE YOU, MAN.
LIKEWISE.
THE TEA'S STILL WARM.
IF YOU'D LIKE A CUP?
THAT'S THE FIRST GOOD NEWS OF THE DAY.

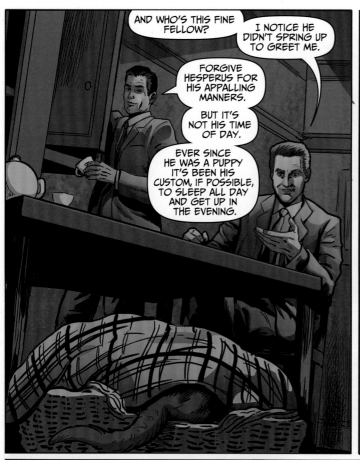

AND WHO'S THIS FINE FELLOW?

I NOTICE HE DIDN'T SPRING UP TO GREET ME.

FORGIVE HESPERUS FOR HIS APPALLING MANNERS.

BUT IT'S NOT HIS TIME OF DAY.

EVER SINCE HE WAS A PUPPY IT'S BEEN HIS CUSTOM, IF POSSIBLE, TO SLEEP ALL DAY AND GET UP IN THE EVENING.

HENCE HIS NAME.

HESPERUS. THE EVENING STAR.

DON'T LOOK SO SURPRISED, THOMAS.

THEY DID TEACH ME SOMETHING AT MANCHESTER GRAMMAR.

EVIDENTLY.

WHEN YOU'VE FINISHED THAT, I'LL POUR US SOMETHING STRONGER.

THAT'S THE SECOND GOOD NEWS OF THE DAY.

SO, ANGUS...

DO YOU WANT TO TELL ME WHAT BROUGHT YOU HERE?

YOU'RE RIGHT. WE'D BETTER GET TO IT.

SINCE THE WAR, STRALLEN HAD ENDED UP FOLLOWING A SIMILAR PATH TO NIGHTINGALE.

I DON'T MEAN HE'D BECOME A WIZARD

I MEAN HE'D JOINED THE JOB.

THE CUMBERLAND AND WESTMORLAND CONSTABULARY, TO BE EXACT.

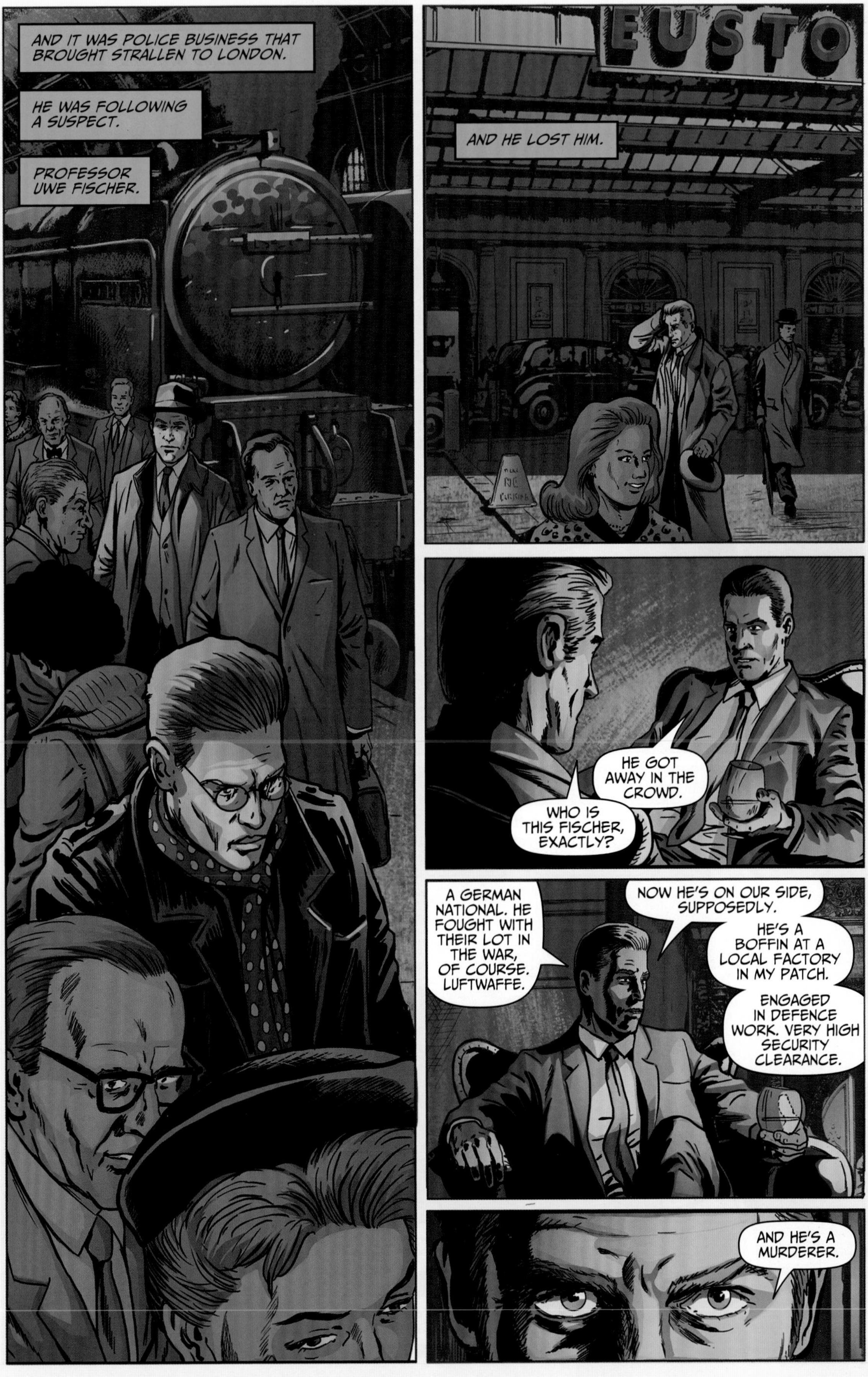
AND IT WAS POLICE BUSINESS THAT BROUGHT STRALLEN TO LONDON.
HE WAS FOLLOWING A SUSPECT.
PROFESSOR UWE FISCHER.
EUSTO
AND HE LOST HIM.
HE GOT AWAY IN THE CROWD.
WHO IS THIS FISCHER, EXACTLY?
A GERMAN NATIONAL. HE FOUGHT WITH THEIR LOT IN THE WAR, OF COURSE. LUFTWAFFE.
NOW HE'S ON OUR SIDE, SUPPOSEDLY.
HE'S A BOFFIN AT A LOCAL FACTORY IN MY PATCH.
ENGAGED IN DEFENCE WORK. VERY HIGH SECURITY CLEARANCE.
AND HE'S A MURDERER.

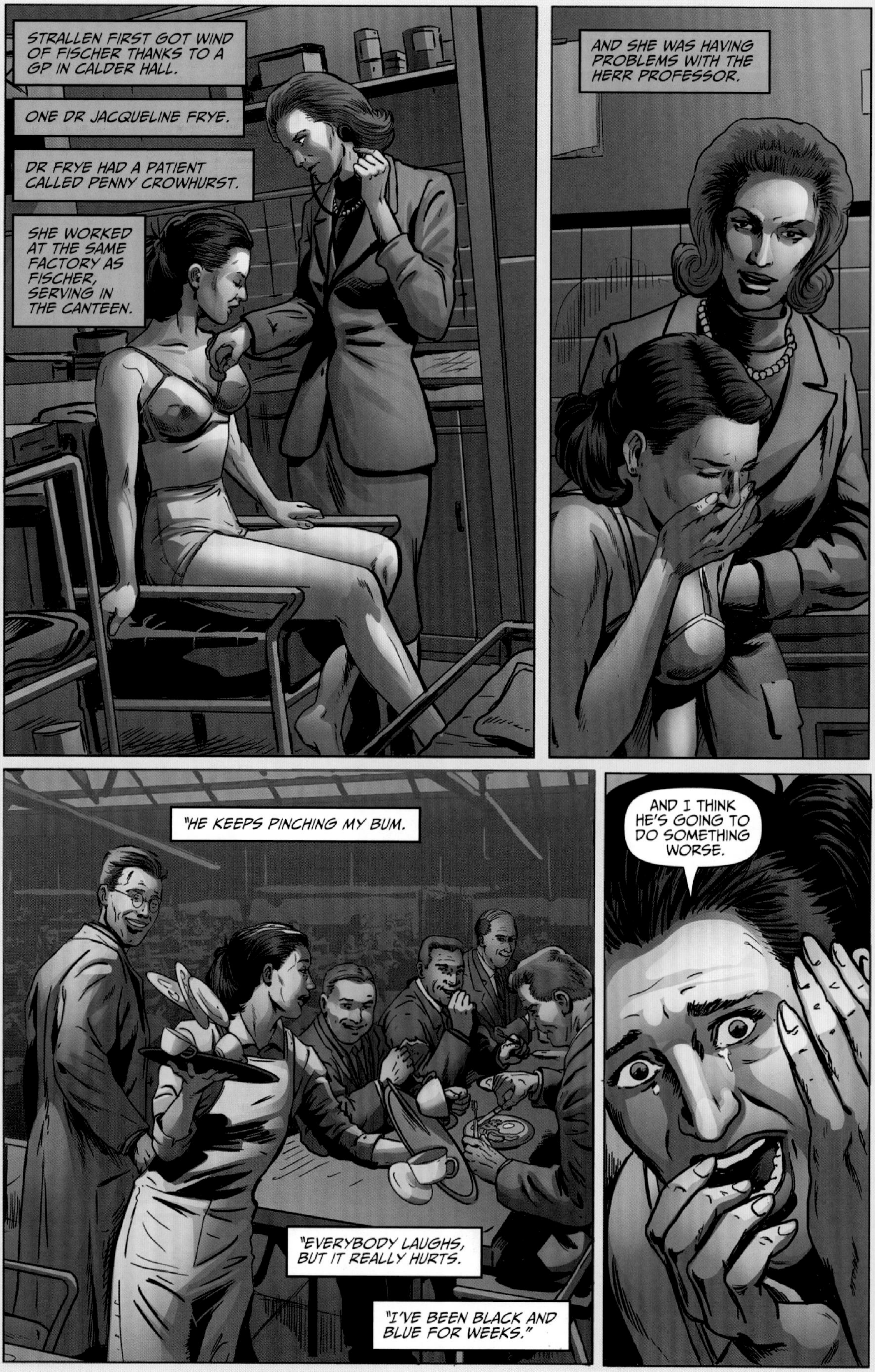
STRALLEN FIRST GOT WIND OF FISCHER THANKS TO A GP IN CALDER HALL.
ONE DR JACQUELINE FRYE.
DR FRYE HAD A PATIENT CALLED PENNY CROWHURST.
SHE WORKED AT THE SAME FACTORY AS FISCHER, SERVING IN THE CANTEEN.
AND SHE WAS HAVING PROBLEMS WITH THE HERR PROFESSOR.
"HE KEEPS PINCHING MY BUM.
"EVERYBODY LAUGHS, BUT IT REALLY HURTS.
"I'VE BEEN BLACK AND BLUE FOR WEEKS."
AND I THINK HE'S GOING TO DO SOMETHING WORSE.

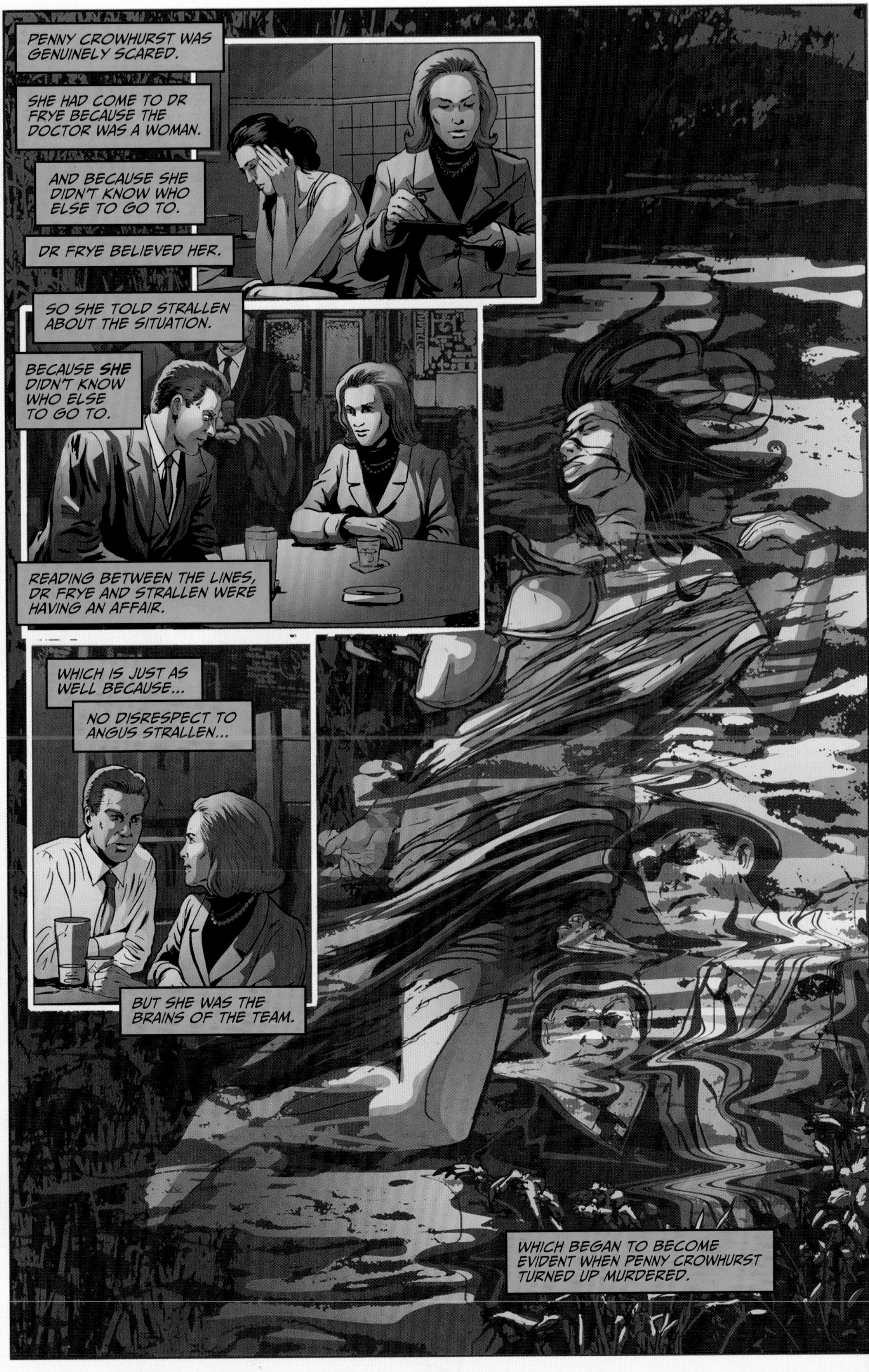
PENNY CROWHURST WAS GENUINELY SCARED.
SHE HAD COME TO DR FRYE BECAUSE THE DOCTOR WAS A WOMAN.
AND BECAUSE SHE DIDN'T KNOW WHO ELSE TO GO TO.
DR FRYE BELIEVED HER.
SO SHE TOLD STRALLEN ABOUT THE SITUATION.
BECAUSE **SHE** DIDN'T KNOW WHO ELSE TO GO TO.
READING BETWEEN THE LINES, DR FRYE AND STRALLEN WERE HAVING AN AFFAIR.
WHICH IS JUST AS WELL BECAUSE...
NO DISRESPECT TO ANGUS STRALLEN...
BUT SHE WAS THE BRAINS OF THE TEAM.
WHICH BEGAN TO BECOME EVIDENT WHEN PENNY CROWHURST TURNED UP MURDERED.

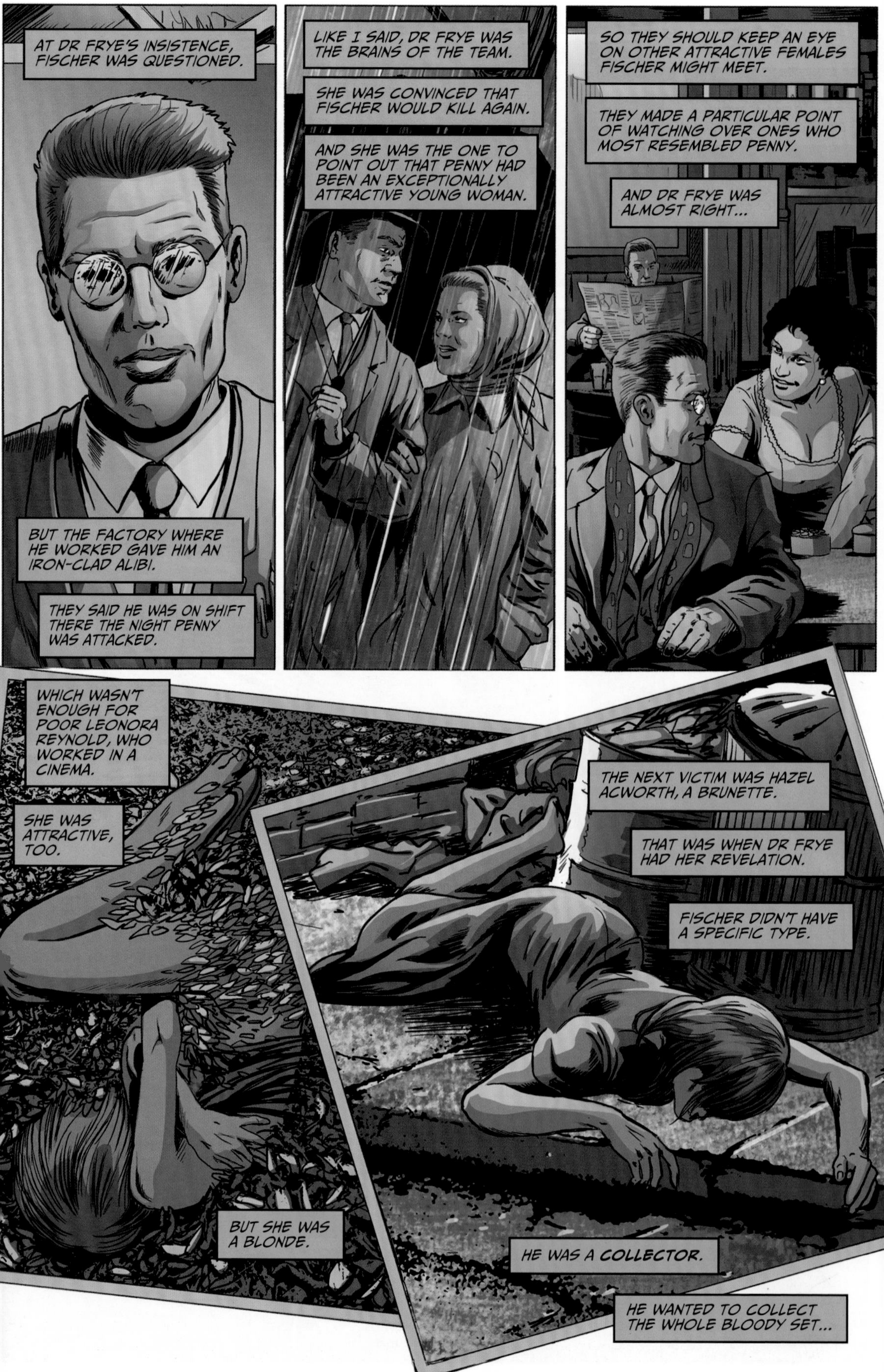
AT DR FRYE'S INSISTENCE, FISCHER WAS QUESTIONED.
BUT THE FACTORY WHERE HE WORKED GAVE HIM AN IRON-CLAD ALIBI.
THEY SAID HE WAS ON SHIFT THERE THE NIGHT PENNY WAS ATTACKED.
LIKE I SAID, DR FRYE WAS THE BRAINS OF THE TEAM.
SHE WAS CONVINCED THAT FISCHER WOULD KILL AGAIN.
AND SHE WAS THE ONE TO POINT OUT THAT PENNY HAD BEEN AN EXCEPTIONALLY ATTRACTIVE YOUNG WOMAN.
SO THEY SHOULD KEEP AN EYE ON OTHER ATTRACTIVE FEMALES FISCHER MIGHT MEET.
THEY MADE A PARTICULAR POINT OF WATCHING OVER ONES WHO MOST RESEMBLED PENNY.
AND DR FRYE WAS ALMOST RIGHT...
WHICH WASN'T ENOUGH FOR POOR LEONORA REYNOLD, WHO WORKED IN A CINEMA.
SHE WAS ATTRACTIVE, TOO.
BUT SHE WAS A BLONDE.
THE NEXT VICTIM WAS HAZEL ACWORTH, A BRUNETTE.
THAT WAS WHEN DR FRYE HAD HER REVELATION.
FISCHER DIDN'T HAVE A SPECIFIC TYPE.
HE WAS A **COLLECTOR**.
HE WANTED TO COLLECT THE WHOLE BLOODY SET...

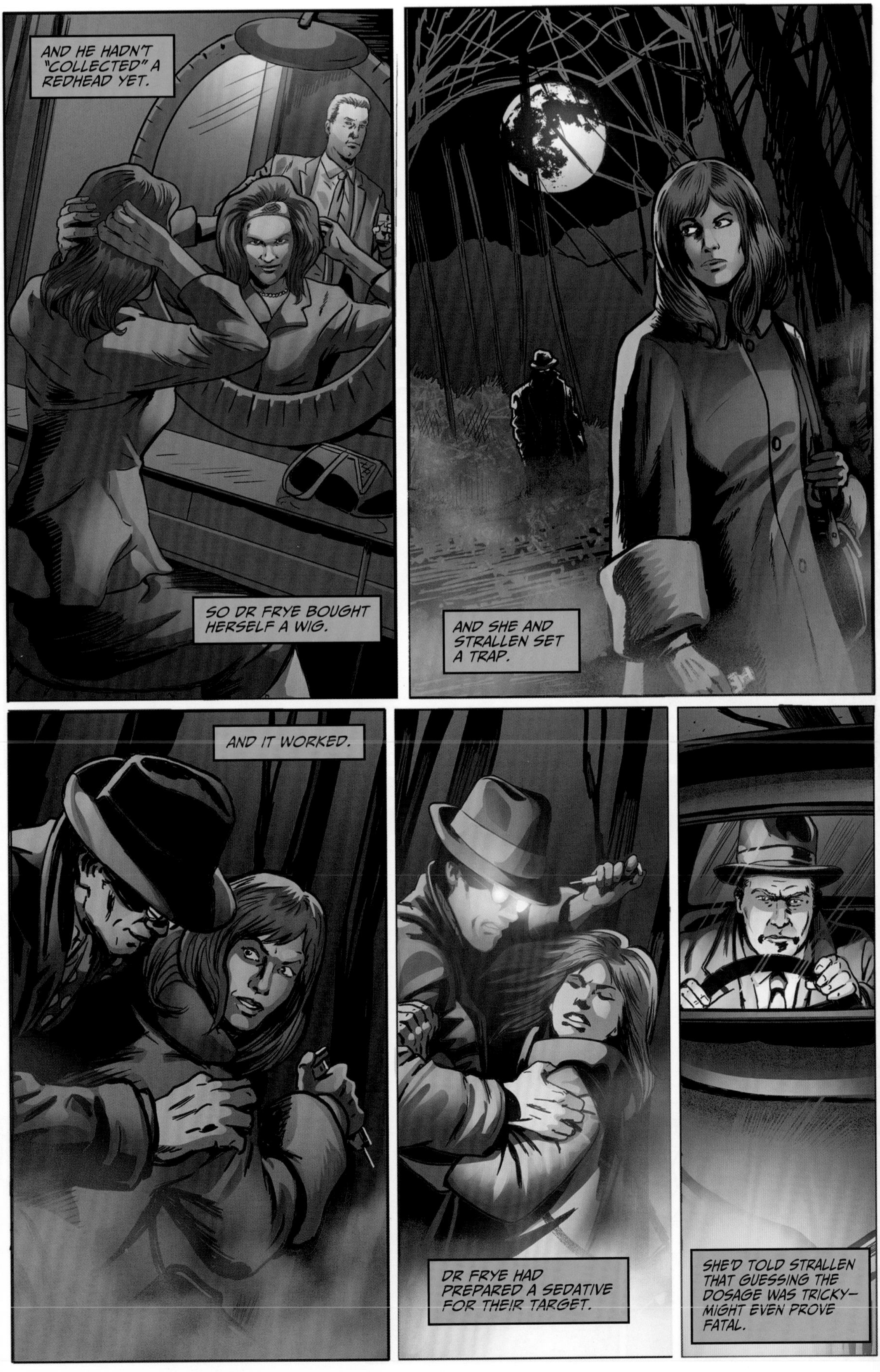
AND HE HADN'T "COLLECTED" A REDHEAD YET.
SO DR FRYE BOUGHT HERSELF A WIG.
AND SHE AND STRALLEN SET A TRAP.
AND IT WORKED.
DR FRYE HAD PREPARED A SEDATIVE FOR THEIR TARGET.
SHE'D TOLD STRALLEN THAT GUESSING THE DOSAGE WAS TRICKY— MIGHT EVEN PROVE FATAL.

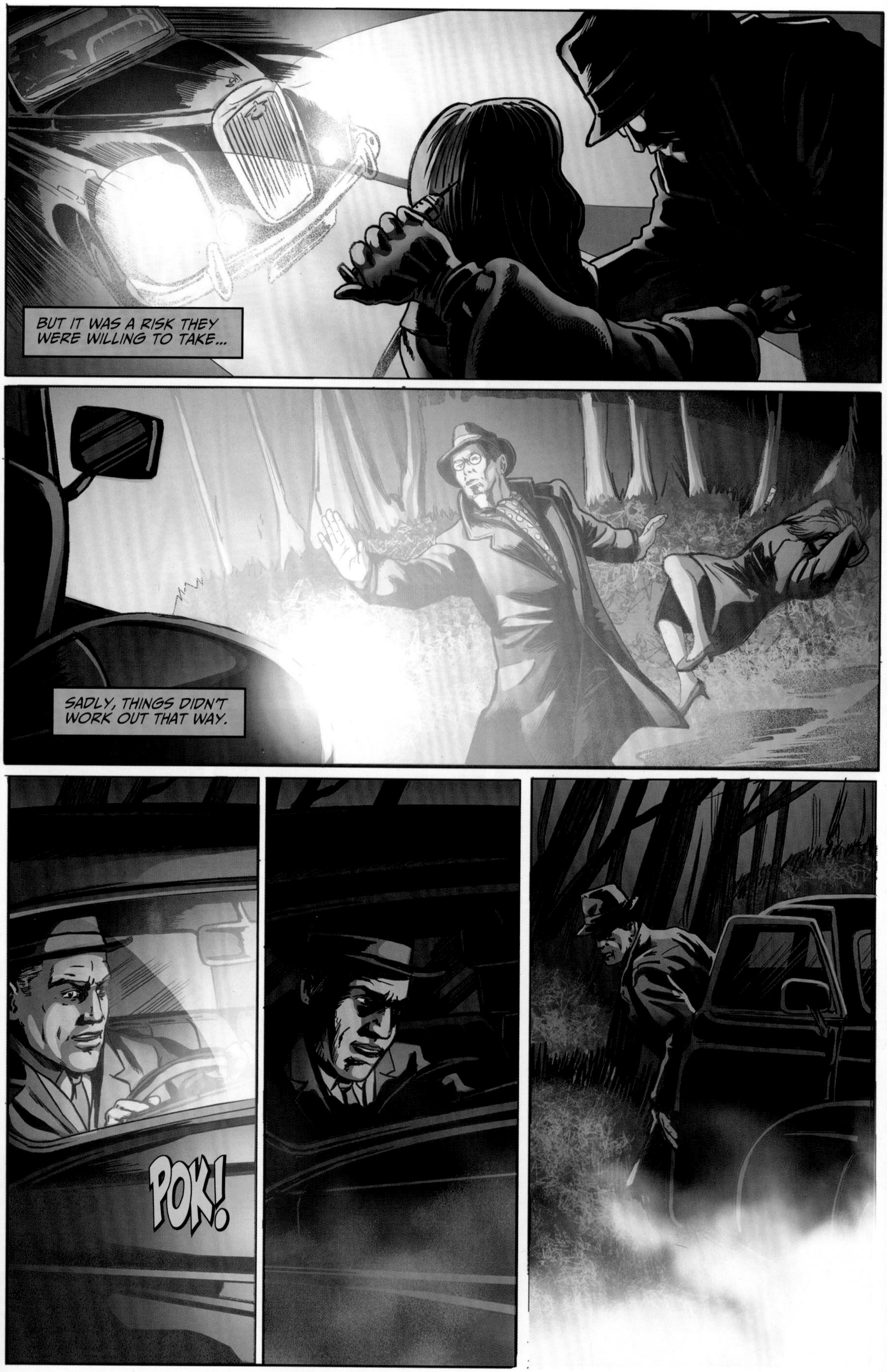
BUT IT WAS A RISK THEY WERE WILLING TO TAKE...
SADLY, THINGS DIDN'T WORK OUT THAT WAY.
POK!

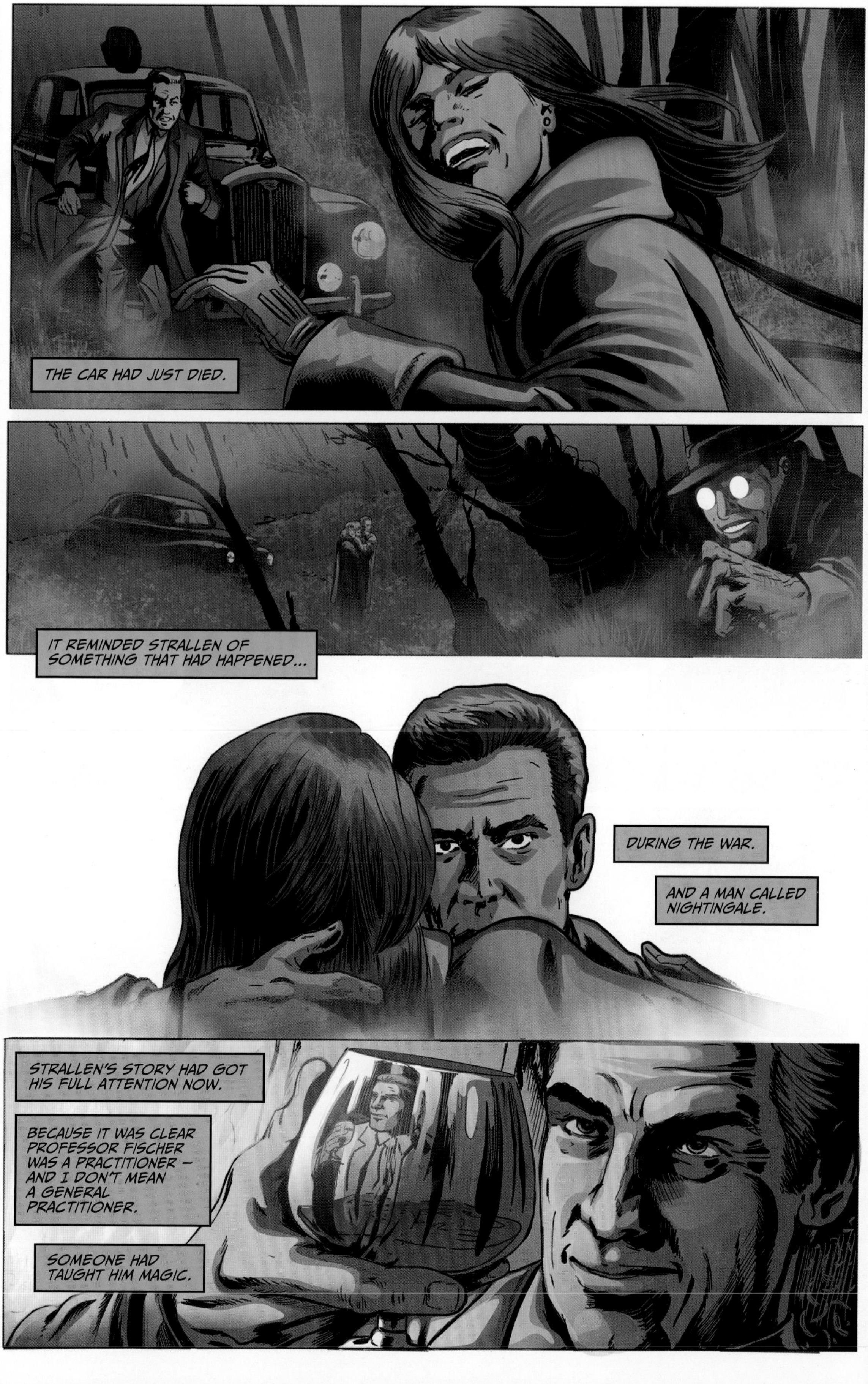
THE CAR HAD JUST DIED.
IT REMINDED STRALLEN OF SOMETHING THAT HAD HAPPENED...
DURING THE WAR.
AND A MAN CALLED NIGHTINGALE.
STRALLEN'S STORY HAD GOT HIS FULL ATTENTION NOW.
BECAUSE IT WAS CLEAR PROFESSOR FISCHER WAS A PRACTITIONER — AND I DON'T MEAN A GENERAL PRACTITIONER.
SOMEONE HAD TAUGHT HIM MAGIC.

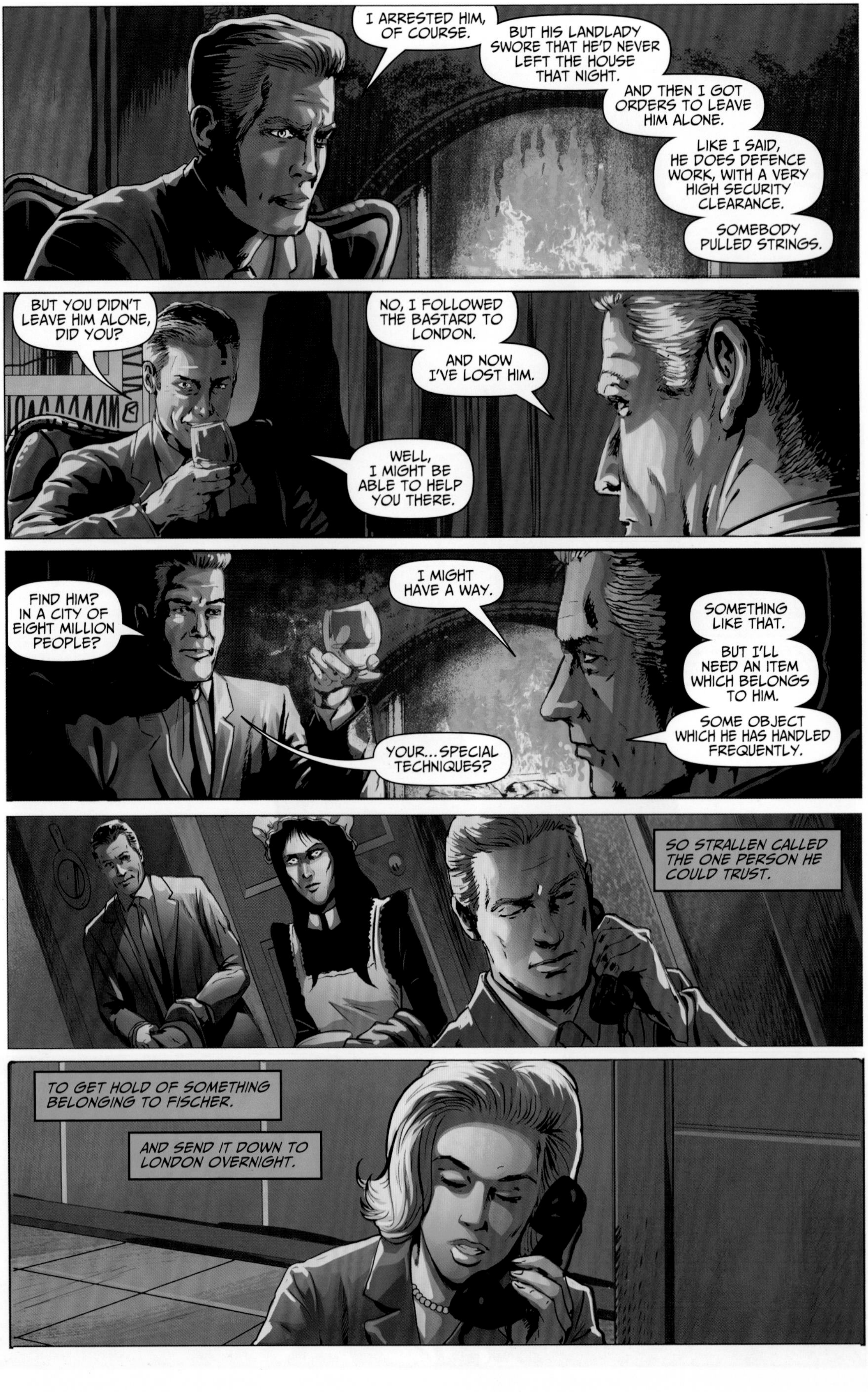
I ARRESTED HIM, OF COURSE.
BUT HIS LANDLADY SWORE THAT HE'D NEVER LEFT THE HOUSE THAT NIGHT.
AND THEN I GOT ORDERS TO LEAVE HIM ALONE.
LIKE I SAID, HE DOES DEFENCE WORK, WITH A VERY HIGH SECURITY CLEARANCE.
SOMEBODY PULLED STRINGS.
BUT YOU DIDN'T LEAVE HIM ALONE, DID YOU?
NO, I FOLLOWED THE BASTARD TO LONDON.
AND NOW I'VE LOST HIM.
WELL, I MIGHT BE ABLE TO HELP YOU THERE.
FIND HIM? IN A CITY OF EIGHT MILLION PEOPLE?
I MIGHT HAVE A WAY.
YOUR...SPECIAL TECHNIQUES?
SOMETHING LIKE THAT.
BUT I'LL NEED AN ITEM WHICH BELONGS TO HIM.
SOME OBJECT WHICH HE HAS HANDLED FREQUENTLY.
SO STRALLEN CALLED THE ONE PERSON HE COULD TRUST.
TO GET HOLD OF SOMETHING BELONGING TO FISCHER.
AND SEND IT DOWN TO LONDON OVERNIGHT.

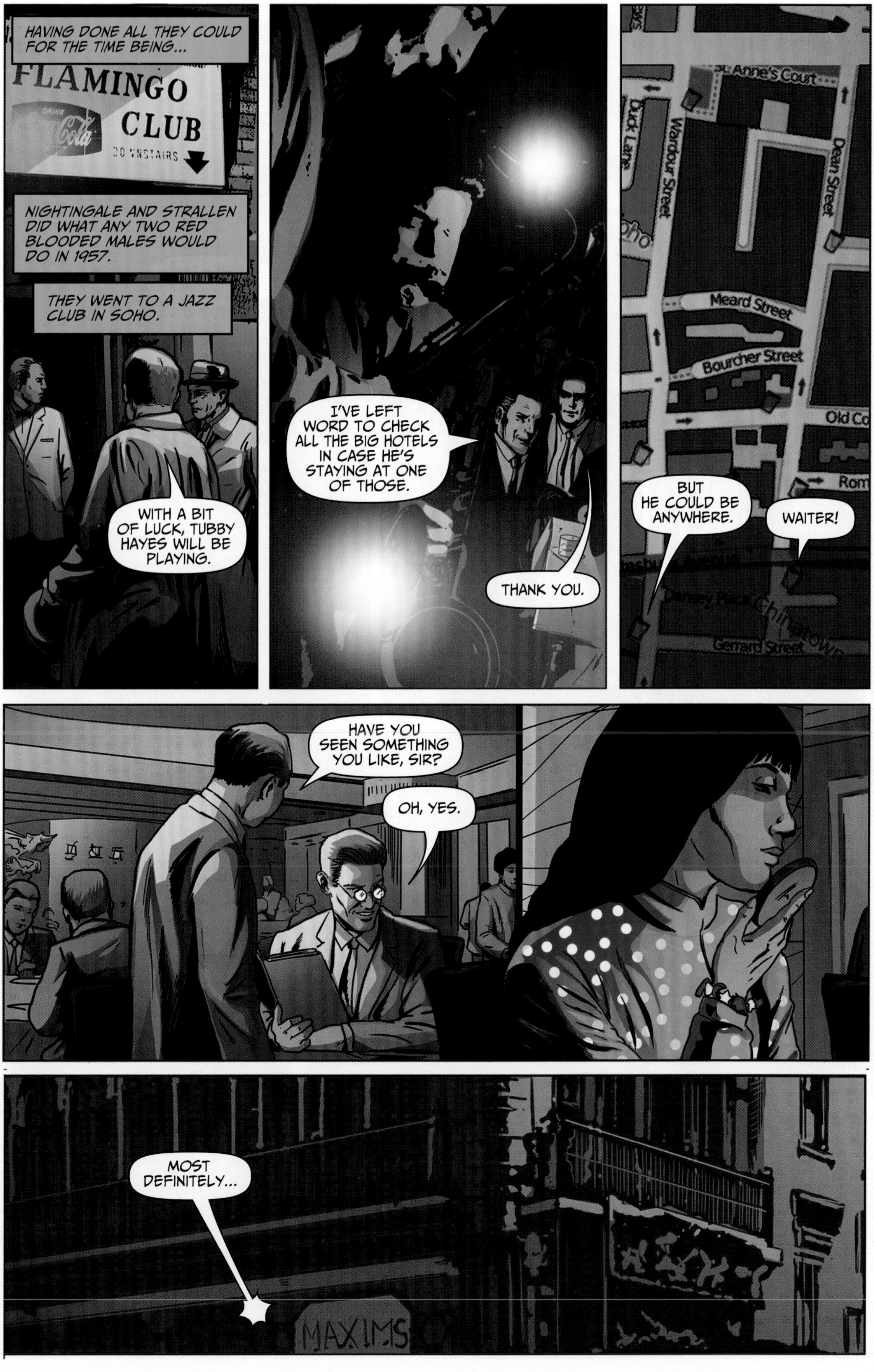
HAVING DONE ALL THEY COULD FOR THE TIME BEING...
FLAMINGO CLUB
Coca-Cola
NIGHTINGALE AND STRALLEN DID WHAT ANY TWO RED BLOODED MALES WOULD DO IN 1957.
THEY WENT TO A JAZZ CLUB IN SOHO.
WITH A BIT OF LUCK, TUBBY HAYES WILL BE PLAYING.
I'VE LEFT WORD TO CHECK ALL THE BIG HOTELS IN CASE HE'S STAYING AT ONE OF THOSE.
THANK YOU.
St. Anne's Court
Duck Lane
Wardour Street
Dean Street
Meard Street
Bourcher Street
BUT HE COULD BE ANYWHERE.
WAITER!
Gerrard Street
HAVE YOU SEEN SOMETHING YOU LIKE, SIR?
OH, YES.
MOST DEFINITELY...
MAXIMS

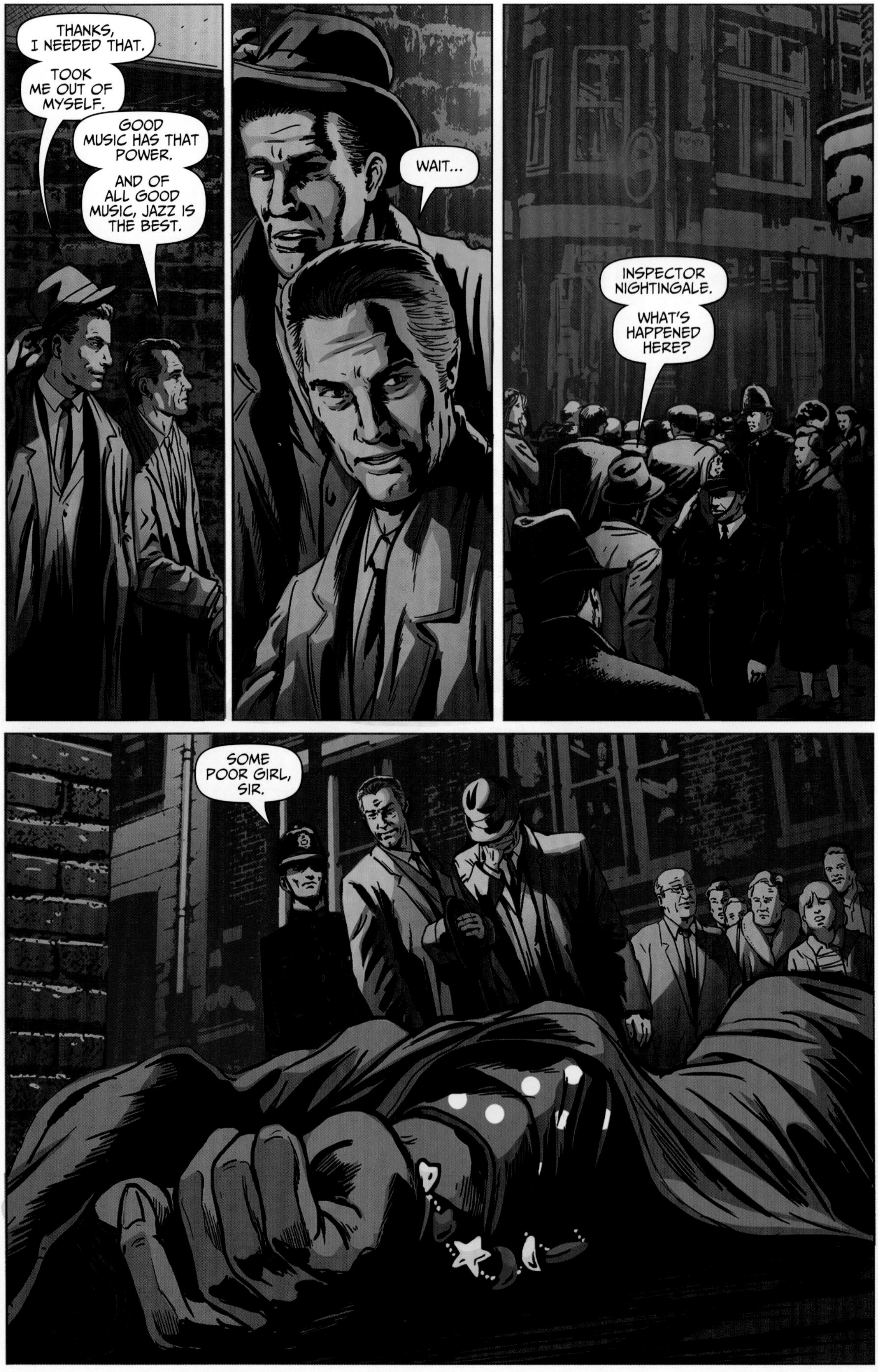
THANKS, I NEEDED THAT.
TOOK ME OUT OF MYSELF.
GOOD MUSIC HAS THAT POWER.
AND OF ALL GOOD MUSIC, JAZZ IS THE BEST.
WAIT...
INSPECTOR NIGHTINGALE.
WHAT'S HAPPENED HERE?
SOME POOR GIRL, SIR.

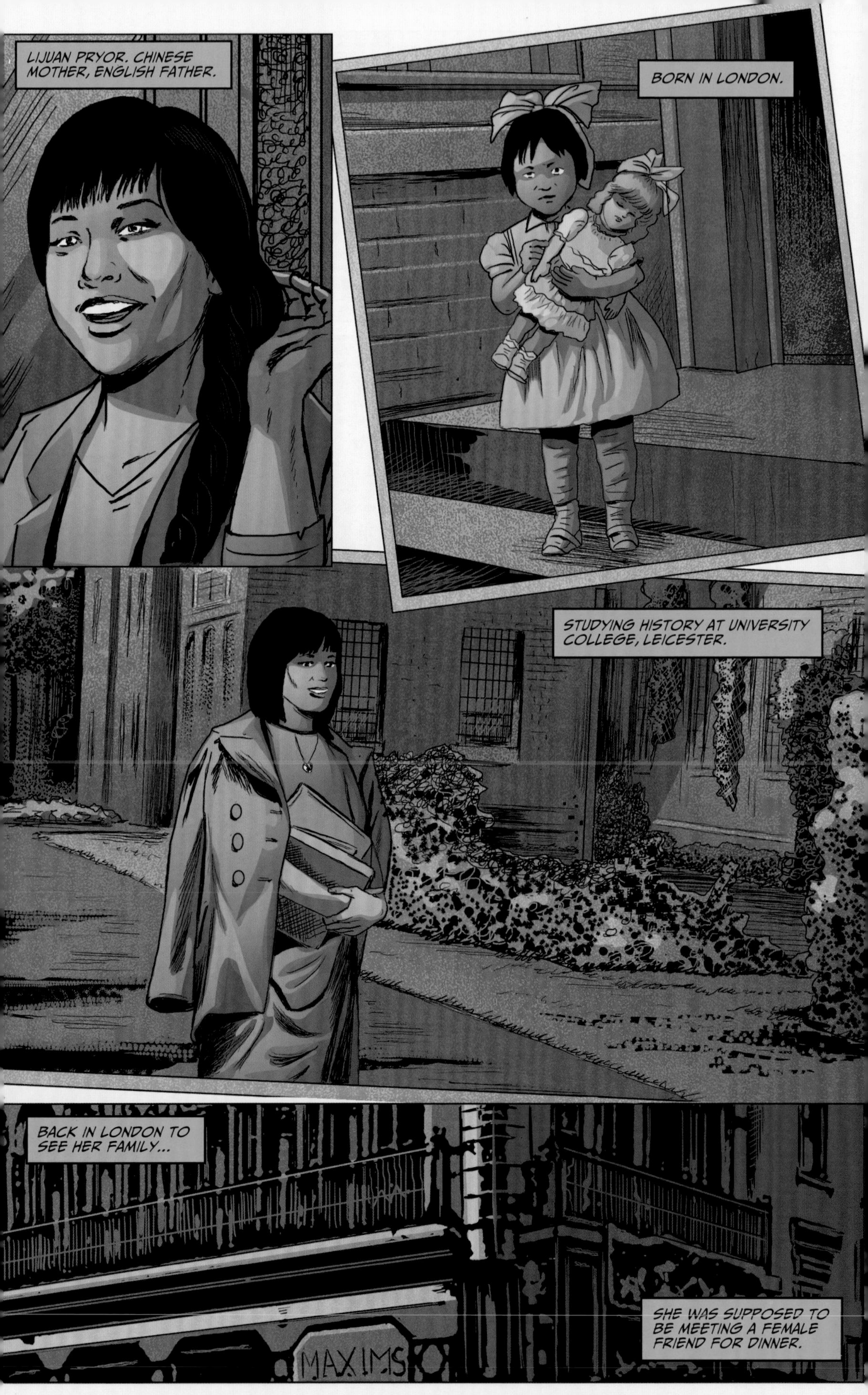

LIJUAN PRYOR. CHINESE MOTHER, ENGLISH FATHER.
BORN IN LONDON.
STUDYING HISTORY AT UNIVERSITY COLLEGE, LEICESTER.
BACK IN LONDON TO SEE HER FAMILY...
SHE WAS SUPPOSED TO BE MEETING A FEMALE FRIEND FOR DINNER.
MAXIMS

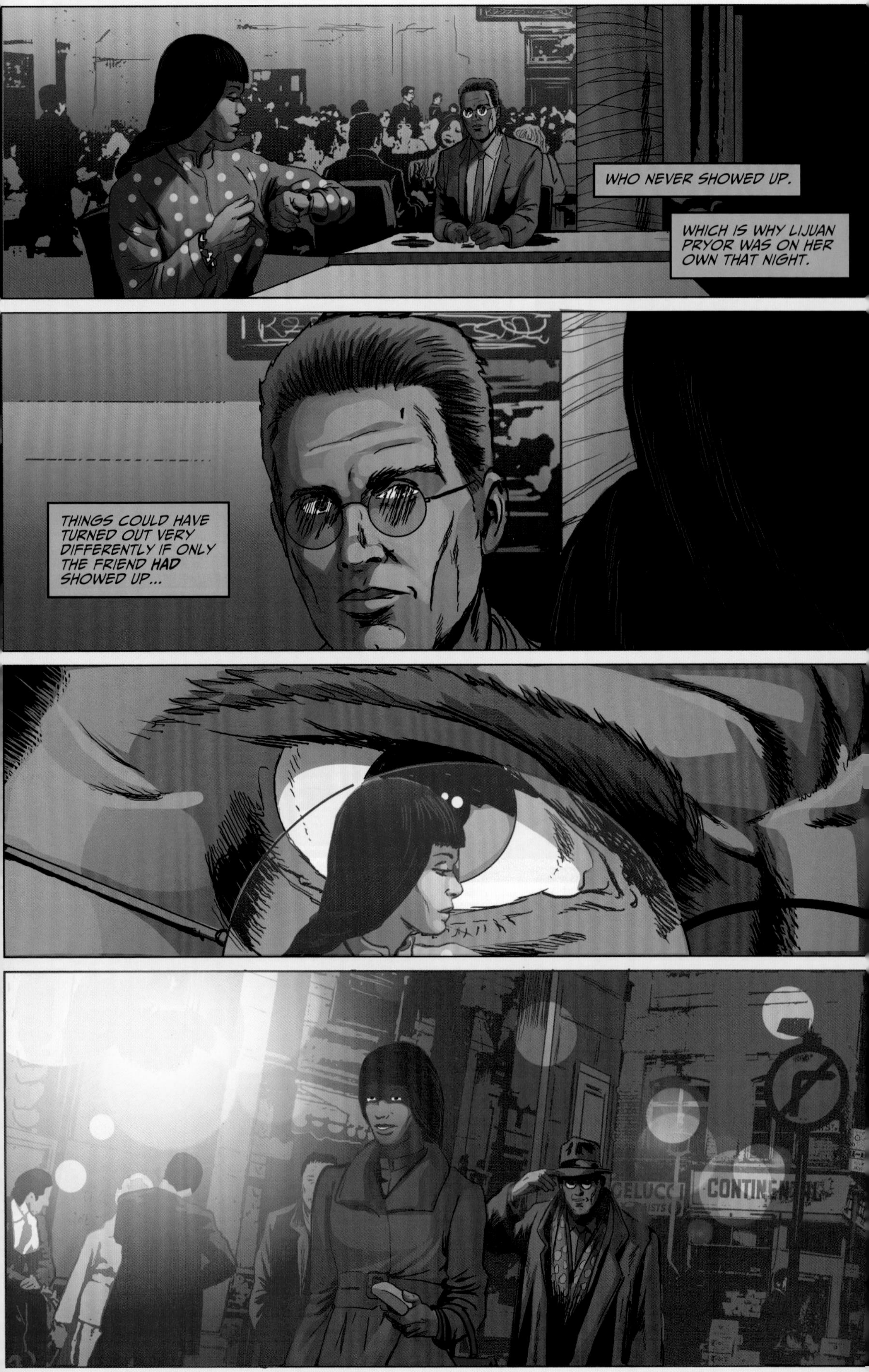
WHO NEVER SHOWED UP.
WHICH IS WHY LIJUAN PRYOR WAS ON HER OWN THAT NIGHT.
THINGS COULD HAVE TURNED OUT VERY DIFFERENTLY IF ONLY THE FRIEND **HAD** SHOWED UP...
CELUCCI
CONTINENTAL

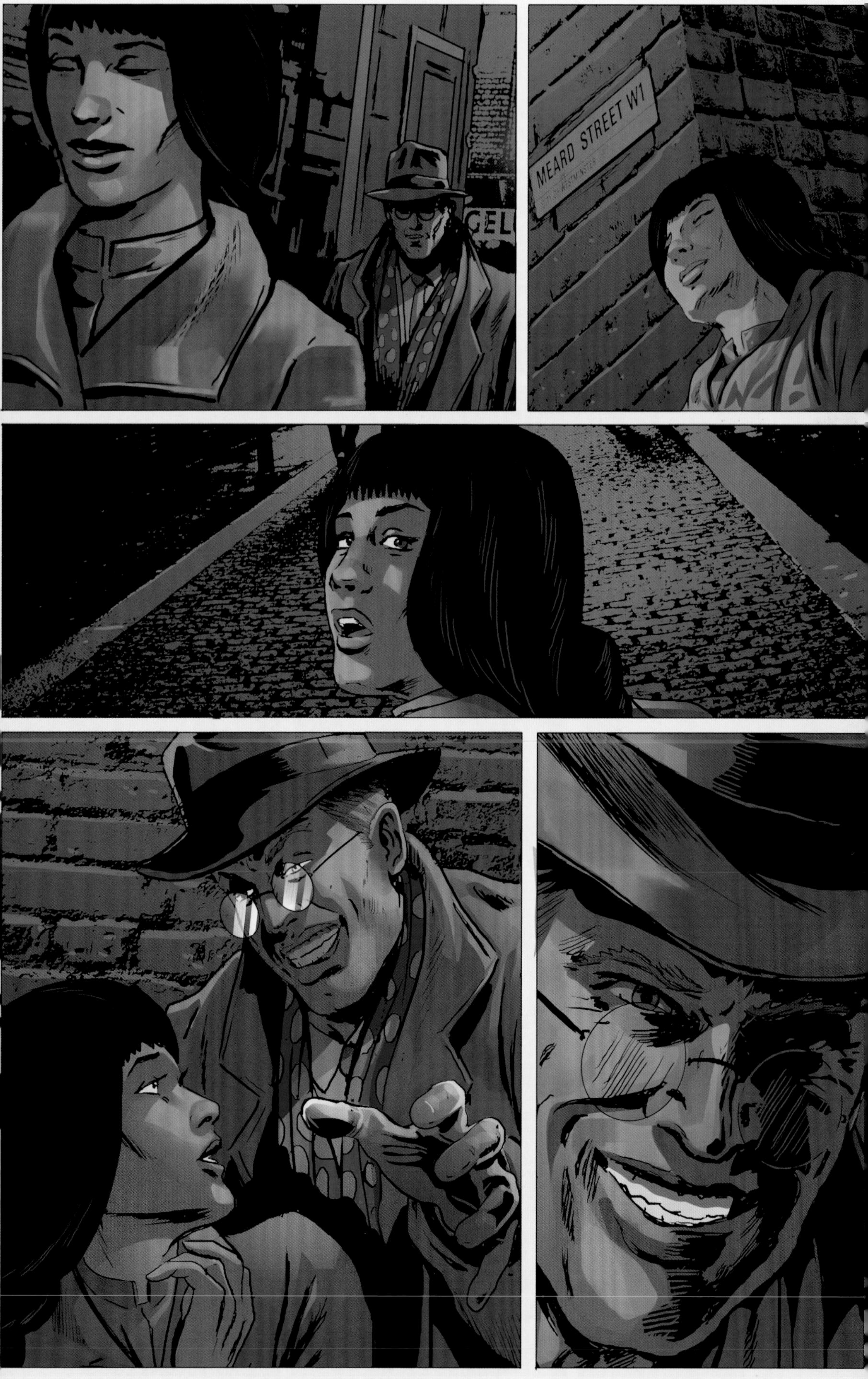
MEARD STREET W1

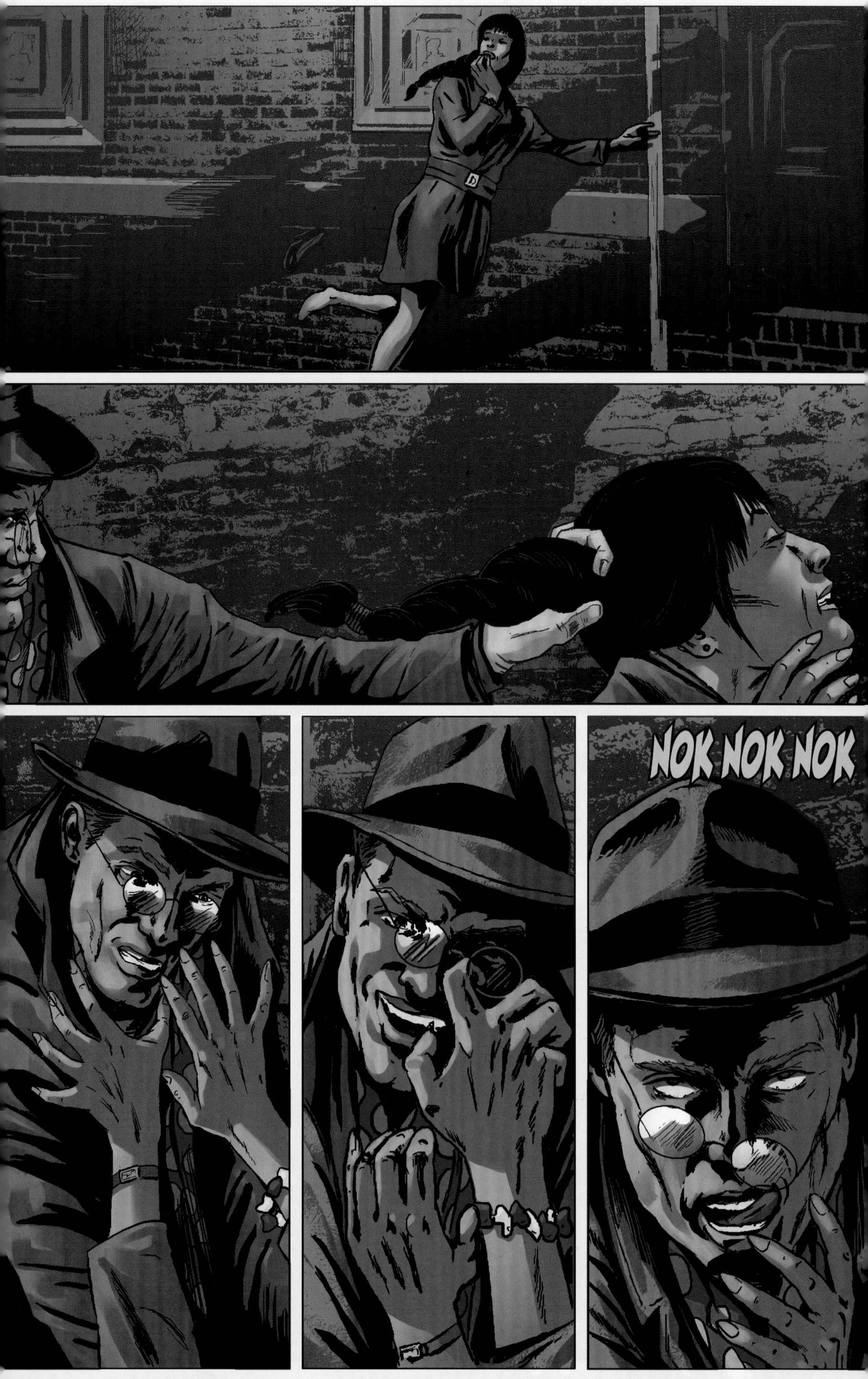
NOK NOK NOK

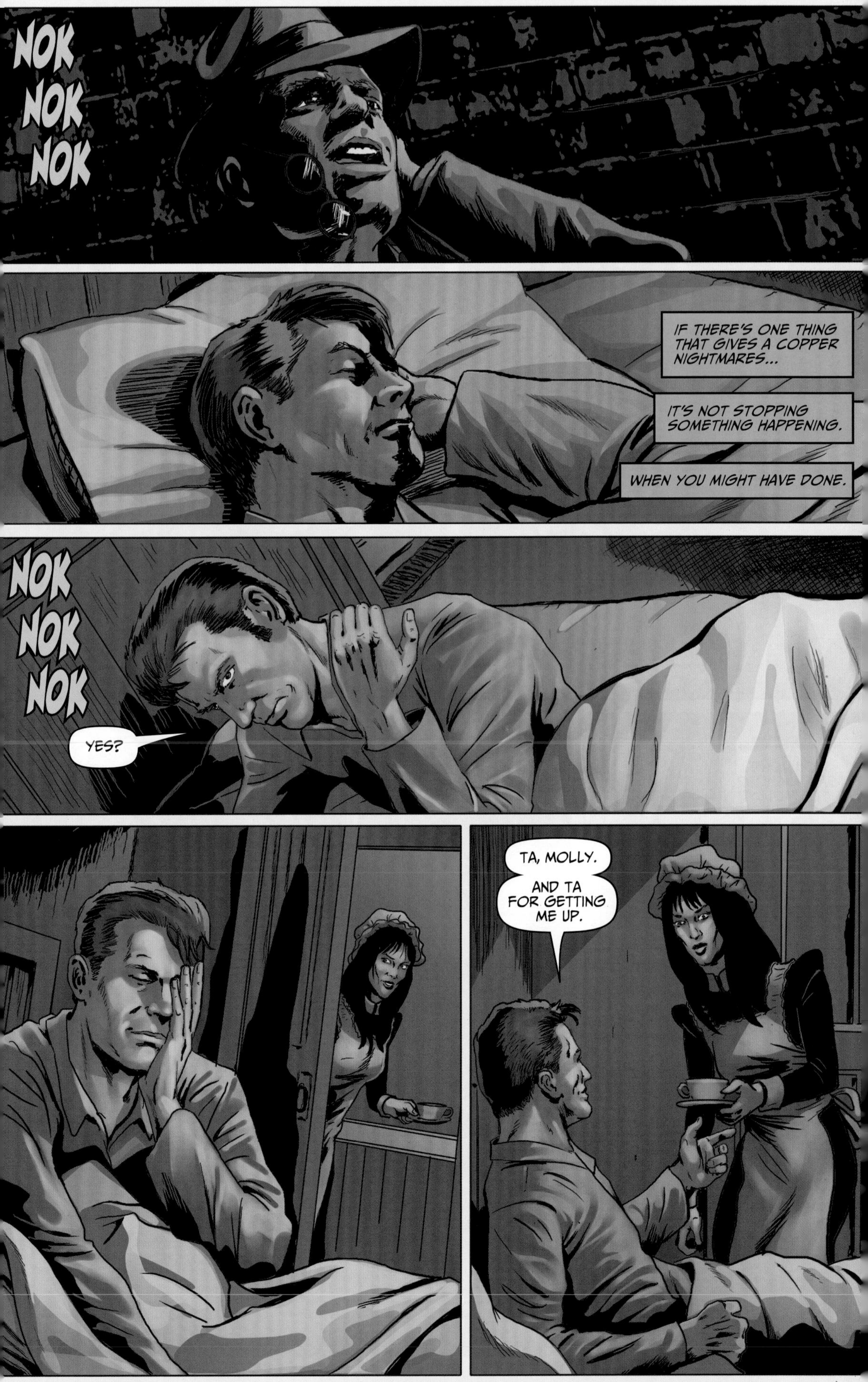
NOK NOK NOK
IF THERE'S ONE THING THAT GIVES A COPPER NIGHTMARES...
IT'S NOT STOPPING SOMETHING HAPPENING.
WHEN YOU MIGHT HAVE DONE.
NOK NOK NOK
YES?
TA, MOLLY.
AND TA FOR GETTING ME UP.

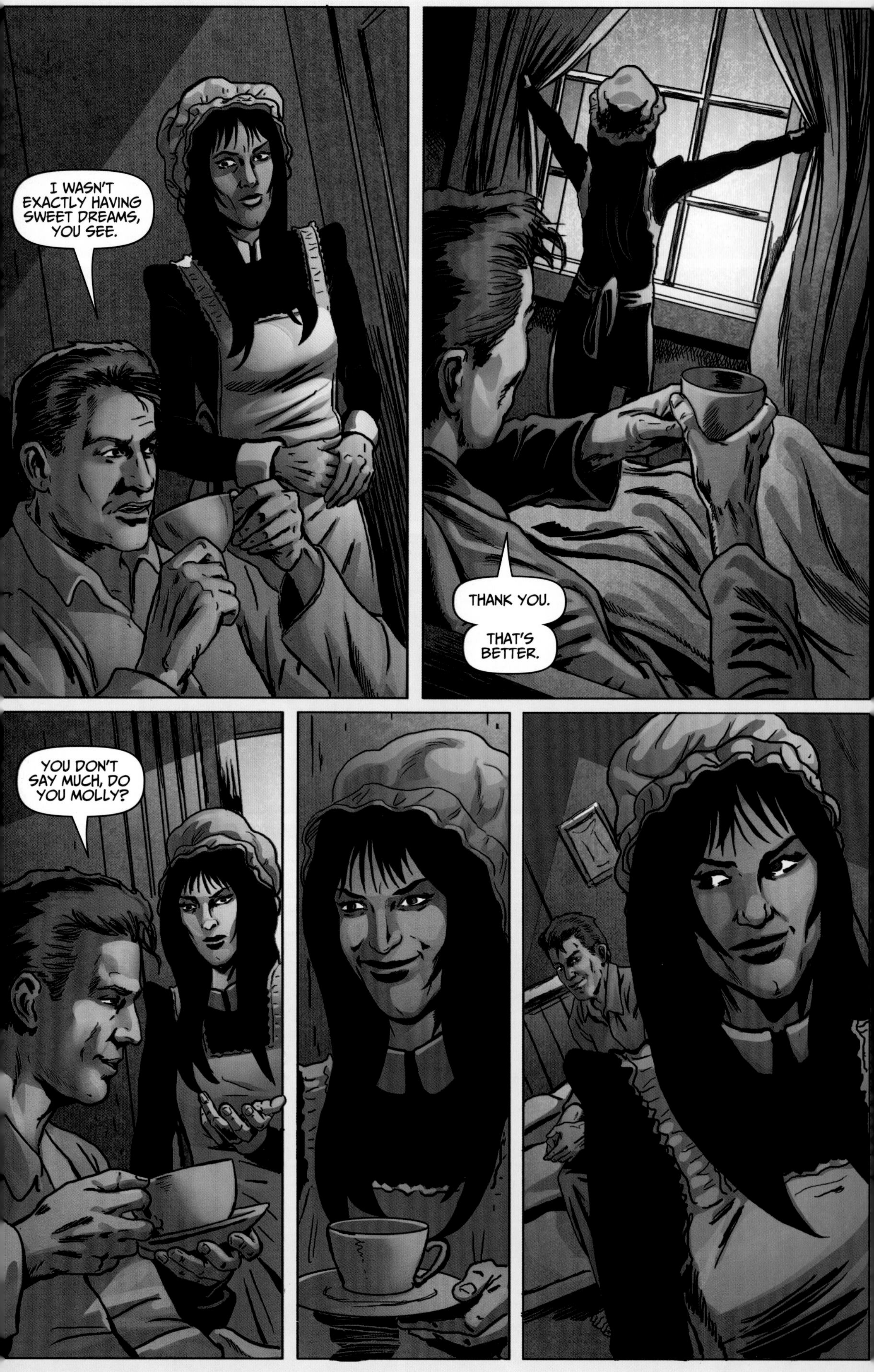
I WASN'T EXACTLY HAVING SWEET DREAMS, YOU SEE.
THANK YOU.
THAT'S BETTER.
YOU DON'T SAY MUCH, DO YOU MOLLY?

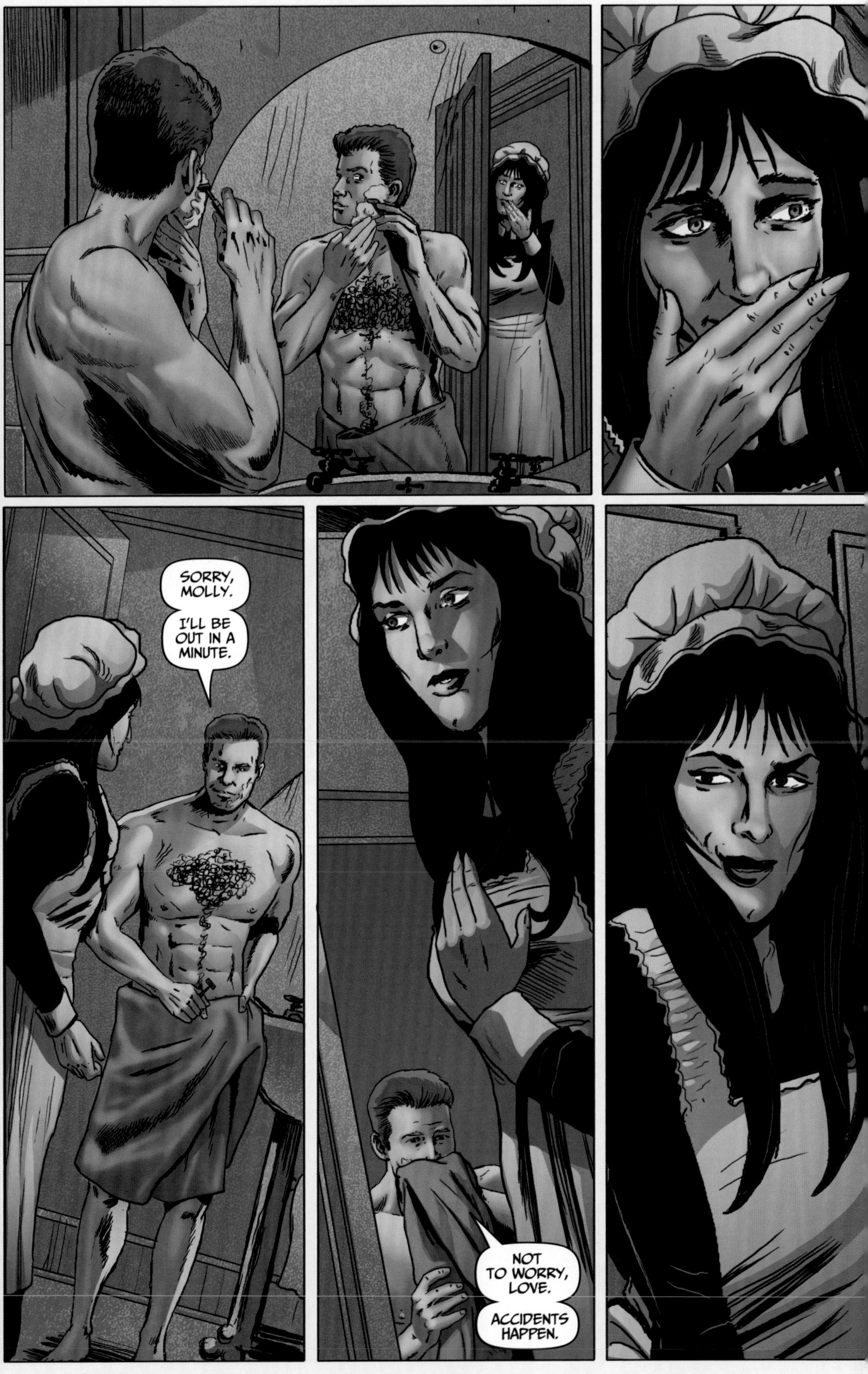
SORRY, MOLLY.
I'LL BE OUT IN A MINUTE.
NOT TO WORRY, LOVE.
ACCIDENTS HAPPEN.

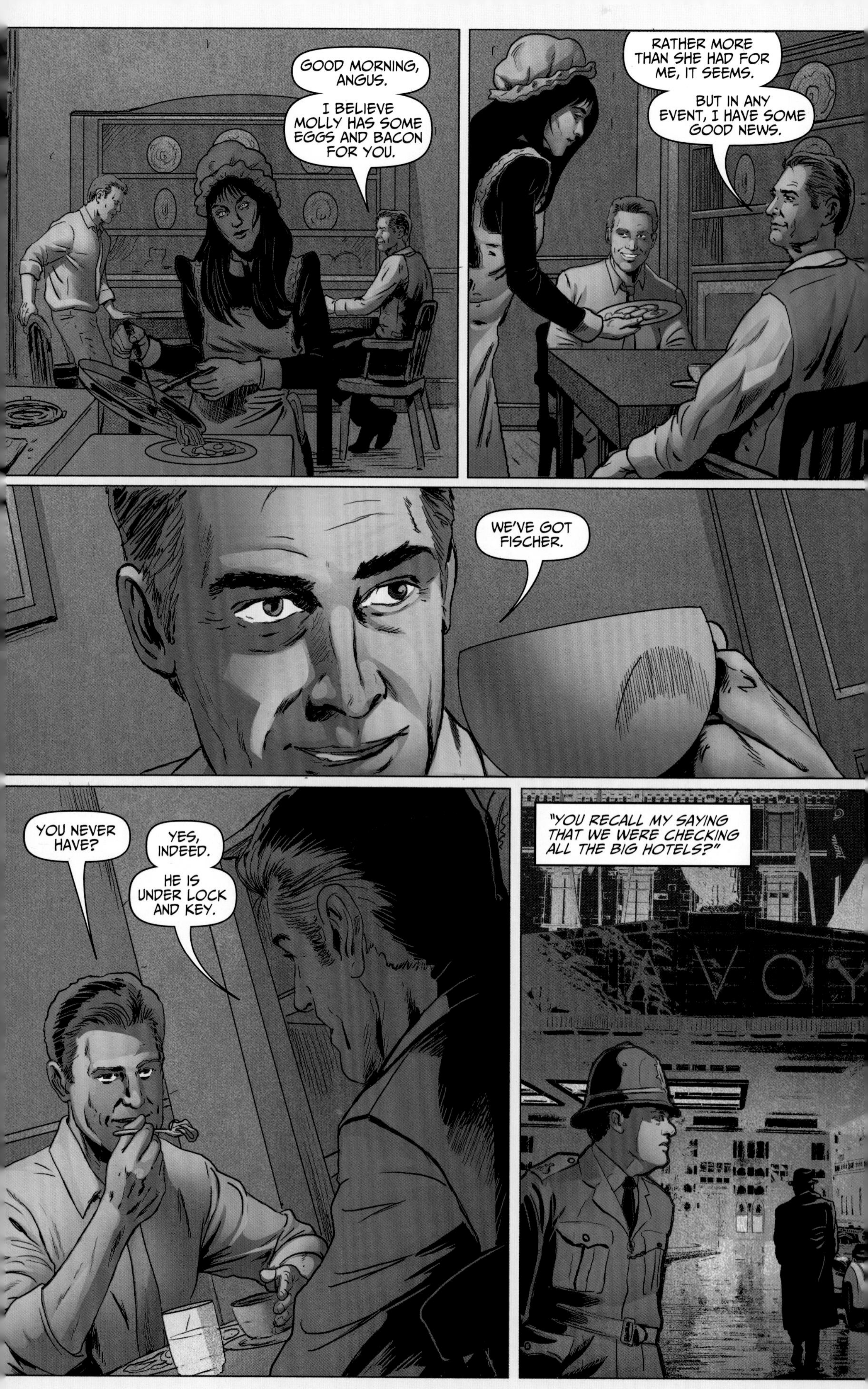
GOOD MORNING, ANGUS.
I BELIEVE MOLLY HAS SOME EGGS AND BACON FOR YOU.
RATHER MORE THAN SHE HAD FOR ME, IT SEEMS.
BUT IN ANY EVENT, I HAVE SOME GOOD NEWS.
WE'VE GOT FISCHER.
YOU NEVER HAVE?
YES, INDEED.
HE IS UNDER LOCK AND KEY.
"YOU RECALL MY SAYING THAT WE WERE CHECKING ALL THE BIG HOTELS?"

"WELL, OUR BOYS TURNED UP TRUMPS."

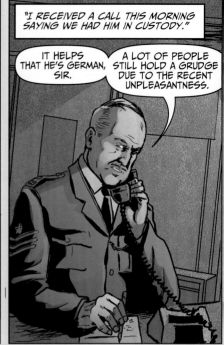

"I RECEIVED A CALL THIS MORNING SAYING WE HAD HIM IN CUSTODY."

IT HELPS THAT HE'S GERMAN, SIR.

A LOT OF PEOPLE STILL HOLD A GRUDGE DUE TO THE RECENT UNPLEASANTNESS.

GREAT WORK, TOM.

GLAD WE COULD HELP.

NOW, I BELIEVE MOLLY HAS SOMETHING SHE WANTS US TO LOOK AT.

OR, RATHER, TO LOOK INTO.

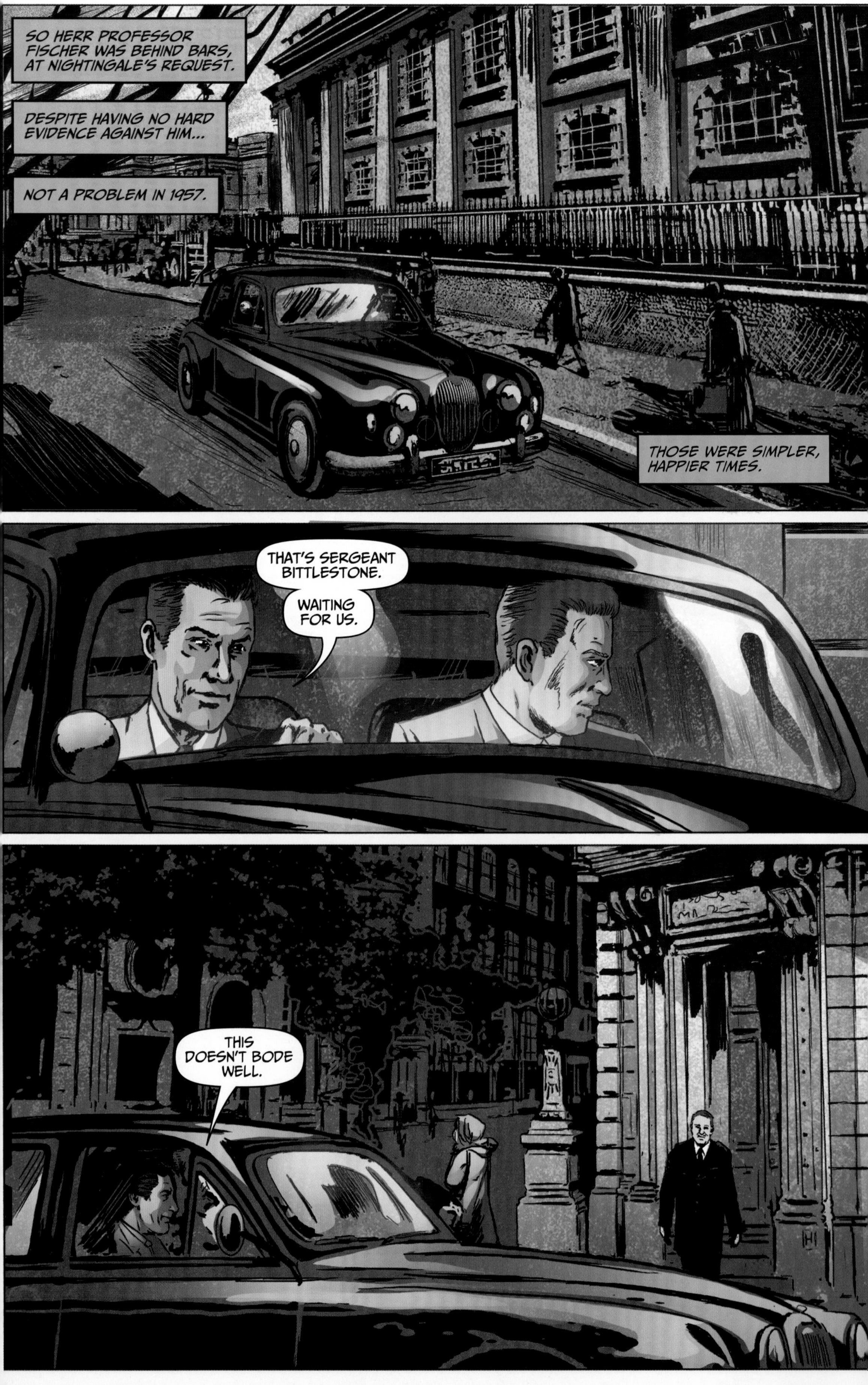
SO HERR PROFESSOR FISCHER WAS BEHIND BARS, AT NIGHTINGALE'S REQUEST.
DESPITE HAVING NO HARD EVIDENCE AGAINST HIM...
NOT A PROBLEM IN 1957.
THOSE WERE SIMPLER, HAPPIER TIMES.
THAT'S SERGEANT BITTLESTONE.
WAITING FOR US.
THIS DOESN'T BODE WELL.

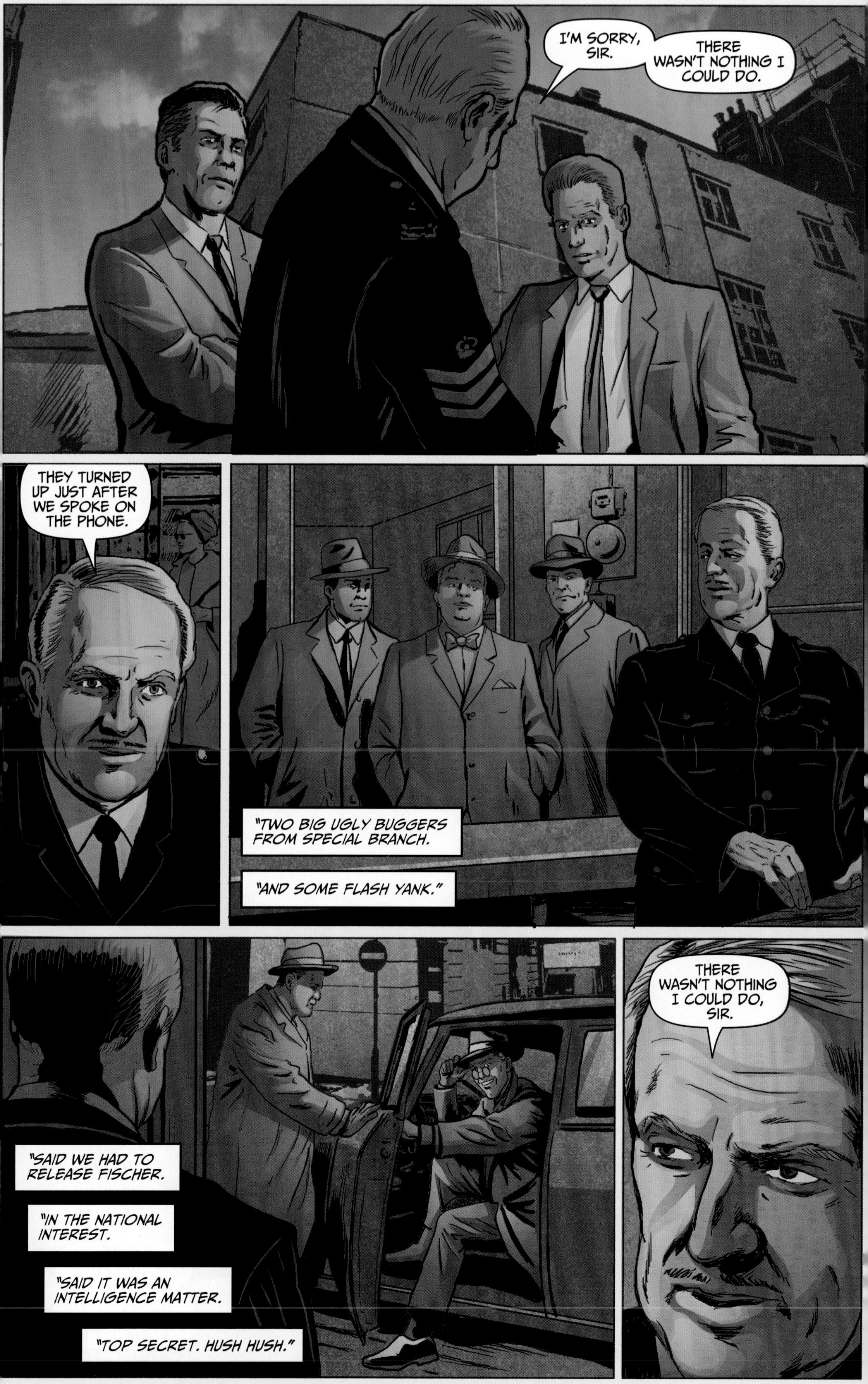
I'M SORRY, SIR.
THERE WASN'T NOTHING I COULD DO.
THEY TURNED UP JUST AFTER WE SPOKE ON THE PHONE.
"TWO BIG UGLY BUGGERS FROM SPECIAL BRANCH.
"AND SOME FLASH YANK."
"SAID WE HAD TO RELEASE FISCHER.
"IN THE NATIONAL INTEREST.
"SAID IT WAS AN INTELLIGENCE MATTER.
"TOP SECRET. HUSH HUSH."
THERE WASN'T NOTHING I COULD DO, SIR.

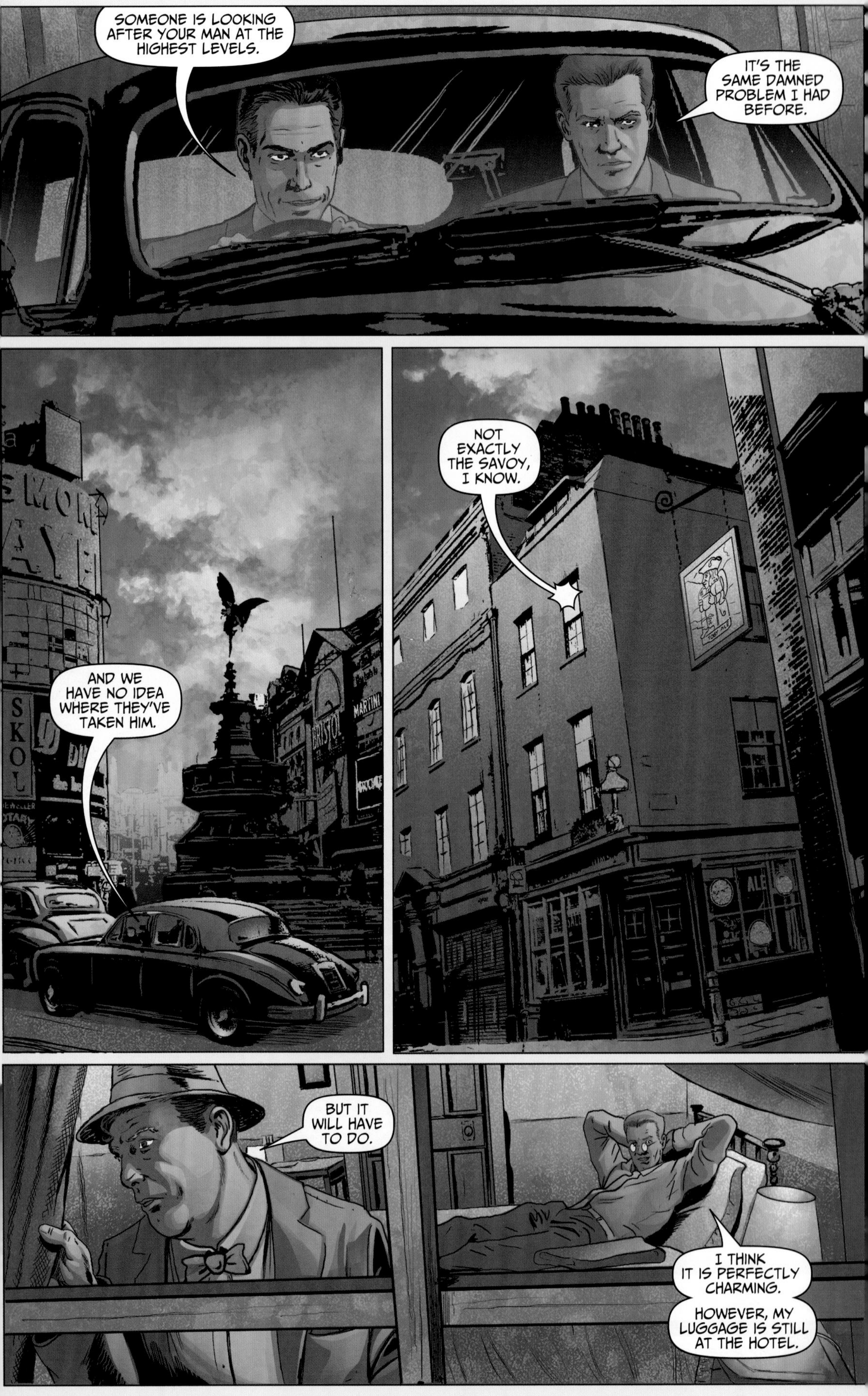
SOMEONE IS LOOKING AFTER YOUR MAN AT THE HIGHEST LEVELS.
IT'S THE SAME DAMNED PROBLEM I HAD BEFORE.
AND WE HAVE NO IDEA WHERE THEY'VE TAKEN HIM.
NOT EXACTLY THE SAVOY, I KNOW.
BUT IT WILL HAVE TO DO.
I THINK IT IS PERFECTLY CHARMING.
HOWEVER, MY LUGGAGE IS STILL AT THE HOTEL.

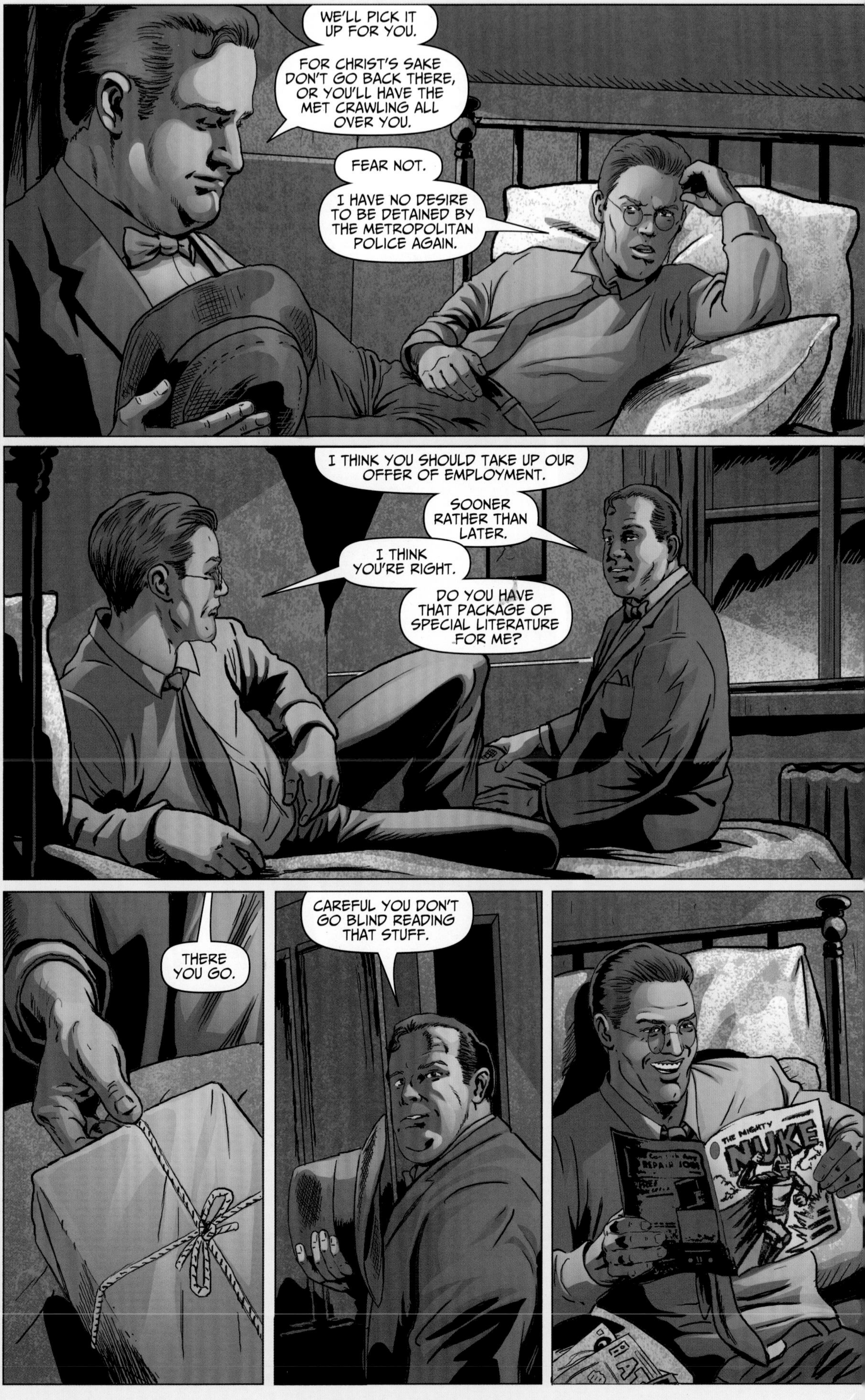
WE'LL PICK IT UP FOR YOU.
FOR CHRIST'S SAKE DON'T GO BACK THERE, OR YOU'LL HAVE THE MET CRAWLING ALL OVER YOU.
FEAR NOT.
I HAVE NO DESIRE TO BE DETAINED BY THE METROPOLITAN POLICE AGAIN.
I THINK YOU SHOULD TAKE UP OUR OFFER OF EMPLOYMENT.
SOONER RATHER THAN LATER.
I THINK YOU'RE RIGHT.
DO YOU HAVE THAT PACKAGE OF SPECIAL LITERATURE FOR ME?
THERE YOU GO.
CAREFUL YOU DON'T GO BLIND READING THAT STUFF.
THE MIGHTY
NUKE

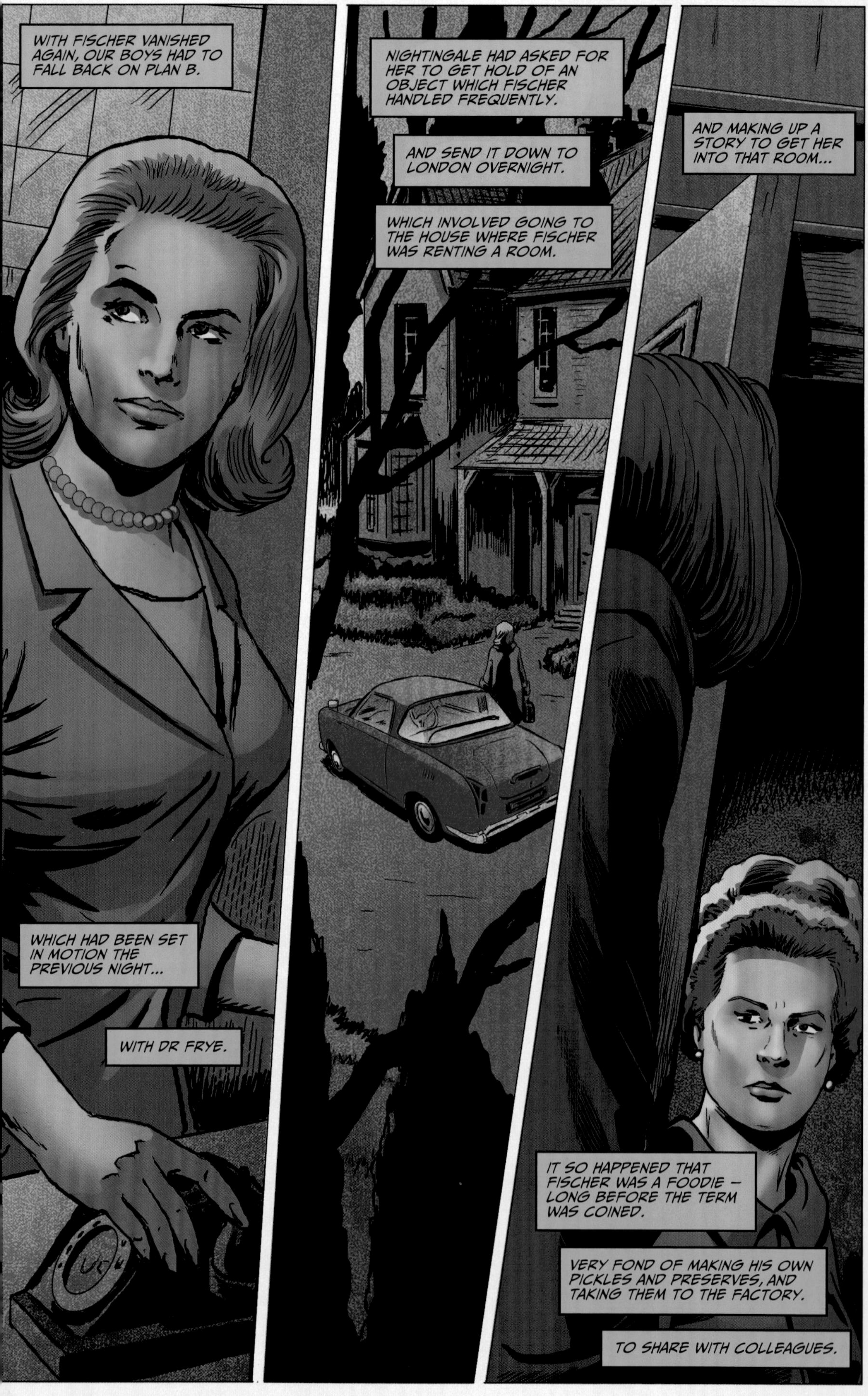
WITH FISCHER VANISHED AGAIN, OUR BOYS HAD TO FALL BACK ON PLAN B.
WHICH HAD BEEN SET IN MOTION THE PREVIOUS NIGHT...
WITH DR FRYE.
NIGHTINGALE HAD ASKED FOR HER TO GET HOLD OF AN OBJECT WHICH FISCHER HANDLED FREQUENTLY.
AND SEND IT DOWN TO LONDON OVERNIGHT.
WHICH INVOLVED GOING TO THE HOUSE WHERE FISCHER WAS RENTING A ROOM.
AND MAKING UP A STORY TO GET HER INTO THAT ROOM...
IT SO HAPPENED THAT FISCHER WAS A FOODIE – LONG BEFORE THE TERM WAS COINED.
VERY FOND OF MAKING HIS OWN PICKLES AND PRESERVES, AND TAKING THEM TO THE FACTORY.
TO SHARE WITH COLLEAGUES.

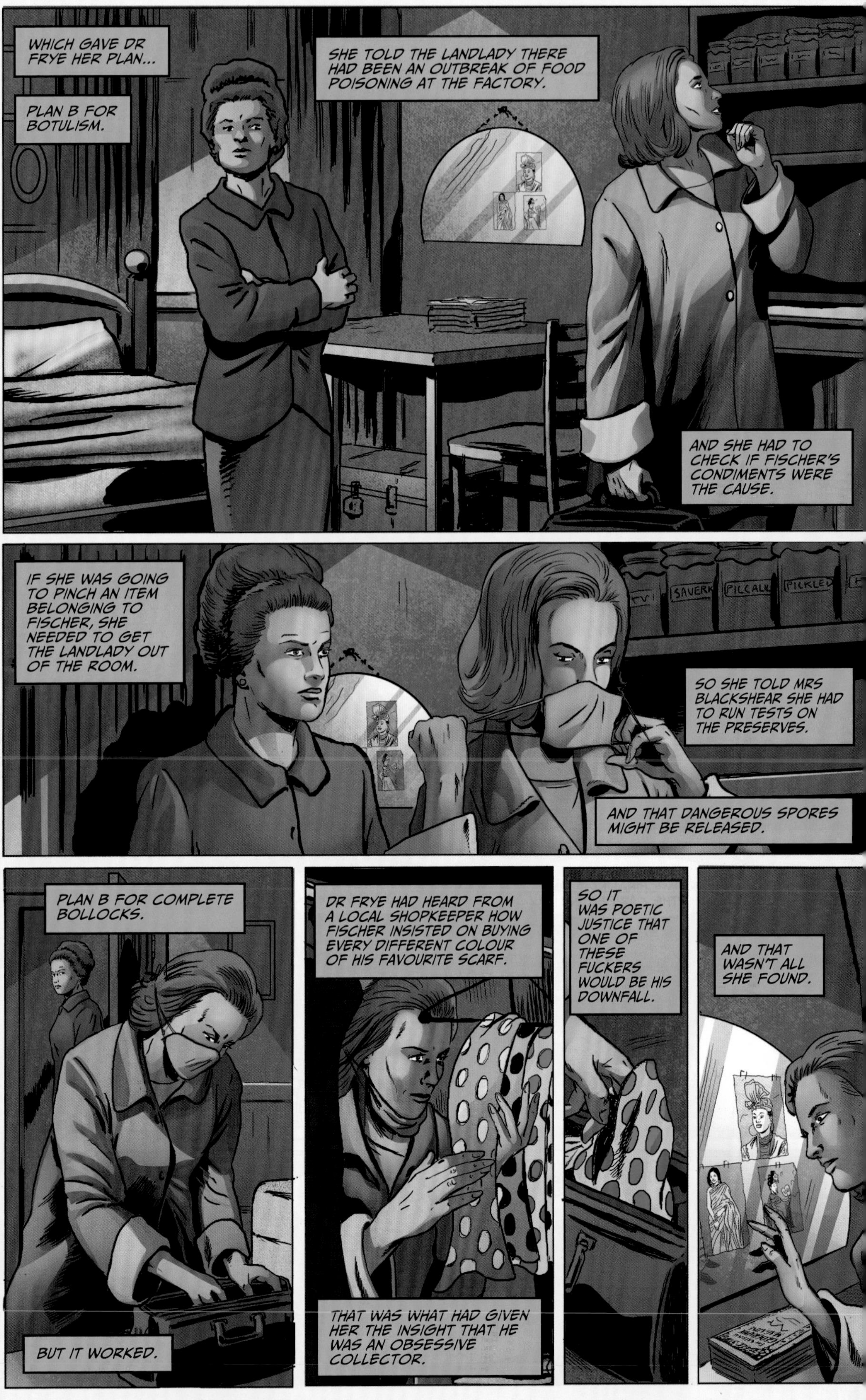
WHICH GAVE DR FRYE HER PLAN...
PLAN B FOR BOTULISM.
SHE TOLD THE LANDLADY THERE HAD BEEN AN OUTBREAK OF FOOD POISONING AT THE FACTORY.
AND SHE HAD TO CHECK IF FISCHER'S CONDIMENTS WERE THE CAUSE.
IF SHE WAS GOING TO PINCH AN ITEM BELONGING TO FISCHER, SHE NEEDED TO GET THE LANDLADY OUT OF THE ROOM.
SAVERK
PICCALILI
PICKLED
SO SHE TOLD MRS BLACKSHEAR SHE HAD TO RUN TESTS ON THE PRESERVES.
AND THAT DANGEROUS SPORES MIGHT BE RELEASED.
PLAN B FOR COMPLETE BOLLOCKS.
BUT IT WORKED.
DR FRYE HAD HEARD FROM A LOCAL SHOPKEEPER HOW FISCHER INSISTED ON BUYING EVERY DIFFERENT COLOUR OF HIS FAVOURITE SCARF.
THAT WAS WHAT HAD GIVEN HER THE INSIGHT THAT HE WAS AN OBSESSIVE COLLECTOR.
SO IT WAS POETIC JUSTICE THAT ONE OF THESE FUCKERS WOULD BE HIS DOWNFALL.
AND THAT WASN'T ALL SHE FOUND.

ANYWAY, THE SCARF DR FRYE HAD NICKED WAS SOON ON ITS WAY TO LONDON...

MEANWHILE SHE PHONED THE FOLLY TO TALK TO STRALLEN.

AND TELL HIM EVERYTHING SHE'D SEEN.

INCLUDING THE CREEPY 'GIRLS OF THE WORLD' COLLAGE...

YOUNG WOMEN FROM CHINA, INDIA, AND THE CARIBBEAN?

PRETTY YOUNG WOMEN.

AND YOU SAY HE'S A FOOD LOVER?

FANCIES HIMSELF A GOURMET.

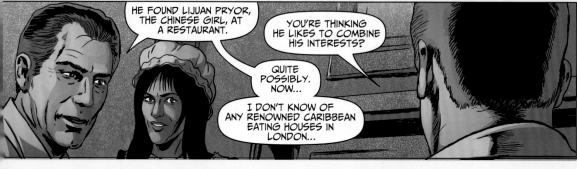

HE FOUND LIJUAN PRYOR, THE CHINESE GIRL, AT A RESTAURANT.

YOU'RE THINKING HE LIKES TO COMBINE HIS INTERESTS?

QUITE POSSIBLY. NOW...

I DON'T KNOW OF ANY RENOWNED CARIBBEAN EATING HOUSES IN LONDON...

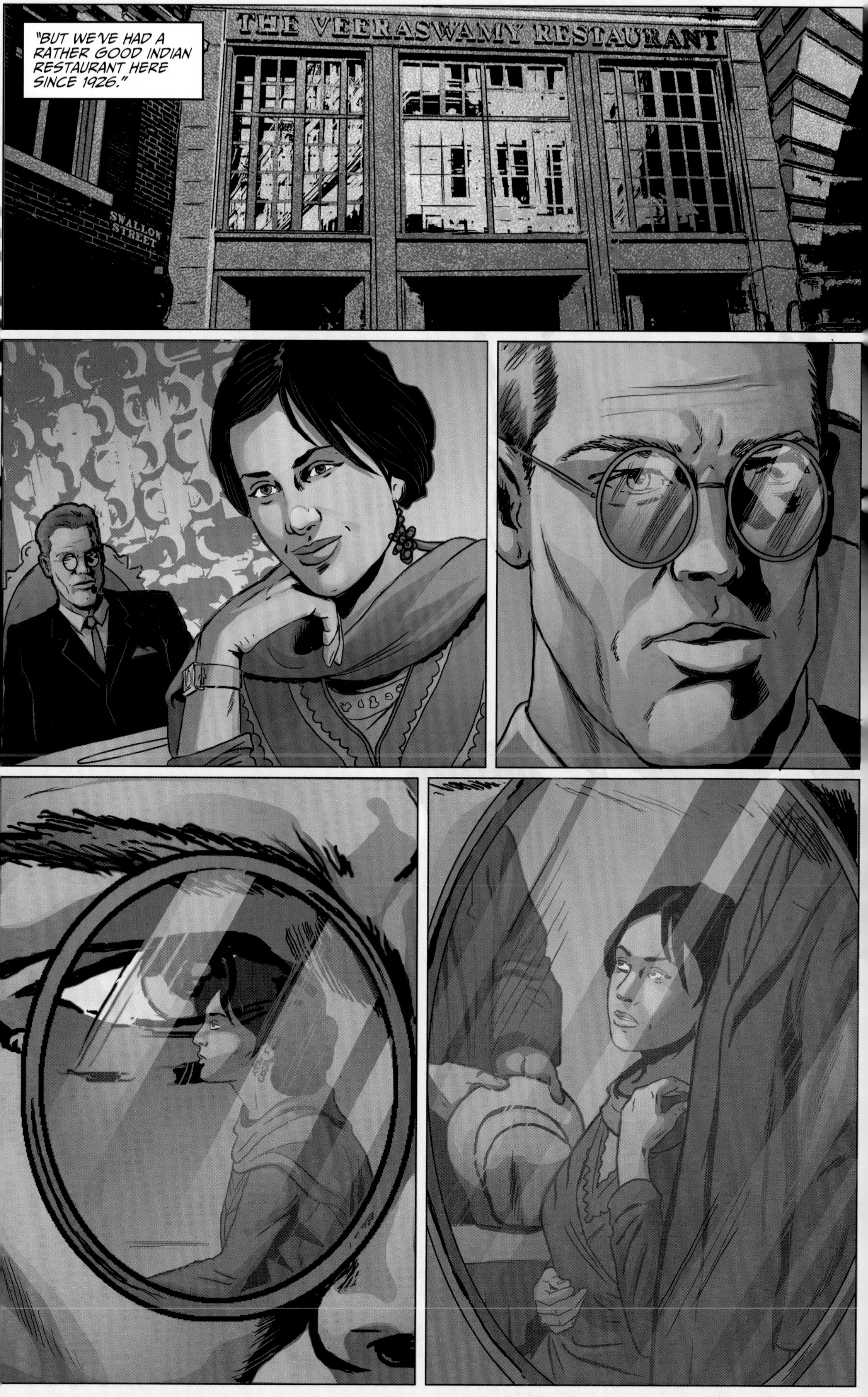
"BUT WE'VE HAD A RATHER GOOD INDIAN RESTAURANT HERE SINCE 1926."
THE VEERASWAMY RESTAURANT
SWALLOW STREET

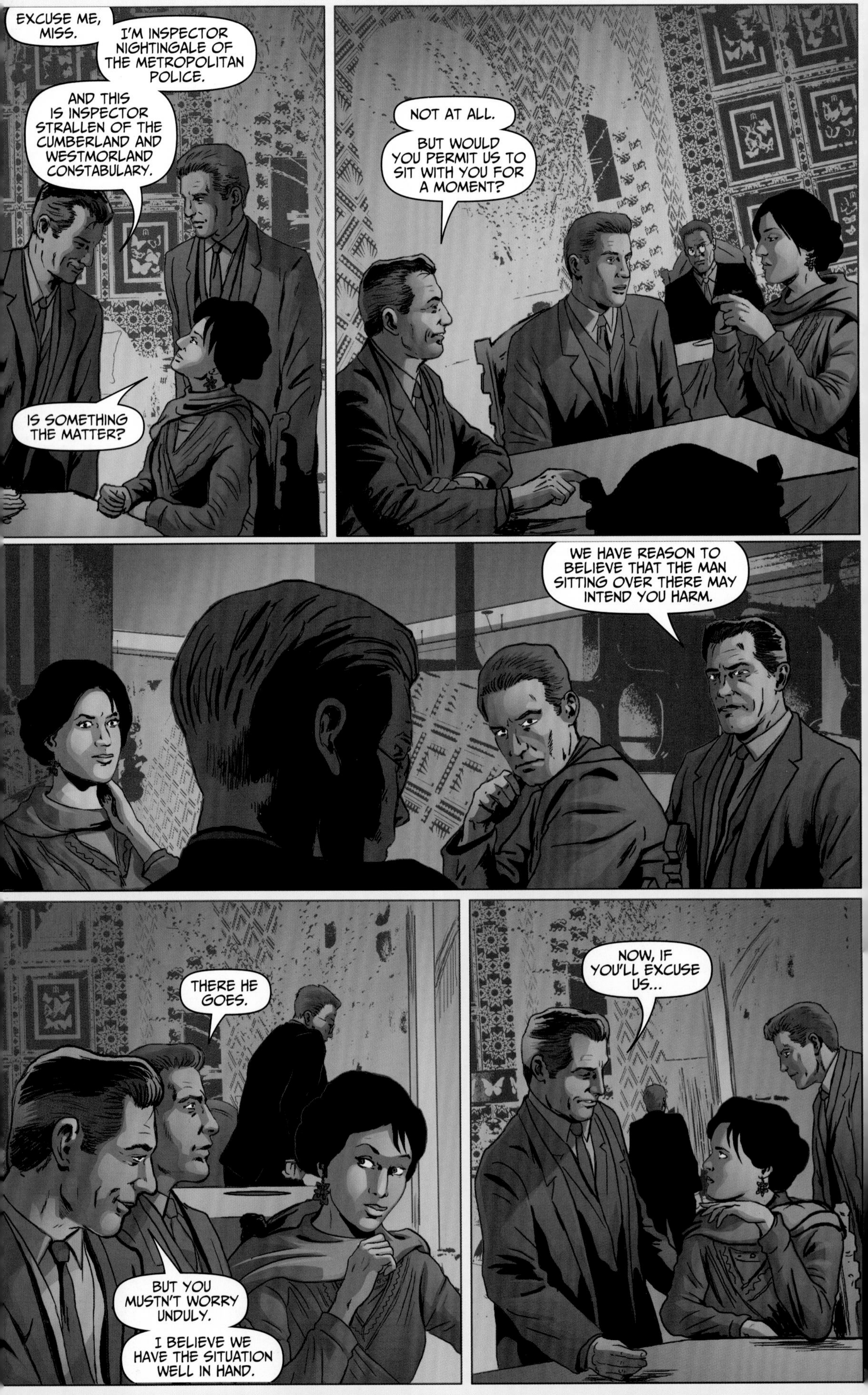
EXCUSE ME, MISS.
I'M INSPECTOR NIGHTINGALE OF THE METROPOLITAN POLICE.
AND THIS IS INSPECTOR STRALLEN OF THE CUMBERLAND AND WESTMORLAND CONSTABULARY.
IS SOMETHING THE MATTER?
NOT AT ALL.
BUT WOULD YOU PERMIT US TO SIT WITH YOU FOR A MOMENT?
WE HAVE REASON TO BELIEVE THAT THE MAN SITTING OVER THERE MAY INTEND YOU HARM.
THERE HE GOES.
BUT YOU MUSTN'T WORRY UNDULY.
I BELIEVE WE HAVE THE SITUATION WELL IN HAND.
NOW, IF YOU'LL EXCUSE US...

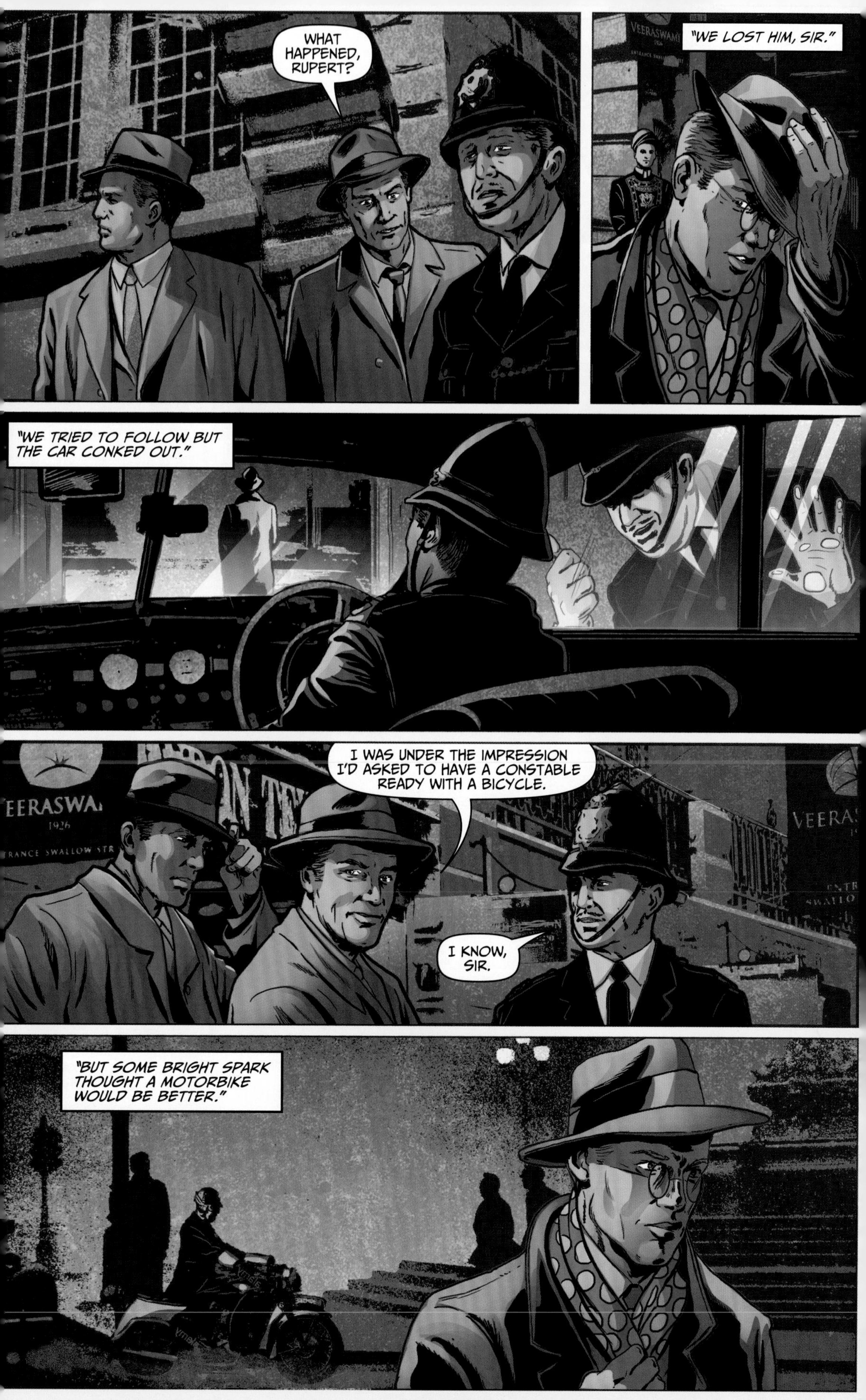
WHAT HAPPENED, RUPERT?
"WE LOST HIM, SIR."
"WE TRIED TO FOLLOW BUT THE CAR CONKED OUT."
I WAS UNDER THE IMPRESSION I'D ASKED TO HAVE A CONSTABLE READY WITH A BICYCLE.
I KNOW, SIR.
"BUT SOME BRIGHT SPARK THOUGHT A MOTORBIKE WOULD BE BETTER."

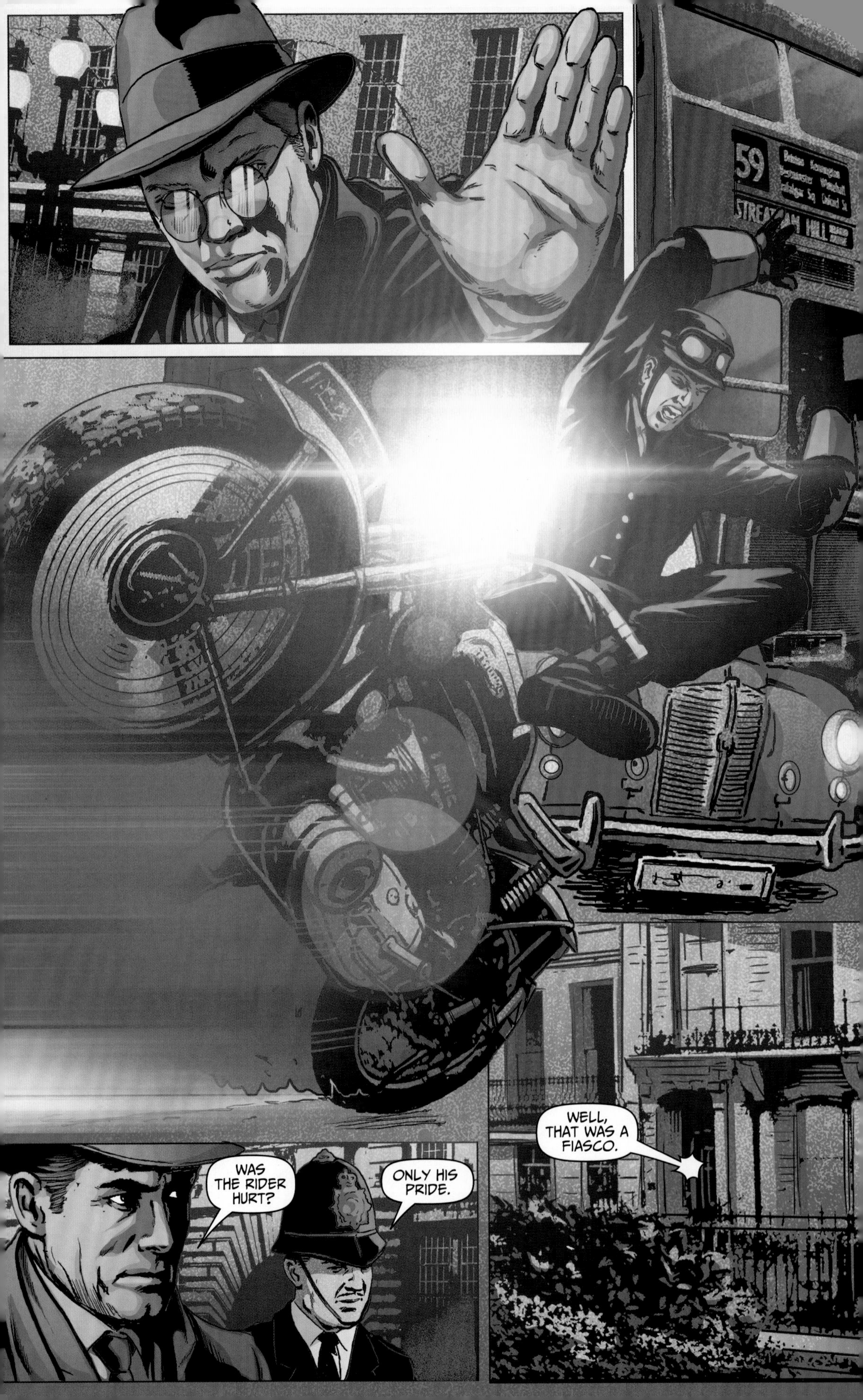
59
WAS THE RIDER HURT?
ONLY HIS PRIDE.
WELL, THAT WAS A FIASCO.

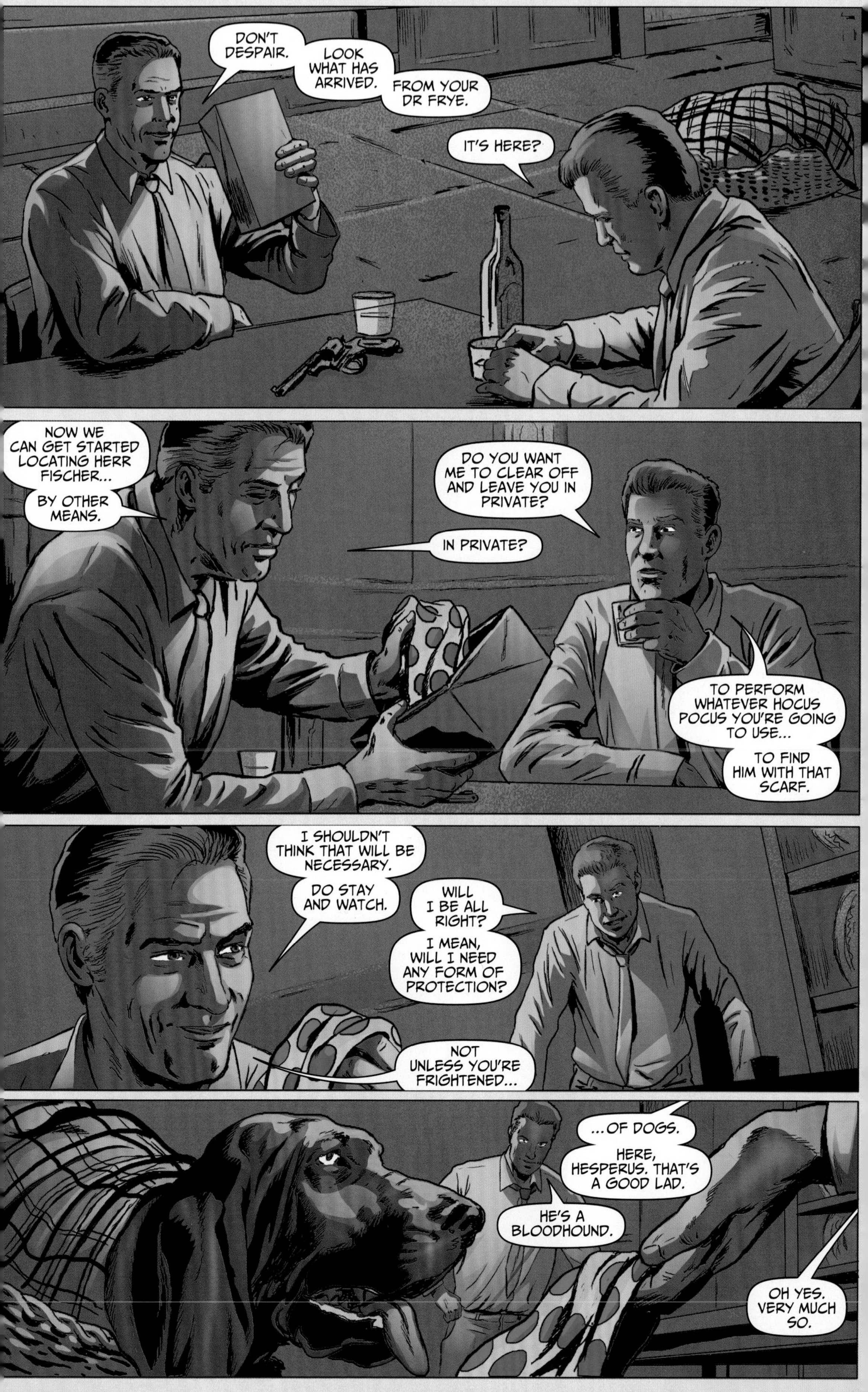
DON'T DESPAIR.
LOOK WHAT HAS ARRIVED.
FROM YOUR DR FRYE.
IT'S HERE?
NOW WE CAN GET STARTED LOCATING HERR FISCHER...
BY OTHER MEANS.
DO YOU WANT ME TO CLEAR OFF AND LEAVE YOU IN PRIVATE?
IN PRIVATE?
TO PERFORM WHATEVER HOCUS POCUS YOU'RE GOING TO USE...
TO FIND HIM WITH THAT SCARF.
I SHOULDN'T THINK THAT WILL BE NECESSARY.
DO STAY AND WATCH.
WILL I BE ALL RIGHT?
I MEAN, WILL I NEED ANY FORM OF PROTECTION?
NOT UNLESS YOU'RE FRIGHTENED...
...OF DOGS.
HERE, HESPERUS. THAT'S A GOOD LAD.
HE'S A BLOODHOUND.
OH YES. VERY MUCH SO.

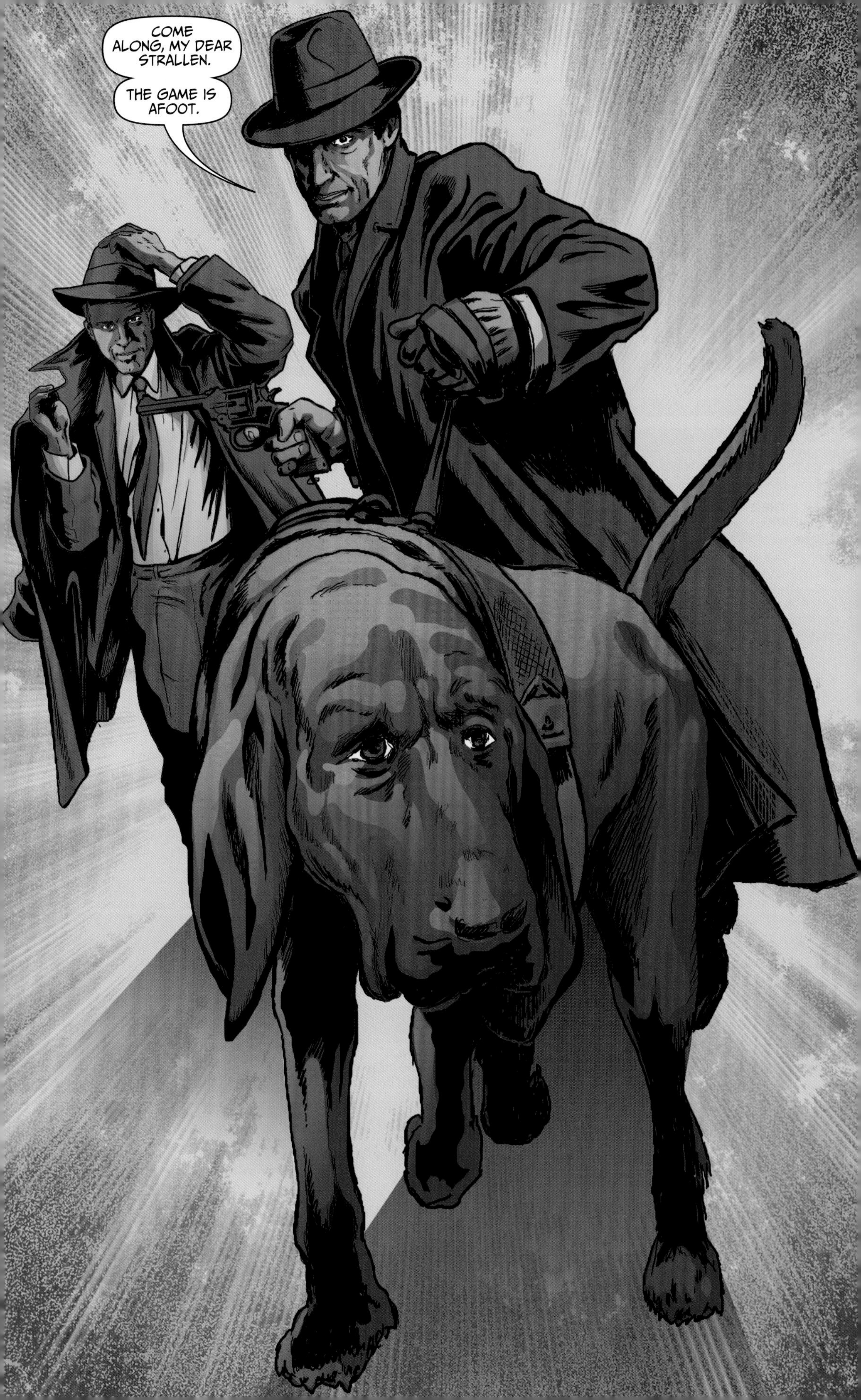
COME ALONG, MY DEAR STRALLEN.
THE GAME IS AFOOT.

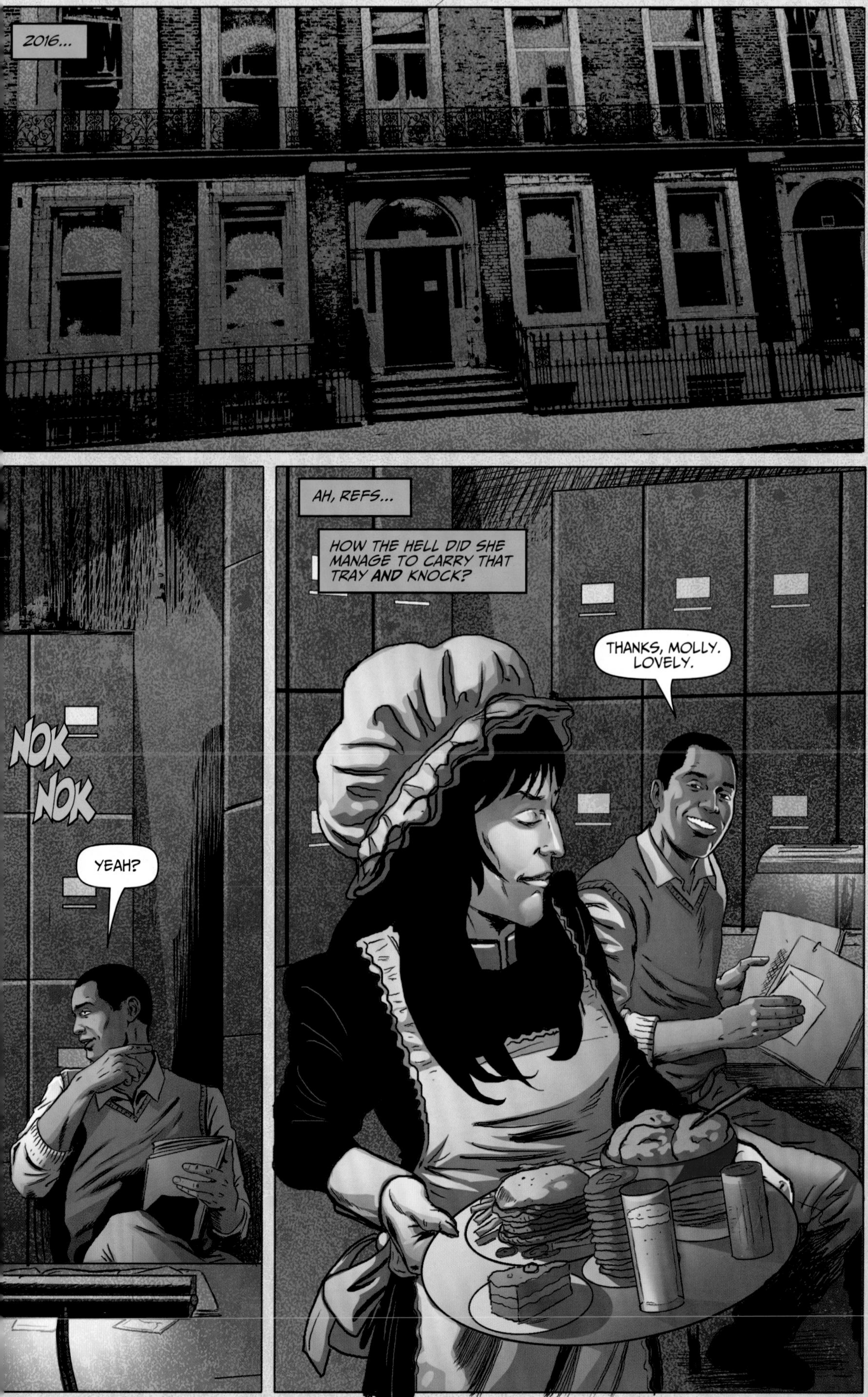
2016...
NOK NOK
YEAH?
AH, REFS...
HOW THE HELL DID SHE MANAGE TO CARRY THAT TRAY AND KNOCK?
THANKS, MOLLY. LOVELY.

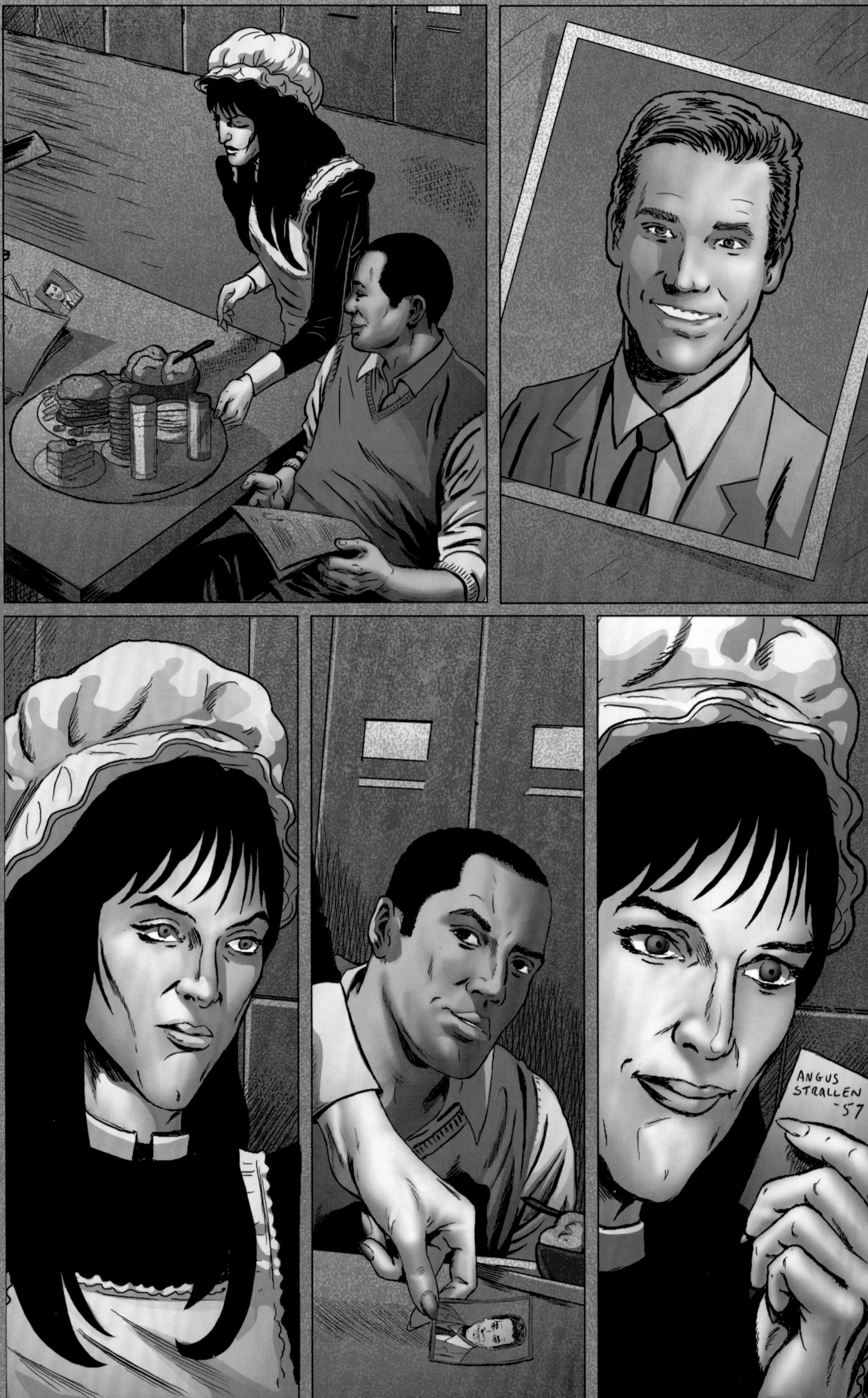
ANGUS
STRALLEN
-57

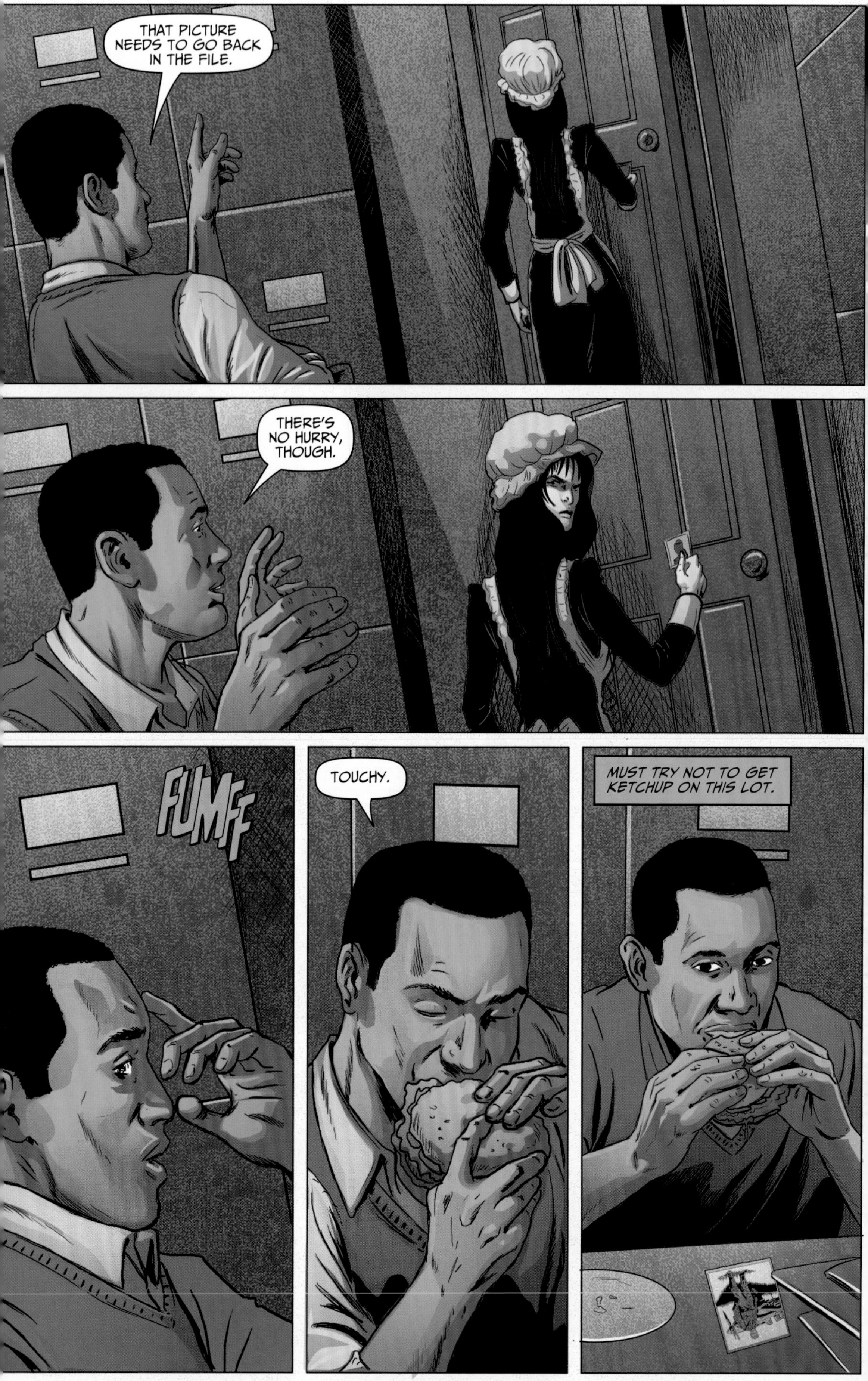
THAT PICTURE NEEDS TO GO BACK IN THE FILE.
THERE'S NO HURRY, THOUGH.
FUMFF
TOUCHY.
MUST TRY NOT TO GET KETCHUP ON THIS LOT.

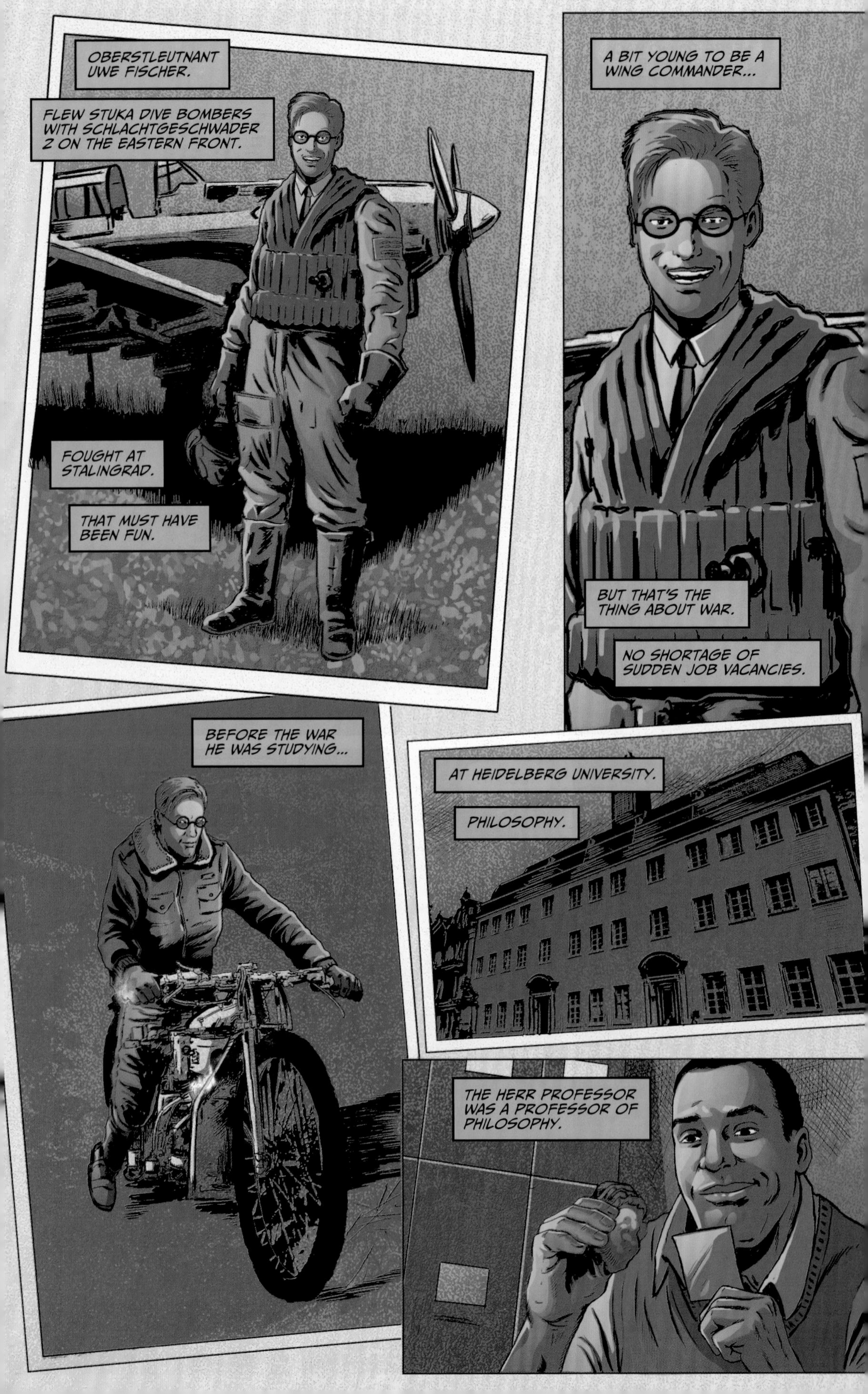
OBERSTLEUTNANT UWE FISCHER.
FLEW STUKA DIVE BOMBERS WITH SCHLACHTGESCHWADER 2 ON THE EASTERN FRONT.
FOUGHT AT STALINGRAD.
THAT MUST HAVE BEEN FUN.
A BIT YOUNG TO BE A WING COMMANDER...
BUT THAT'S THE THING ABOUT WAR.
NO SHORTAGE OF SUDDEN JOB VACANCIES.
BEFORE THE WAR HE WAS STUDYING...
AT HEIDELBERG UNIVERSITY.
PHILOSOPHY.
THE HERR PROFESSOR WAS A PROFESSOR OF PHILOSOPHY.

NOT PHYSICS OR CHEMISTRY OR MATHEMATICS.

PHILOSOPHY.

WHICH SUGGESTS THAT HIS "HIGH SECURITY CLEARANCE DEFENCE WORK" WAS NOTHING TO DO WITH HIS ACADEMIC BACKGROUND...

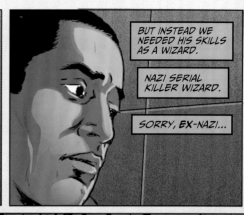

BUT INSTEAD WE NEEDED HIS SKILLS AS A WIZARD.

NAZI SERIAL KILLER WIZARD.

SORRY, EX-NAZI...

NO WONDER THE GOVERNOR WAS SO EAGER TO NAIL THE BASTARD.

NEVER MESS WITH THE NIGHTINGALE.

ESPECIALLY WHEN HE HAS HELP FROM MAN'S BEST FRIEND.

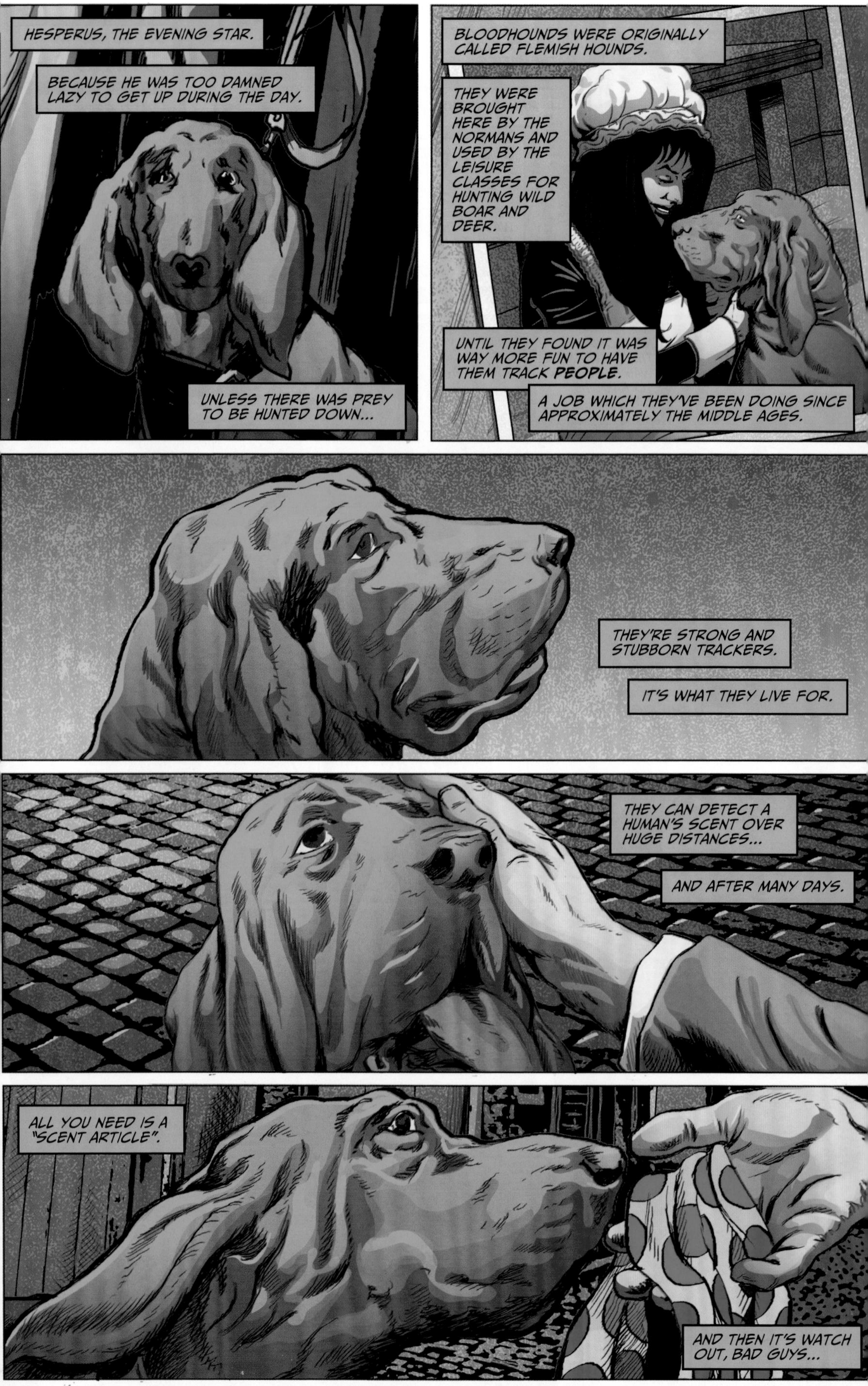
HESPERUS, THE EVENING STAR.
BECAUSE HE WAS TOO DAMNED LAZY TO GET UP DURING THE DAY.
UNLESS THERE WAS PREY TO BE HUNTED DOWN...
BLOODHOUNDS WERE ORIGINALLY CALLED FLEMISH HOUNDS.
THEY WERE BROUGHT HERE BY THE NORMANS AND USED BY THE LEISURE CLASSES FOR HUNTING WILD BOAR AND DEER.
UNTIL THEY FOUND IT WAS WAY MORE FUN TO HAVE THEM TRACK **PEOPLE**.
A JOB WHICH THEY'VE BEEN DOING SINCE APPROXIMATELY THE MIDDLE AGES.
THEY'RE STRONG AND STUBBORN TRACKERS.
IT'S WHAT THEY LIVE FOR.
THEY CAN DETECT A HUMAN'S SCENT OVER HUGE DISTANCES...
AND AFTER MANY DAYS.
ALL YOU NEED IS A "SCENT ARTICLE".
AND THEN IT'S WATCH OUT, BAD GUYS...

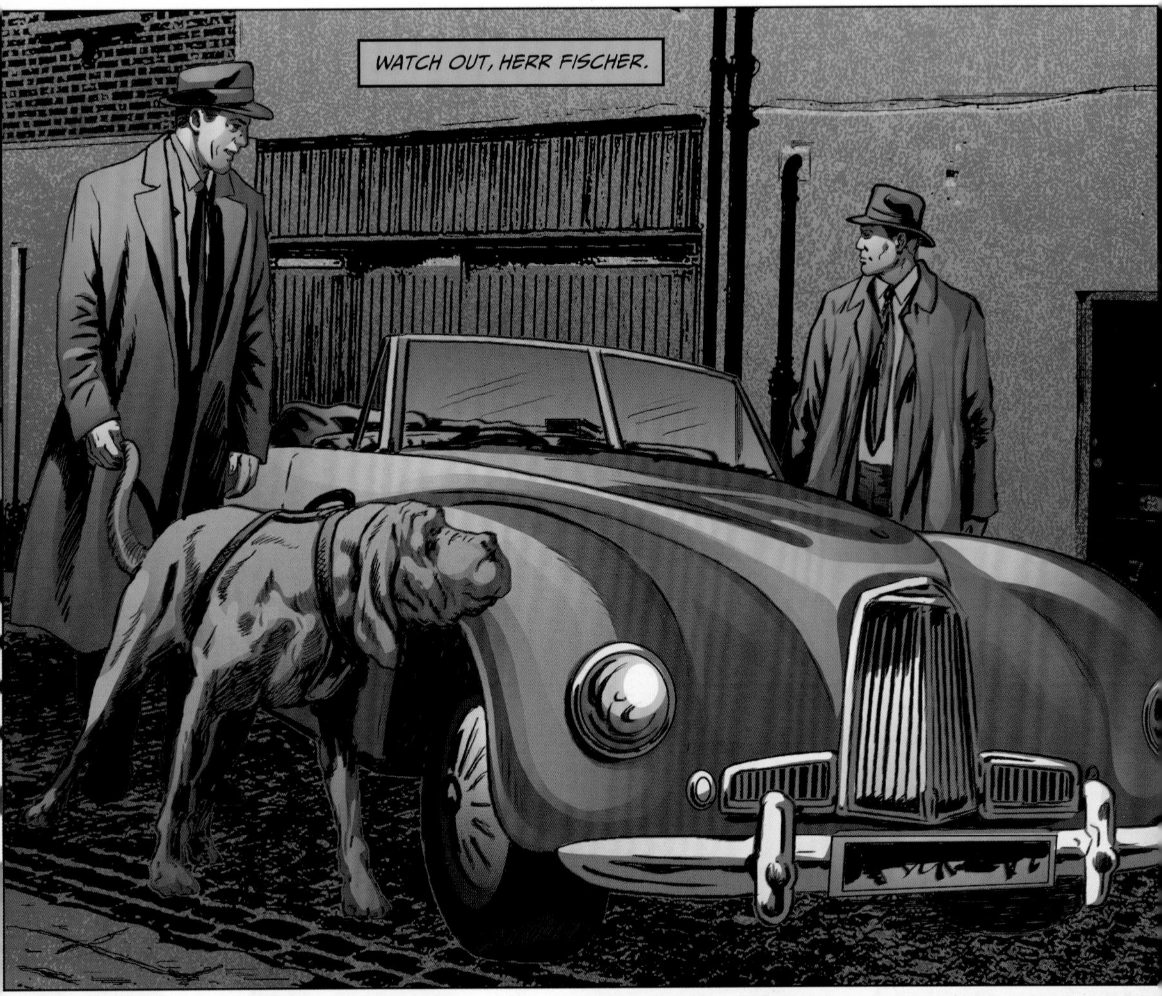
WATCH OUT, HERR FISCHER.

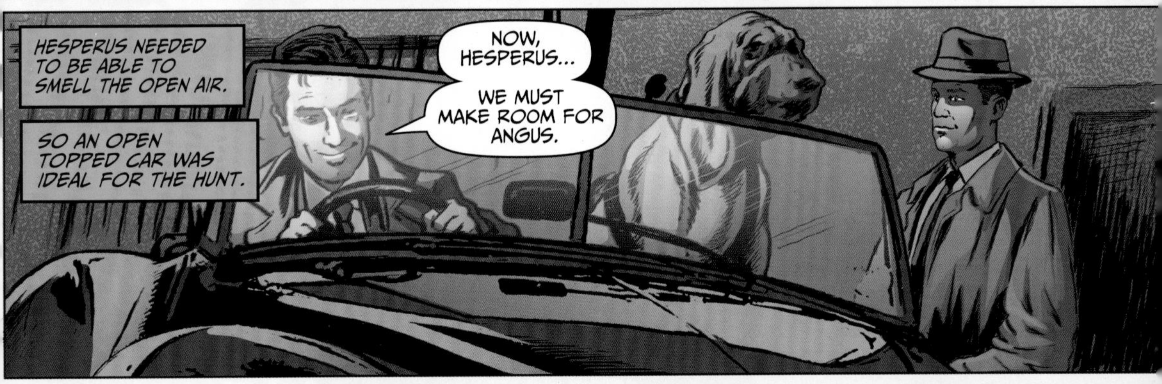
HESPERUS NEEDED TO BE ABLE TO SMELL THE OPEN AIR.
SO AN OPEN TOPPED CAR WAS IDEAL FOR THE HUNT.
NOW, HESPERUS...
WE MUST MAKE ROOM FOR ANGUS.

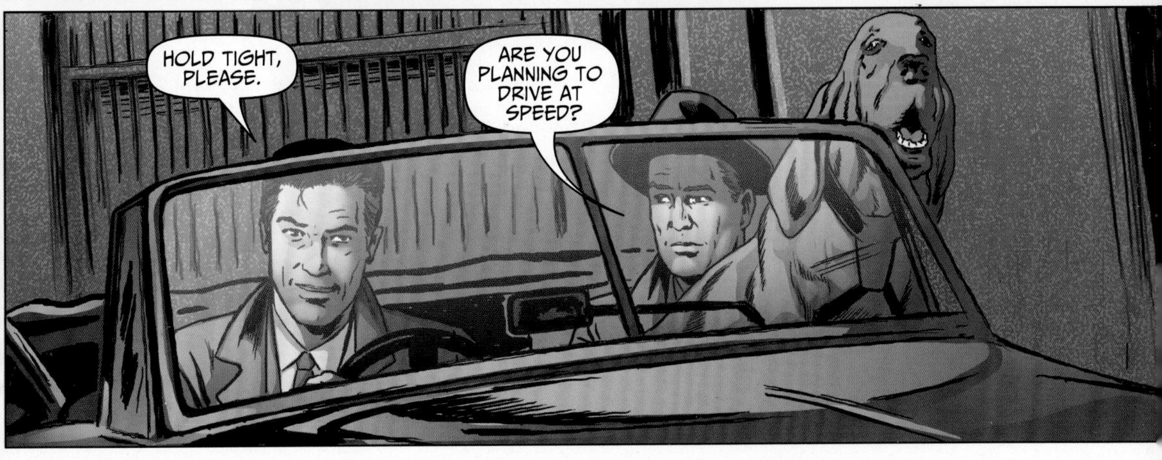
HOLD TIGHT, PLEASE.
ARE YOU PLANNING TO DRIVE AT SPEED?

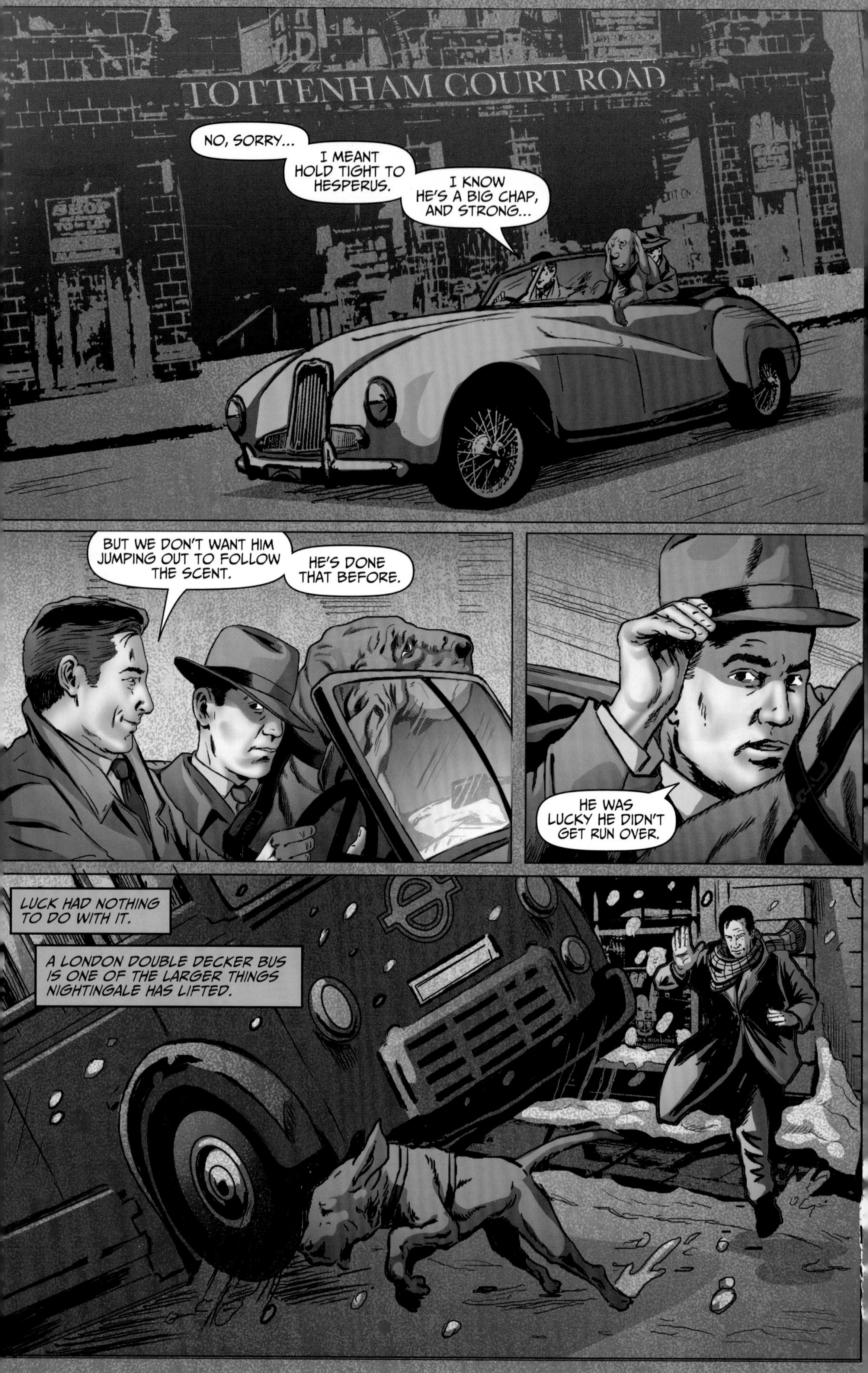

TOTTENHAM COURT ROAD
NO, SORRY...
I MEANT HOLD TIGHT TO HESPERUS.
I KNOW HE'S A BIG CHAP, AND STRONG...
BUT WE DON'T WANT HIM JUMPING OUT TO FOLLOW THE SCENT.
HE'S DONE THAT BEFORE.
HE WAS LUCKY HE DIDN'T GET RUN OVER.
LUCK HAD NOTHING TO DO WITH IT.
A LONDON DOUBLE DECKER BUS IS ONE OF THE LARGER THINGS NIGHTINGALE HAS LIFTED.

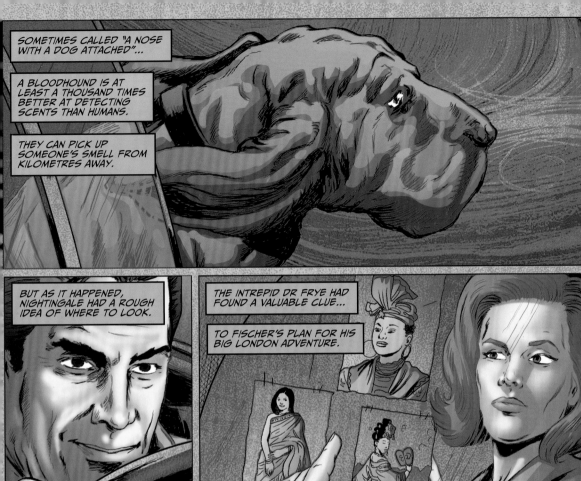

SOMETIMES CALLED "A NOSE WITH A DOG ATTACHED"...

A BLOODHOUND IS AT LEAST A THOUSAND TIMES BETTER AT DETECTING SCENTS THAN HUMANS.

THEY CAN PICK UP SOMEONE'S SMELL FROM KILOMETRES AWAY.

BUT AS IT HAPPENED, NIGHTINGALE HAD A ROUGH IDEA OF WHERE TO LOOK.

THE INTREPID DR FRYE HAD FOUND A VALUABLE CLUE...

TO FISCHER'S PLAN FOR HIS BIG LONDON ADVENTURE.

THERE WAS GOING TO BE A CHINESE WOMAN.

UNLUCKY LIJUAN PRYOR...

AND ONE FROM INDIA...

LUCKY SIMA REDDY.

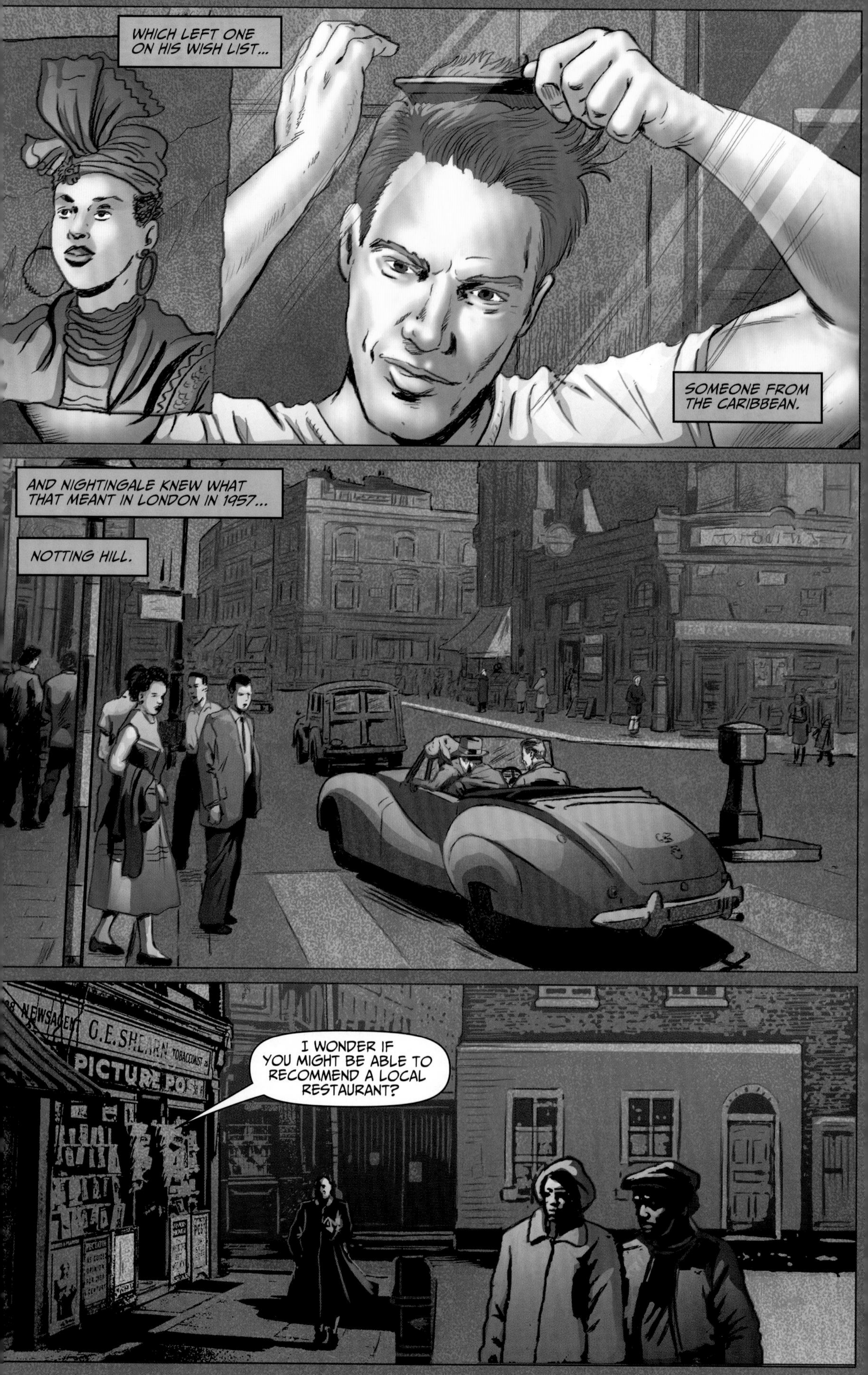
WHICH LEFT ONE ON HIS WISH LIST...
SOMEONE FROM THE CARIBBEAN.
AND NIGHTINGALE KNEW WHAT THAT MEANT IN LONDON IN 1957...
NOTTING HILL.
NEWSAGENT G.E.SHEARN TOBACCONIST
I WONDER IF YOU MIGHT BE ABLE TO RECOMMEND A LOCAL RESTAURANT?

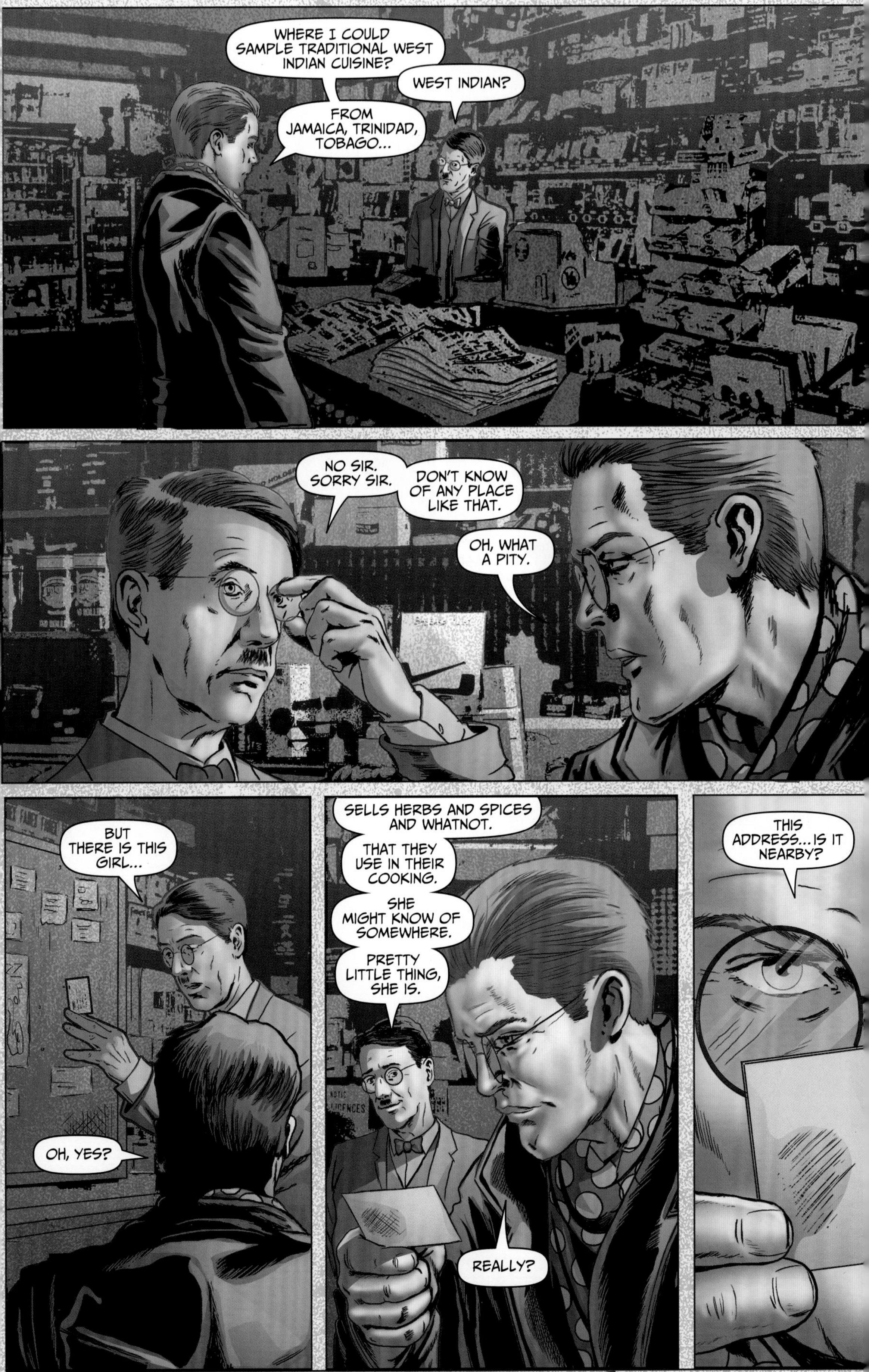
WHERE I COULD SAMPLE TRADITIONAL WEST INDIAN CUISINE?
WEST INDIAN?
FROM JAMAICA, TRINIDAD, TOBAGO...
NO SIR. SORRY SIR.
DON'T KNOW OF ANY PLACE LIKE THAT.
OH, WHAT A PITY.
BUT THERE IS THIS GIRL...
OH, YES?
SELLS HERBS AND SPICES AND WHATNOT.
THAT THEY USE IN THEIR COOKING.
SHE MIGHT KNOW OF SOMEWHERE.
PRETTY LITTLE THING, SHE IS.
REALLY?
THIS ADDRESS...IS IT NEARBY?

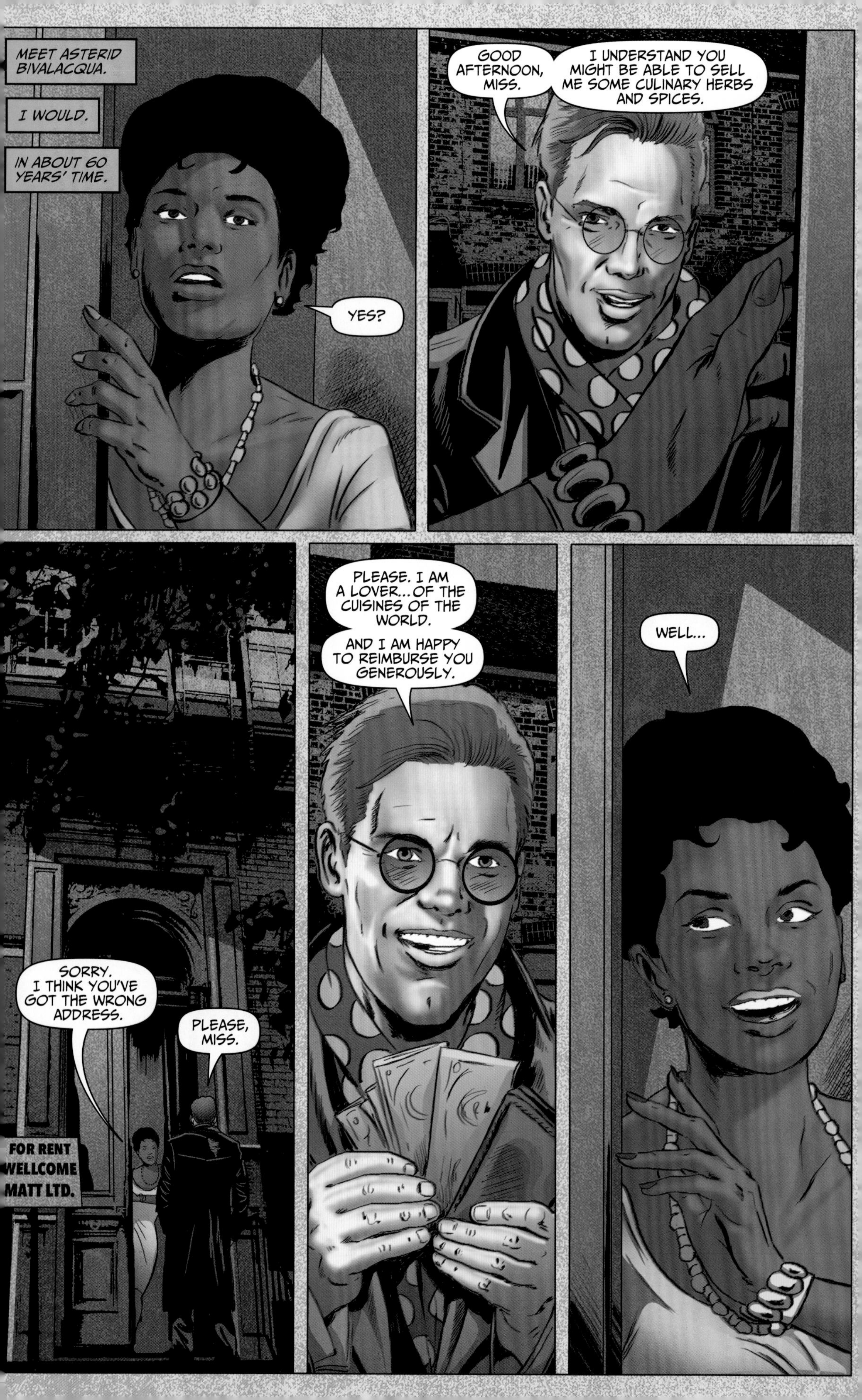
MEET ASTERID BIVALACQUA.
I WOULD.
IN ABOUT 60 YEARS' TIME.
YES?
GOOD AFTERNOON, MISS.
I UNDERSTAND YOU MIGHT BE ABLE TO SELL ME SOME CULINARY HERBS AND SPICES.
SORRY. I THINK YOU'VE GOT THE WRONG ADDRESS.
PLEASE, MISS.
FOR RENT WELLCOME MATT LTD.
PLEASE. I AM A LOVER...OF THE CUISINES OF THE WORLD.
AND I AM HAPPY TO REIMBURSE YOU GENEROUSLY.
WELL...

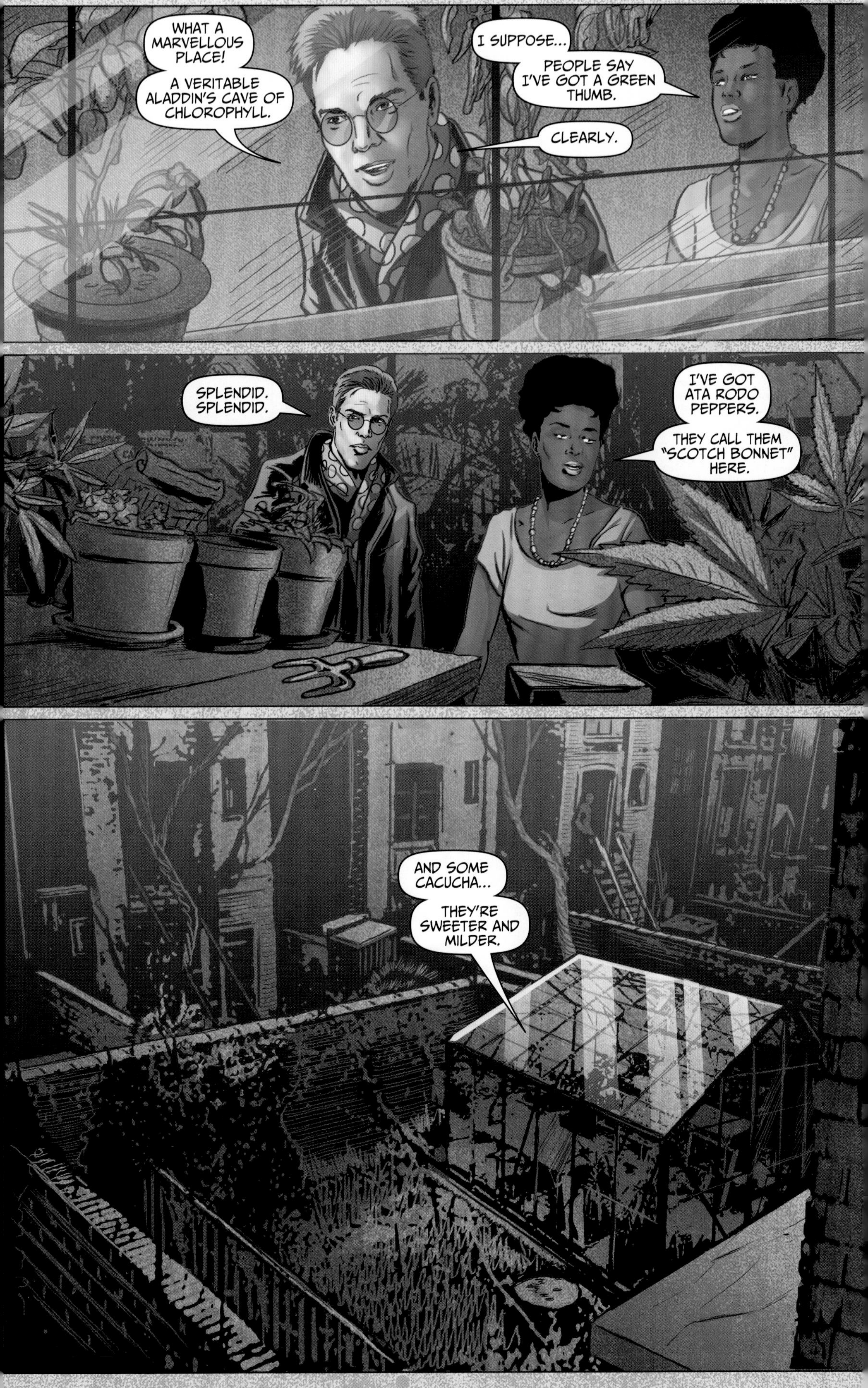
WHAT A MARVELLOUS PLACE!
A VERITABLE ALADDIN'S CAVE OF CHLOROPHYLL.
I SUPPOSE...
PEOPLE SAY I'VE GOT A GREEN THUMB.
CLEARLY.
SPLENDID. SPLENDID.
I'VE GOT ATA RODO PEPPERS.
THEY CALL THEM "SCOTCH BONNET" HERE.
AND SOME CACUCHA...
THEY'RE SWEETER AND MILDER.

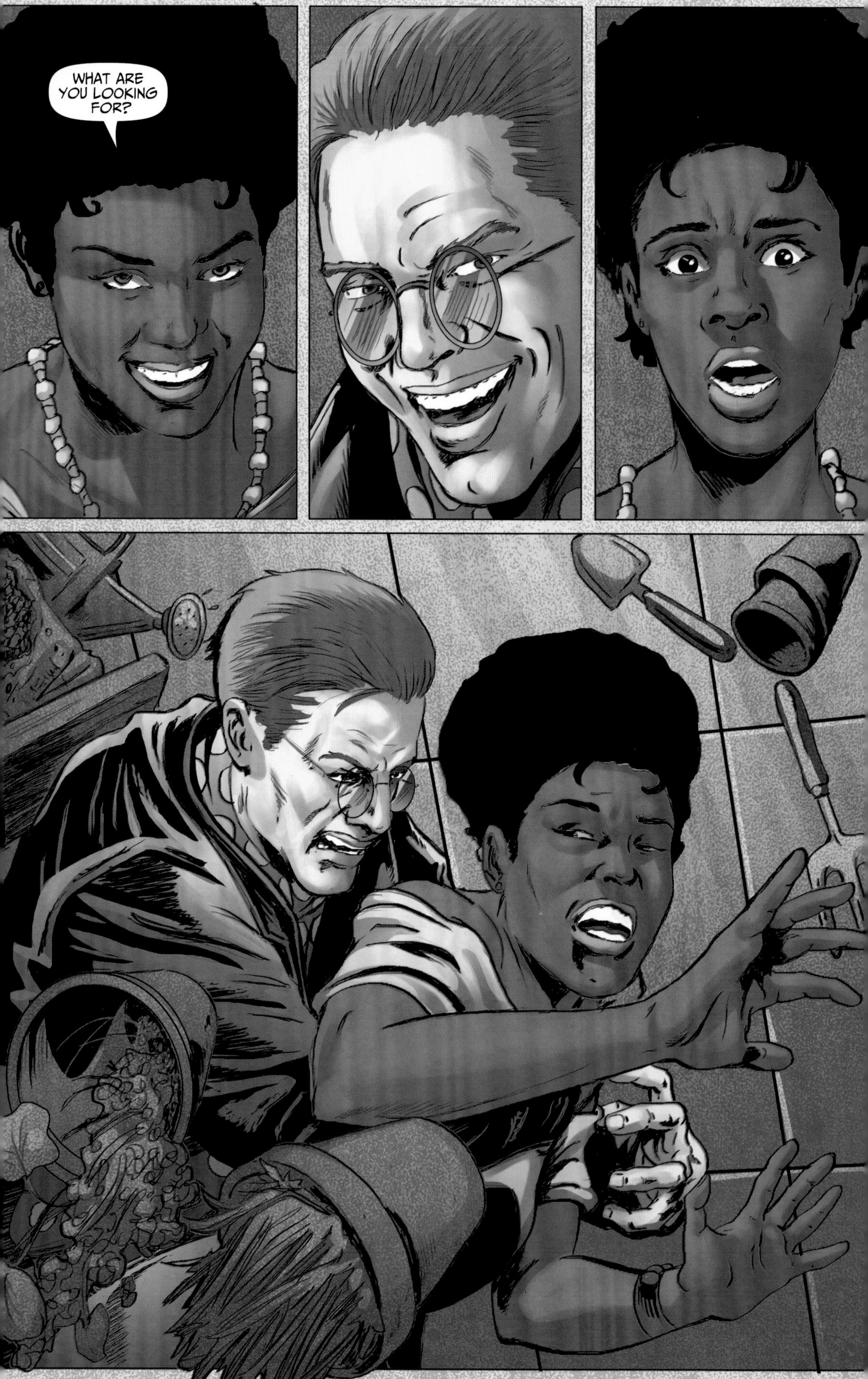
WHAT ARE YOU LOOKING FOR?

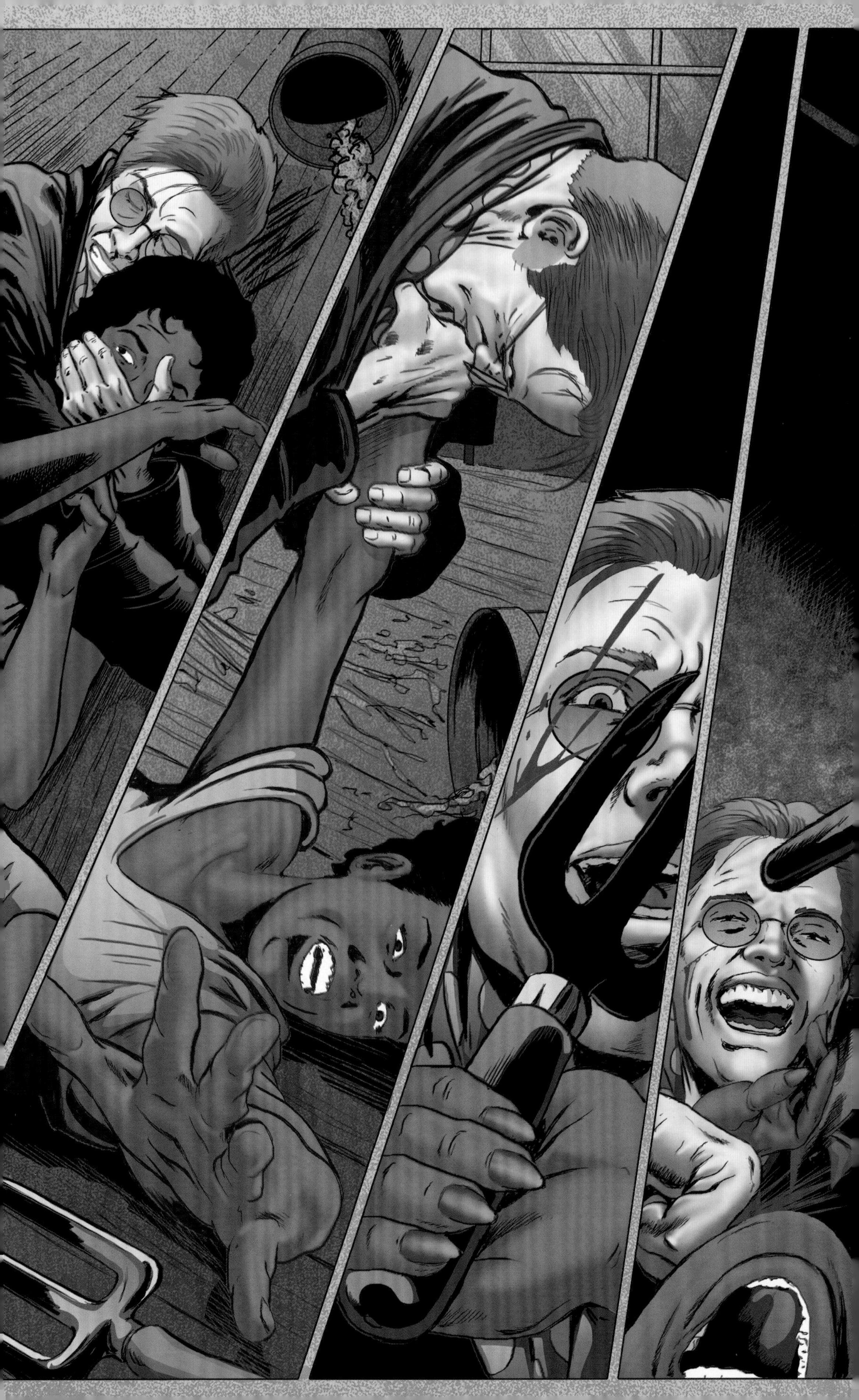

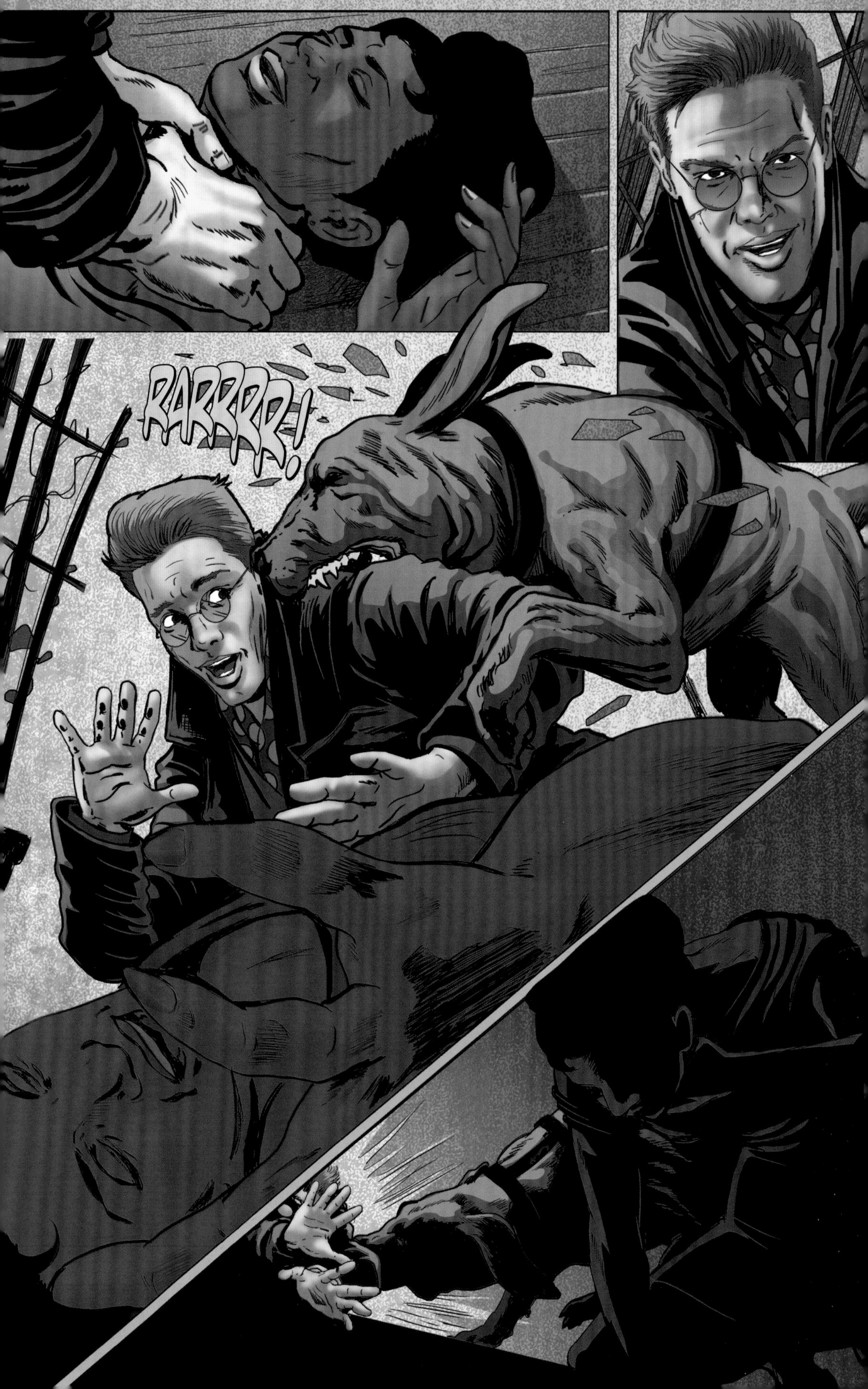
RARRRR!

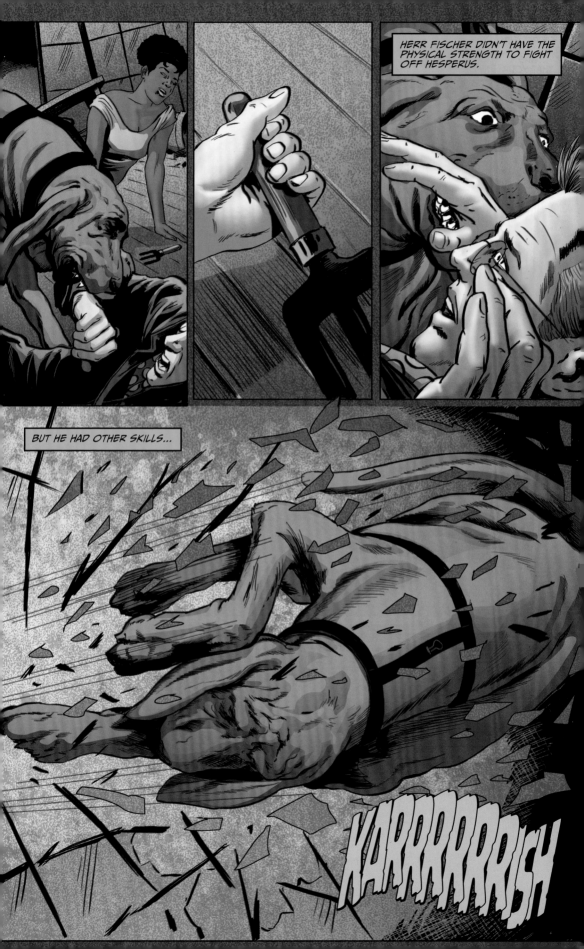

HERR FISCHER DIDN'T HAVE THE PHYSICAL STRENGTH TO FIGHT OFF HESPERUS.

BUT HE HAD OTHER SKILLS...

KARRRRRRISH

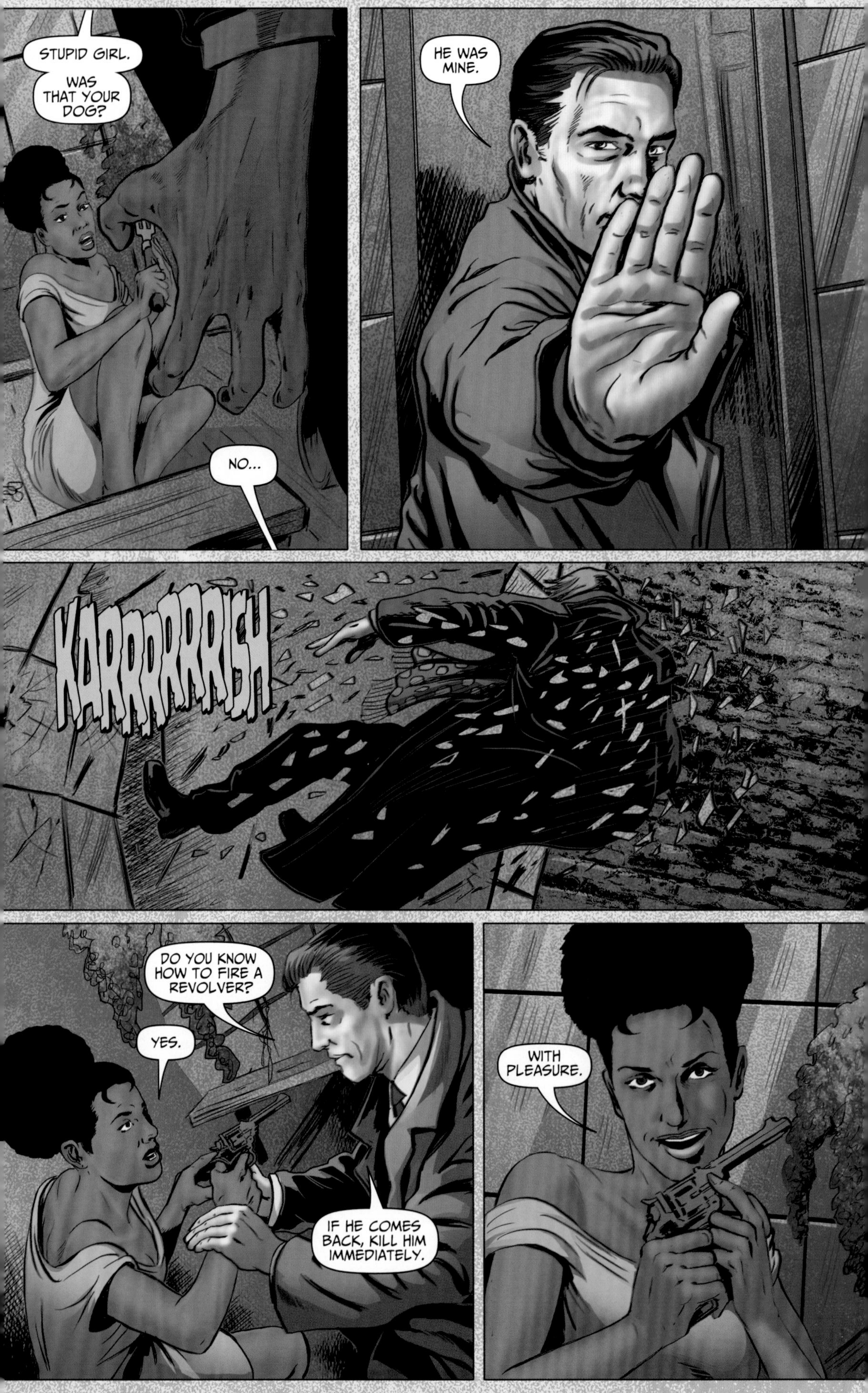
STUPID GIRL.
WAS THAT YOUR DOG?
NO...
HE WAS MINE.
KARRRRRRISH
DO YOU KNOW HOW TO FIRE A REVOLVER?
YES.
IF HE COMES BACK, KILL HIM IMMEDIATELY.
WITH PLEASURE.

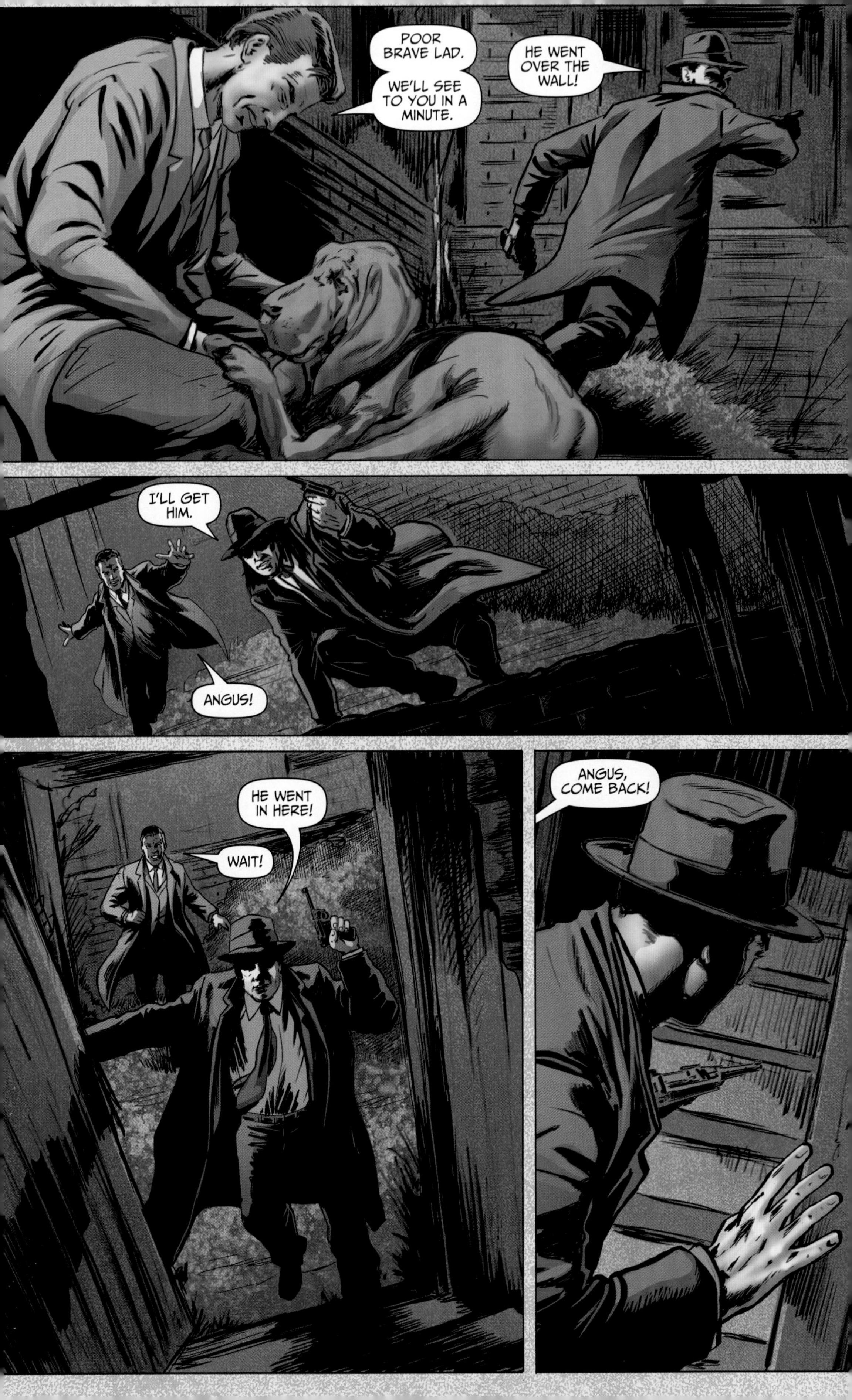
POOR BRAVE LAD.
WE'LL SEE TO YOU IN A MINUTE.
HE WENT OVER THE WALL!
I'LL GET HIM.
ANGUS!
HE WENT IN HERE!
WAIT!
ANGUS, COME BACK!

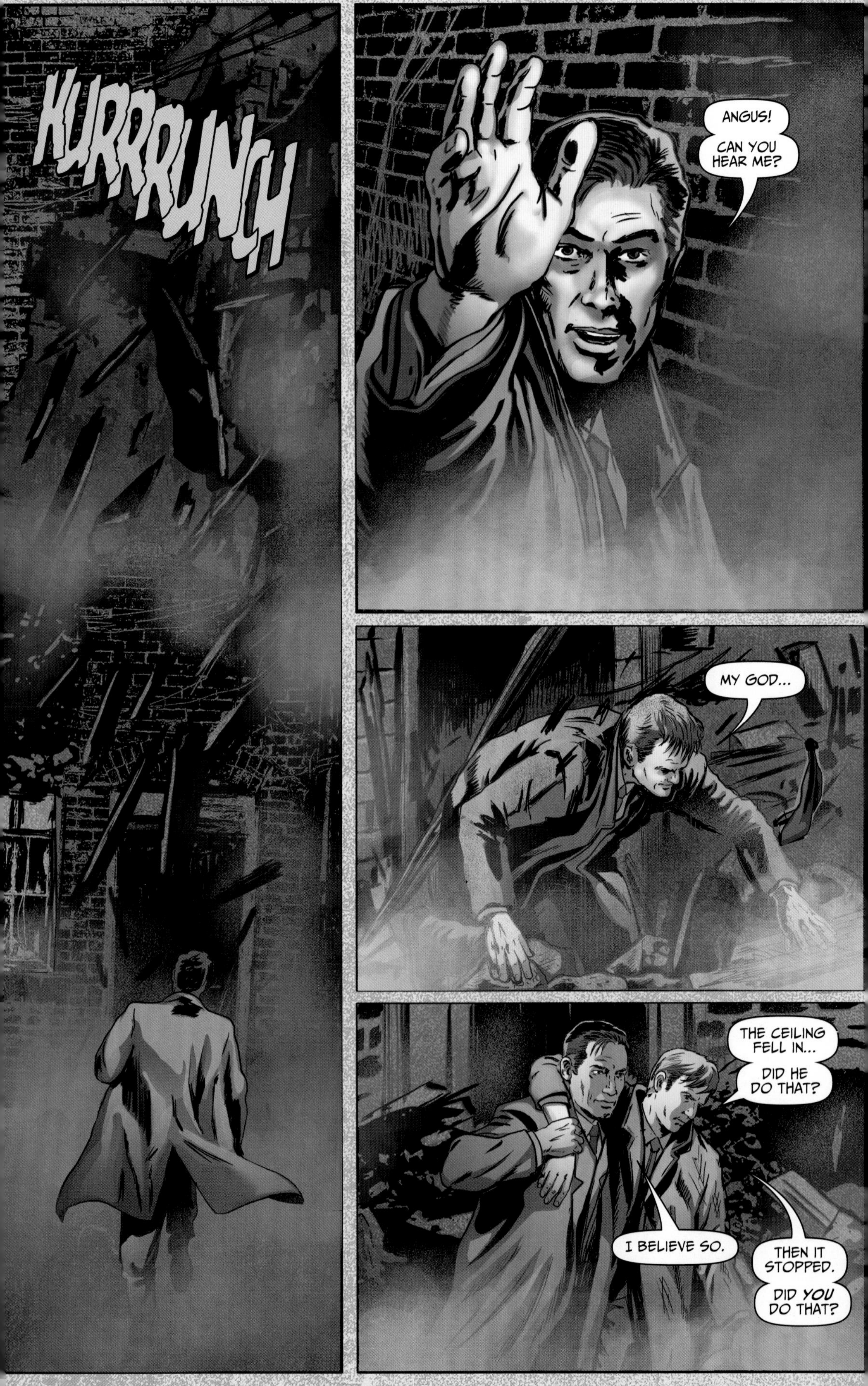
KURRRUNCH
ANGUS!
CAN YOU HEAR ME?
MY GOD...
THE CEILING FELL IN...
DID HE DO THAT?
I BELIEVE SO.
THEN IT STOPPED.
DID *YOU* DO THAT?

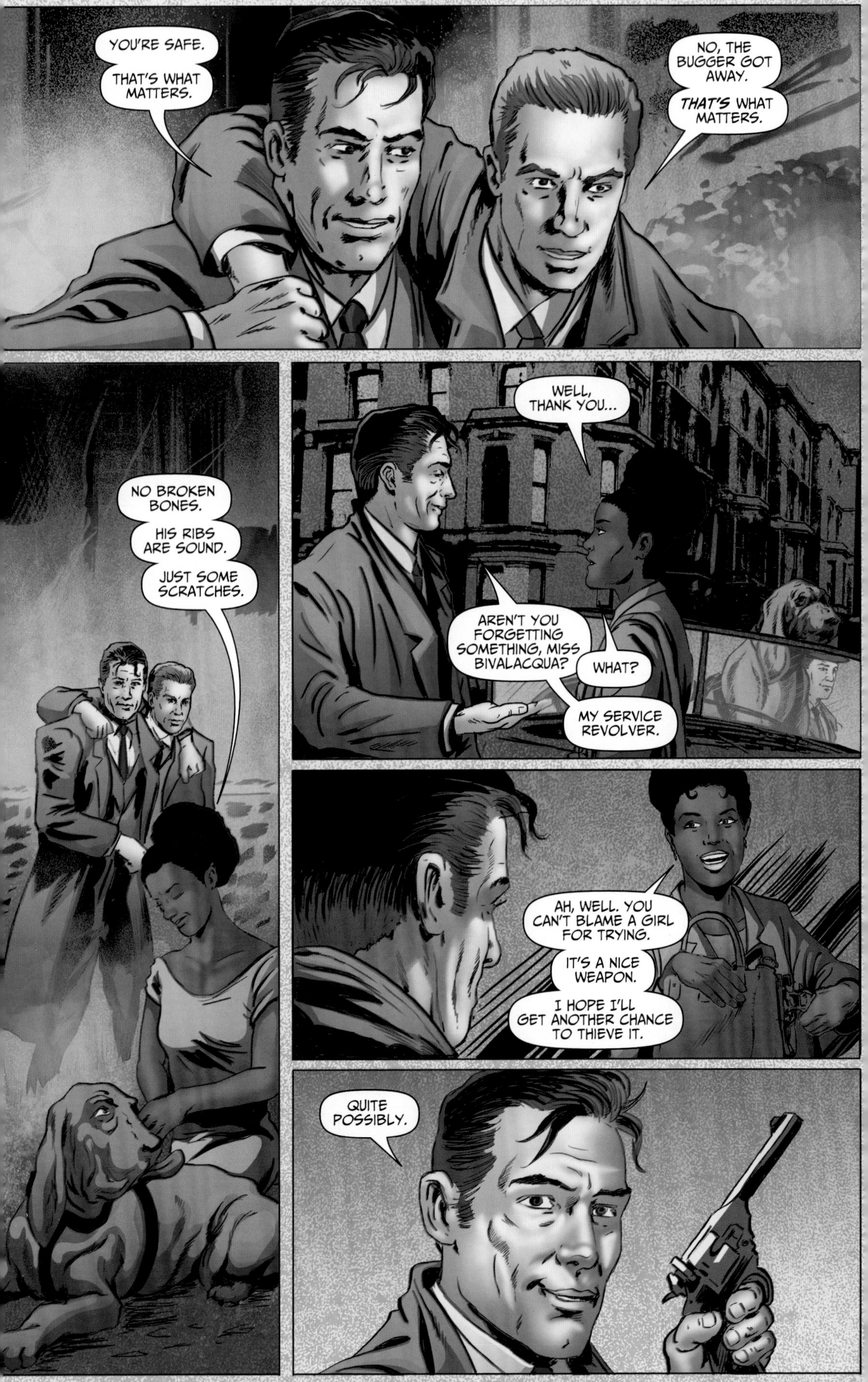
YOU'RE SAFE.
THAT'S WHAT MATTERS.
NO, THE BUGGER GOT AWAY.
THAT'S WHAT MATTERS.
NO BROKEN BONES.
HIS RIBS ARE SOUND.
JUST SOME SCRATCHES.
WELL, THANK YOU...
AREN'T YOU FORGETTING SOMETHING, MISS BIVALACQUA?
WHAT?
MY SERVICE REVOLVER.
AH, WELL. YOU CAN'T BLAME A GIRL FOR TRYING.
IT'S A NICE WEAPON.
I HOPE I'LL GET ANOTHER CHANCE TO THIEVE IT.
QUITE POSSIBLY.

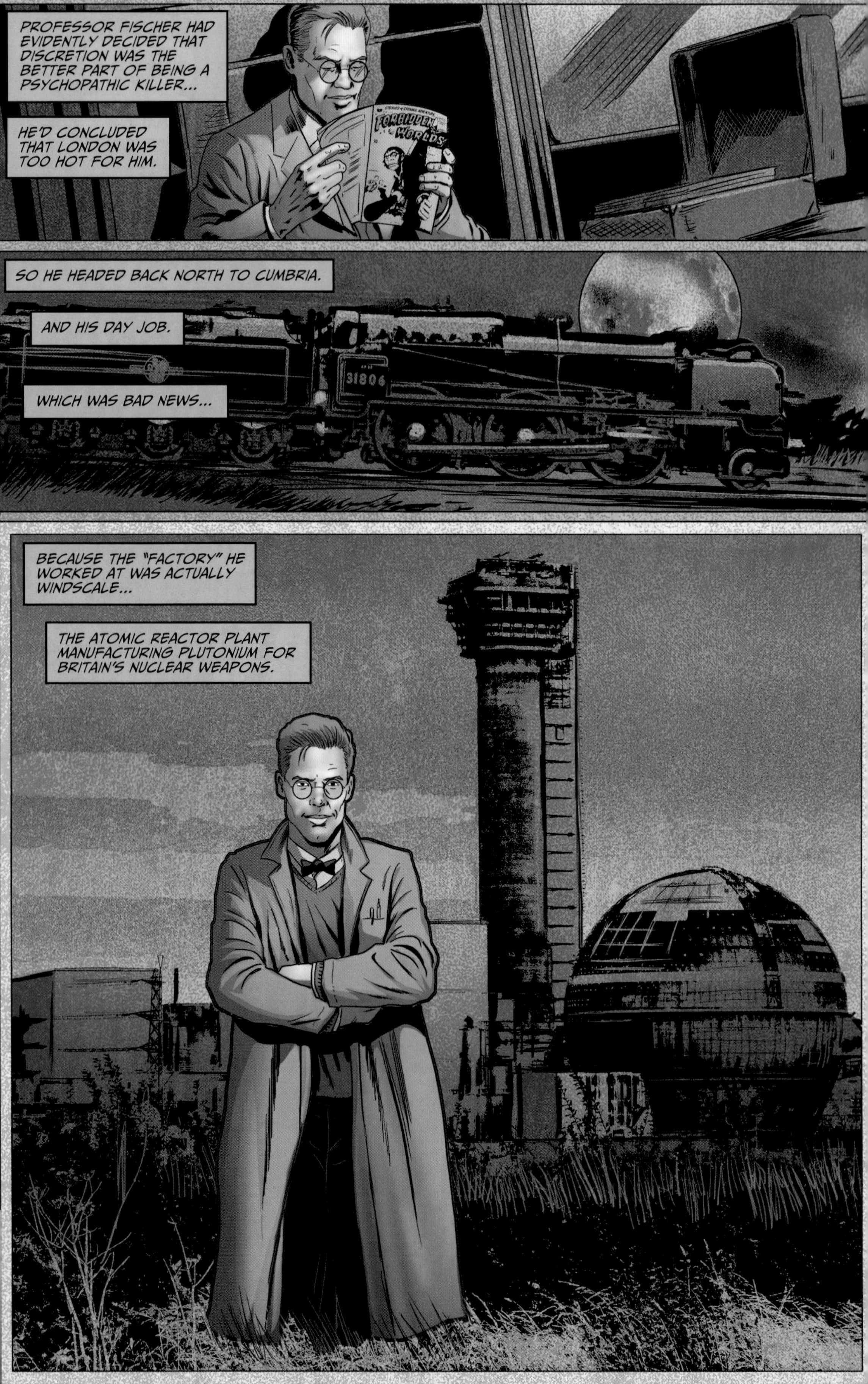
PROFESSOR FISCHER HAD EVIDENTLY DECIDED THAT DISCRETION WAS THE BETTER PART OF BEING A PSYCHOPATHIC KILLER...
HE'D CONCLUDED THAT LONDON WAS TOO HOT FOR HIM.
SO HE HEADED BACK NORTH TO CUMBRIA.
AND HIS DAY JOB.
31806
WHICH WAS BAD NEWS...
BECAUSE THE "FACTORY" HE WORKED AT WAS ACTUALLY WINDSCALE...
THE ATOMIC REACTOR PLANT MANUFACTURING PLUTONIUM FOR BRITAIN'S NUCLEAR WEAPONS.

SAMUEL DALSTON CROYLE.

SERVED WITH AMERICAN INTELLIGENCE DURING WORLD WAR 2 — THE OSS.

OFFICIALLY, AFTER THE WAR HE BECAME AN INSURANCE EXECUTIVE.

UNOFFICIALLY, THE NOTES IN OUR FILE INDICATE HE WAS WORKING FOR THE CIA.

WHICH IS WHAT THE OSS MORPHED INTO WHEN IT RAN OUT OF NAZIS TO FIGHT.

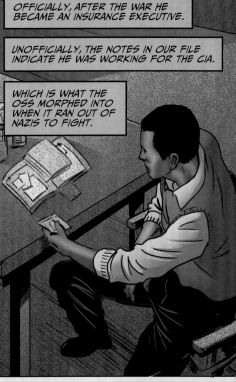

AND APPARENTLY THE CIA SENT HIM OVER HERE TO POACH SOME OF OUR SPECIAL TALENT.

IN THE SHAPE OF ONE PROFESSOR UWE FISCHER.

FISCHER WAS HAVING LOTS OF FUN AND WAS IN NO HURRY TO LEAVE.

BUT EVENTS TOOK THE DECISION OUT OF HIS HAND.

TIME FOR PASTURES NEW.

SO IT WOULD APPEAR.

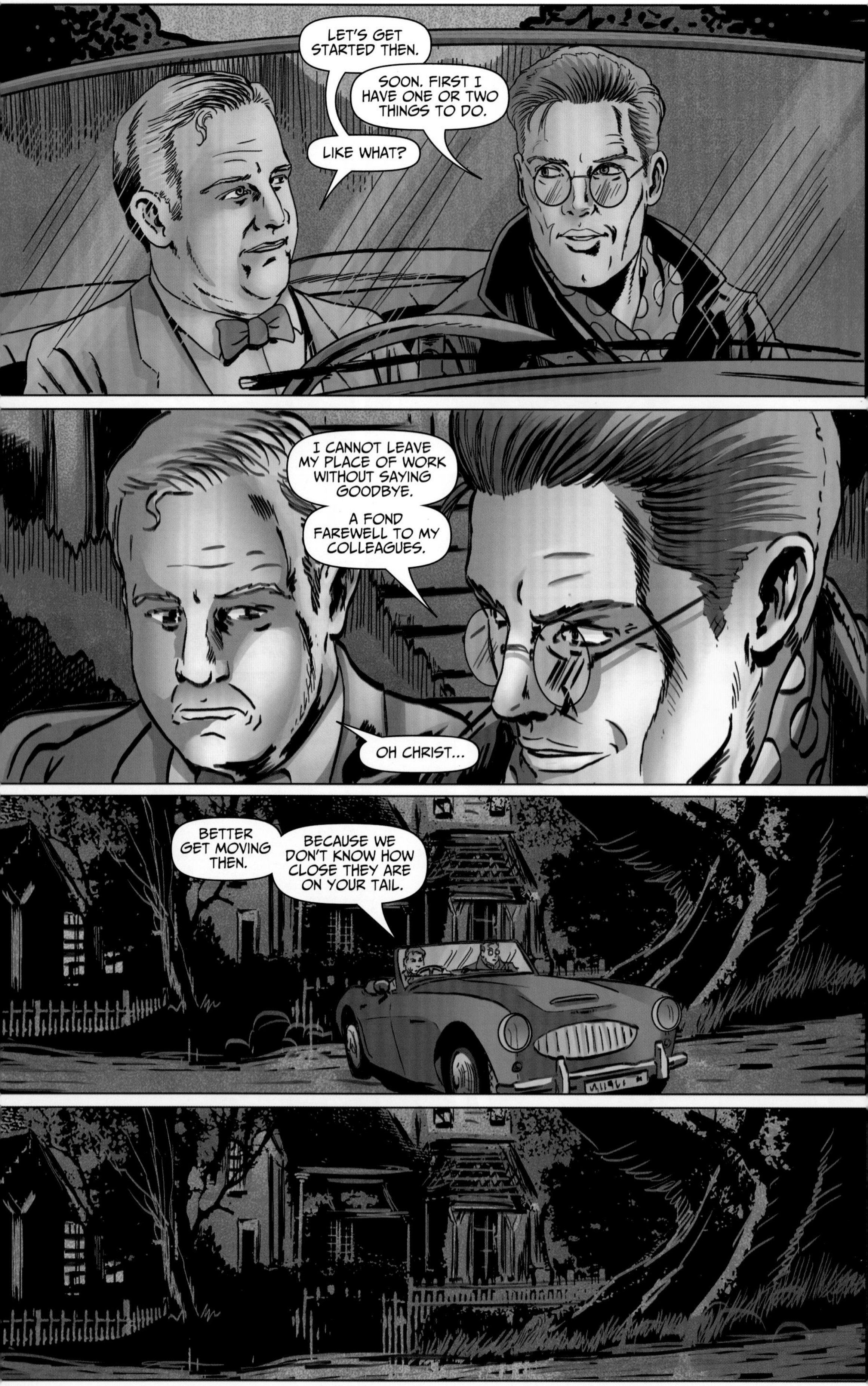
LET'S GET STARTED THEN.
SOON. FIRST I HAVE ONE OR TWO THINGS TO DO.
LIKE WHAT?
I CANNOT LEAVE MY PLACE OF WORK WITHOUT SAYING GOODBYE.
A FOND FAREWELL TO MY COLLEAGUES.
OH CHRIST...
BETTER GET MOVING THEN.
BECAUSE WE DON'T KNOW HOW CLOSE THEY ARE ON YOUR TAIL.

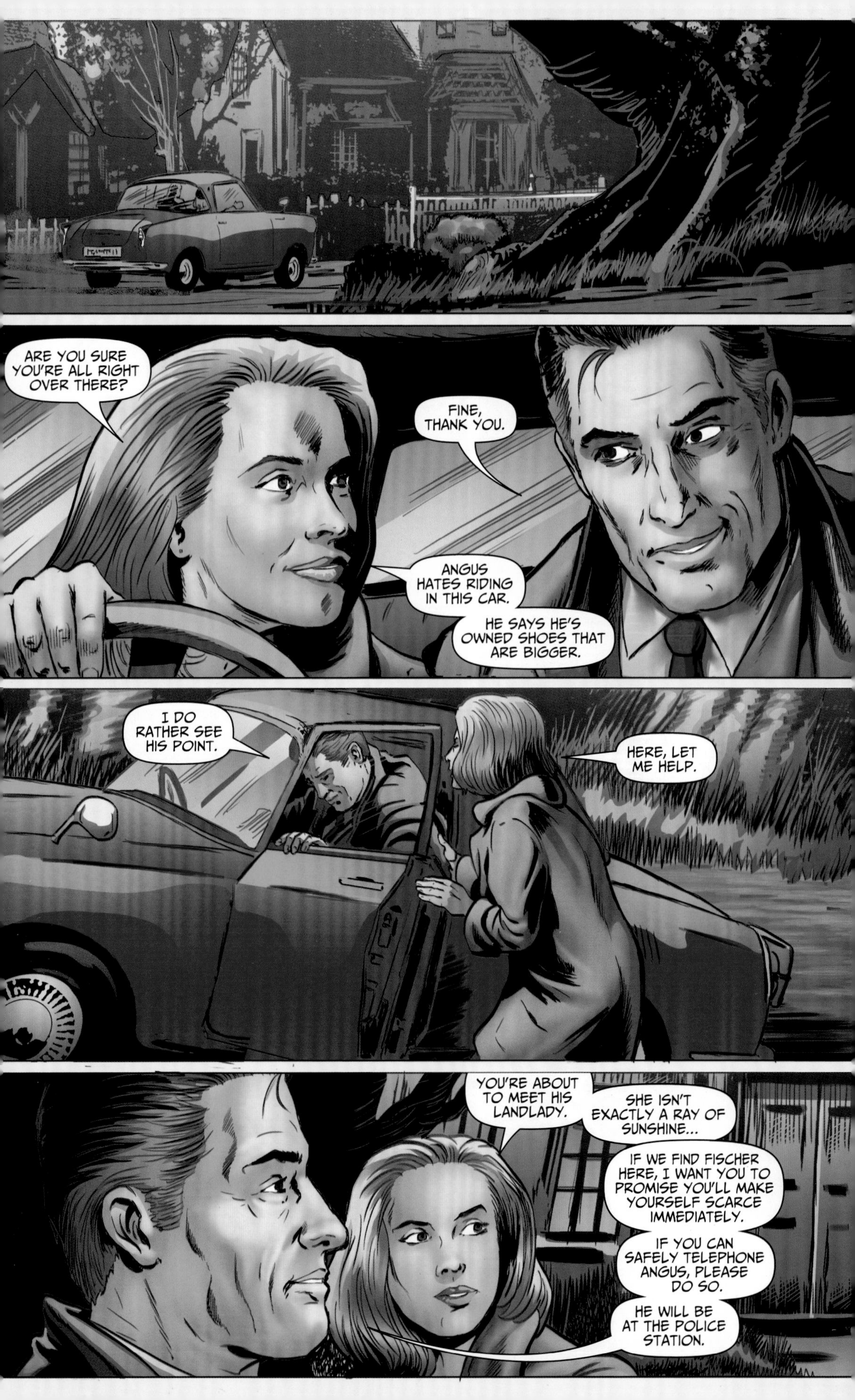
ARE YOU SURE YOU'RE ALL RIGHT OVER THERE?
FINE, THANK YOU.
ANGUS HATES RIDING IN THIS CAR.
HE SAYS HE'S OWNED SHOES THAT ARE BIGGER.
I DO RATHER SEE HIS POINT.
HERE, LET ME HELP.
YOU'RE ABOUT TO MEET HIS LANDLADY.
SHE ISN'T EXACTLY A RAY OF SUNSHINE...
IF WE FIND FISCHER HERE, I WANT YOU TO PROMISE YOU'LL MAKE YOURSELF SCARCE IMMEDIATELY.
IF YOU CAN SAFELY TELEPHONE ANGUS, PLEASE DO SO.
HE WILL BE AT THE POLICE STATION.

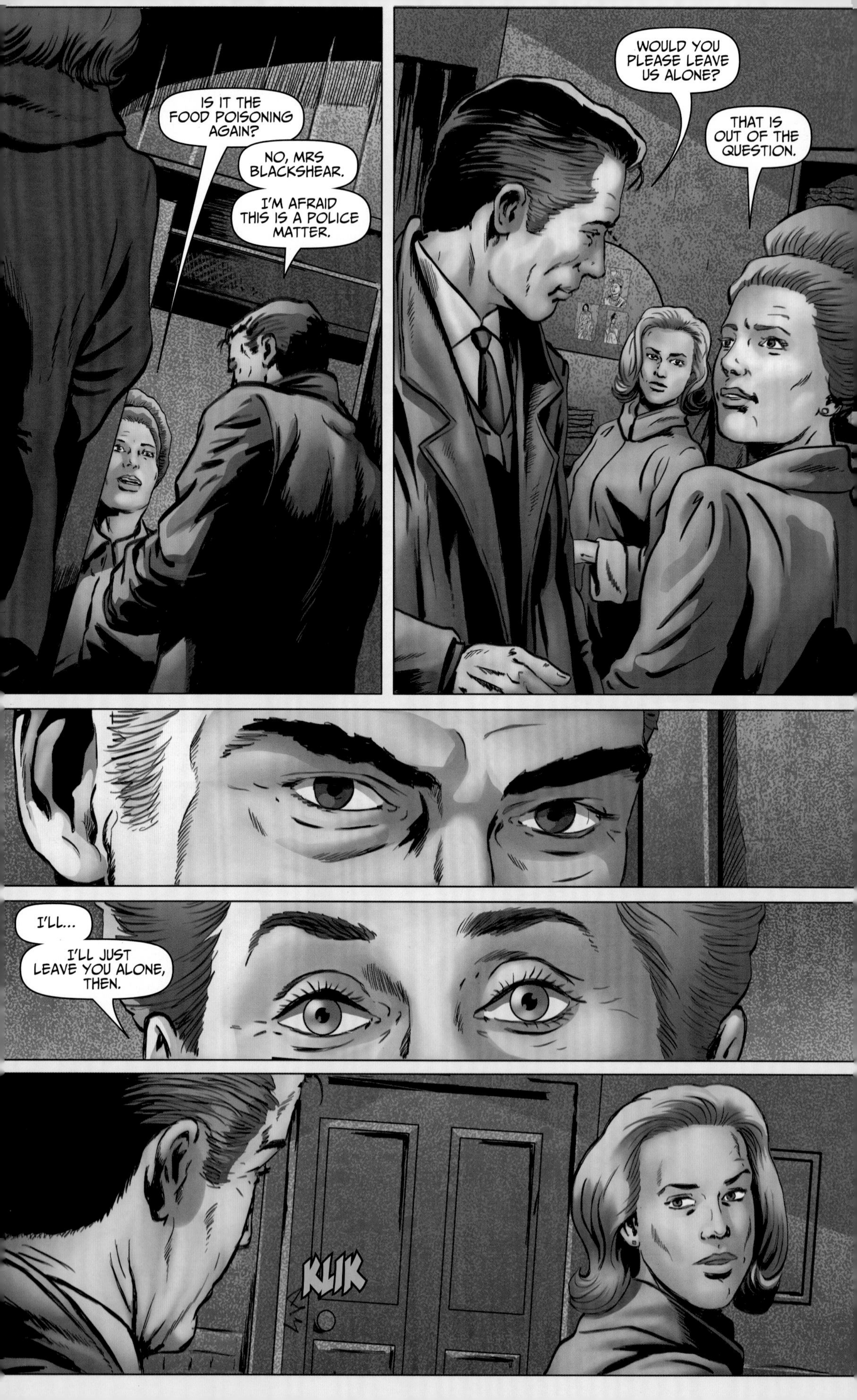
IS IT THE FOOD POISONING AGAIN?
NO, MRS BLACKSHEAR.
I'M AFRAID THIS IS A POLICE MATTER.
WOULD YOU PLEASE LEAVE US ALONE?
THAT IS OUT OF THE QUESTION.
I'LL...
I'LL JUST LEAVE YOU ALONE, THEN.
KLIK

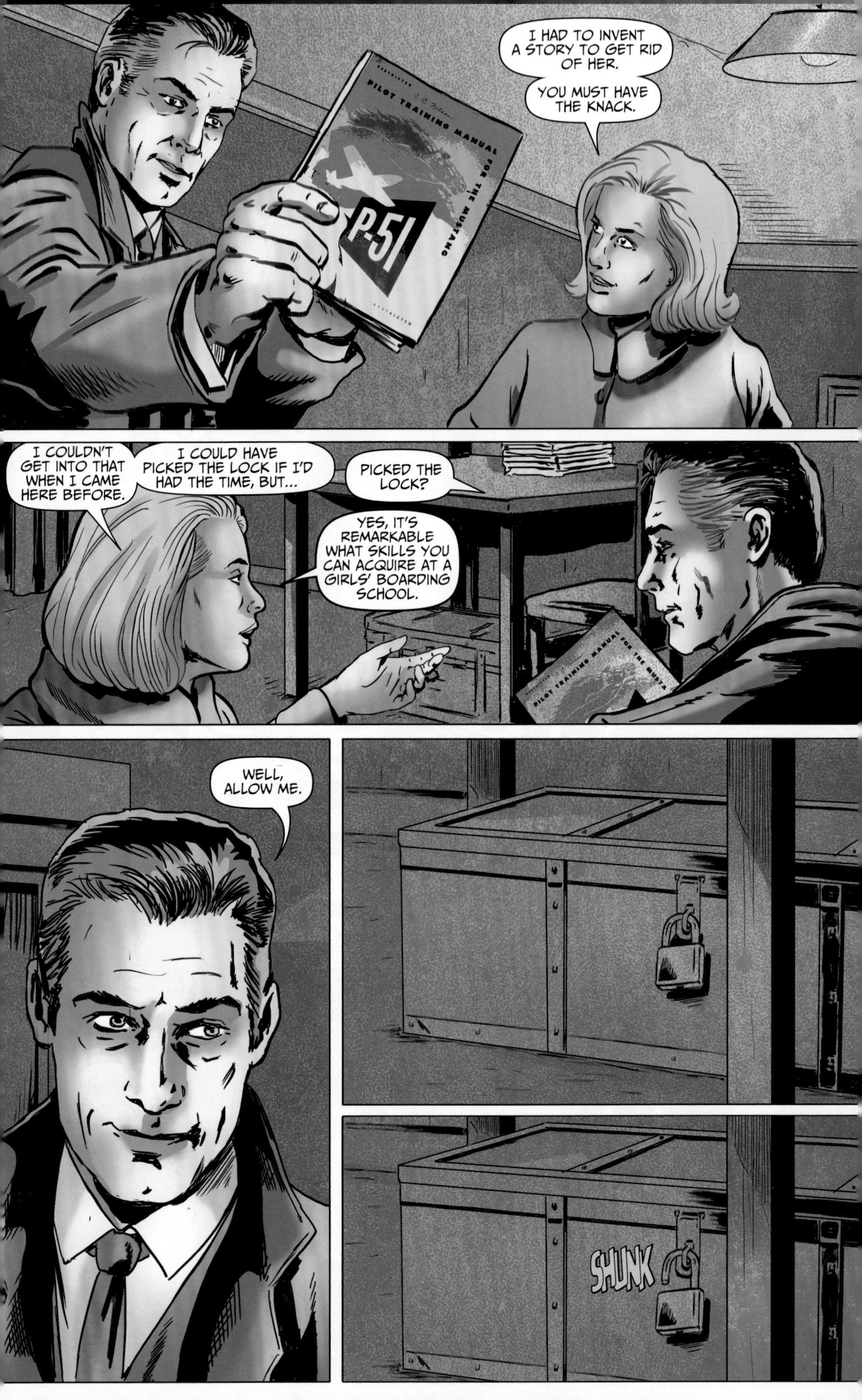
PILOT TRAINING MANUAL FOR THE MUSTANG
P-51
I HAD TO INVENT A STORY TO GET RID OF HER.
YOU MUST HAVE THE KNACK.
I COULDN'T GET INTO THAT WHEN I CAME HERE BEFORE.
I COULD HAVE PICKED THE LOCK IF I'D HAD THE TIME, BUT...
PICKED THE LOCK?
YES, IT'S REMARKABLE WHAT SKILLS YOU CAN ACQUIRE AT A GIRLS' BOARDING SCHOOL.
WELL, ALLOW ME.
SHUNK

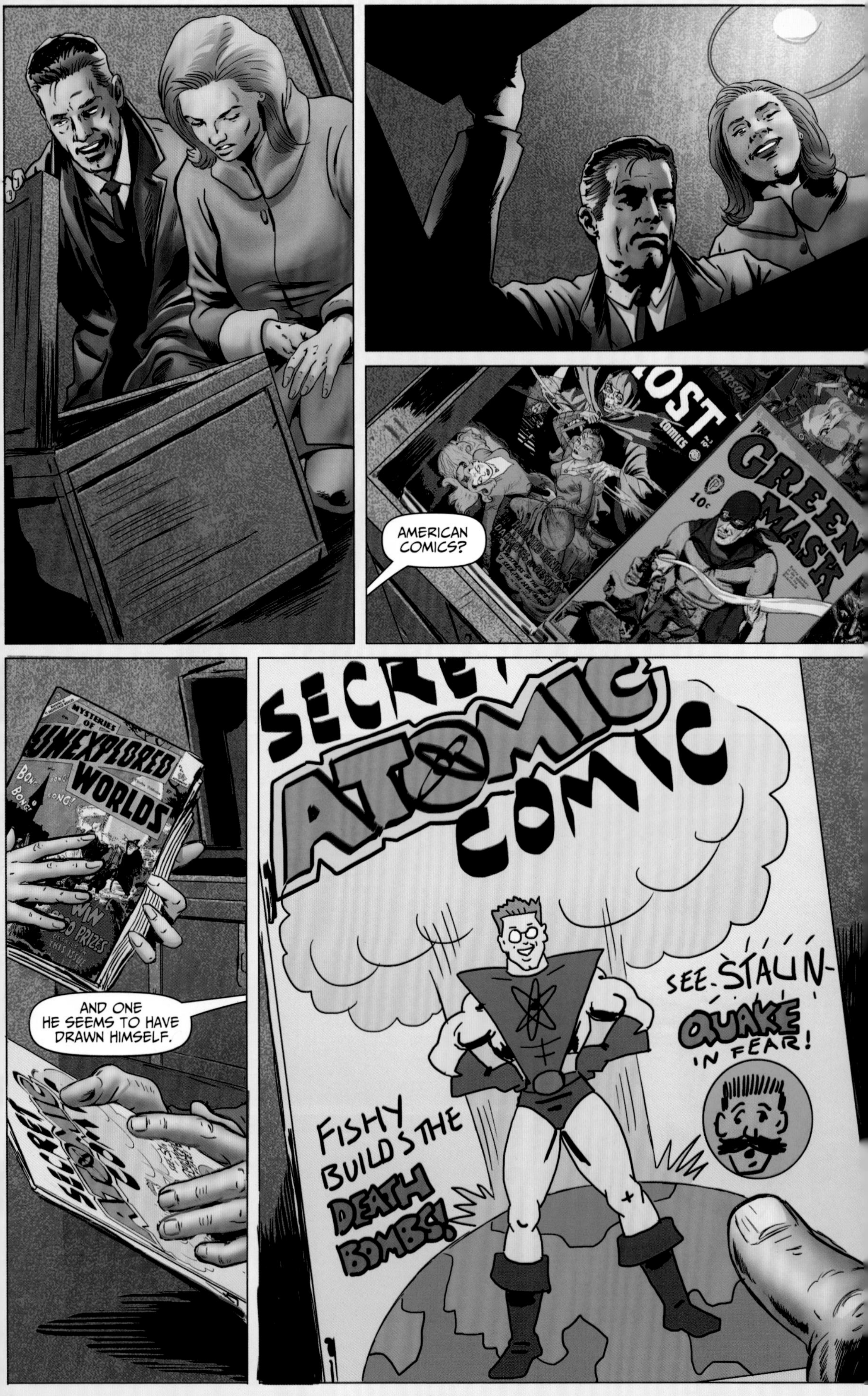
AMERICAN COMICS?
GREEN MASK
10¢
MYSTERIES OF UNEXPLORED WORLDS
BONG! BONG!
AND ONE HE SEEMS TO HAVE DRAWN HIMSELF.
SECRET ATOMIC COMIC
SEE STALIN QUAKE IN FEAR!
FISHY BUILDS THE DEATH BOMBS!

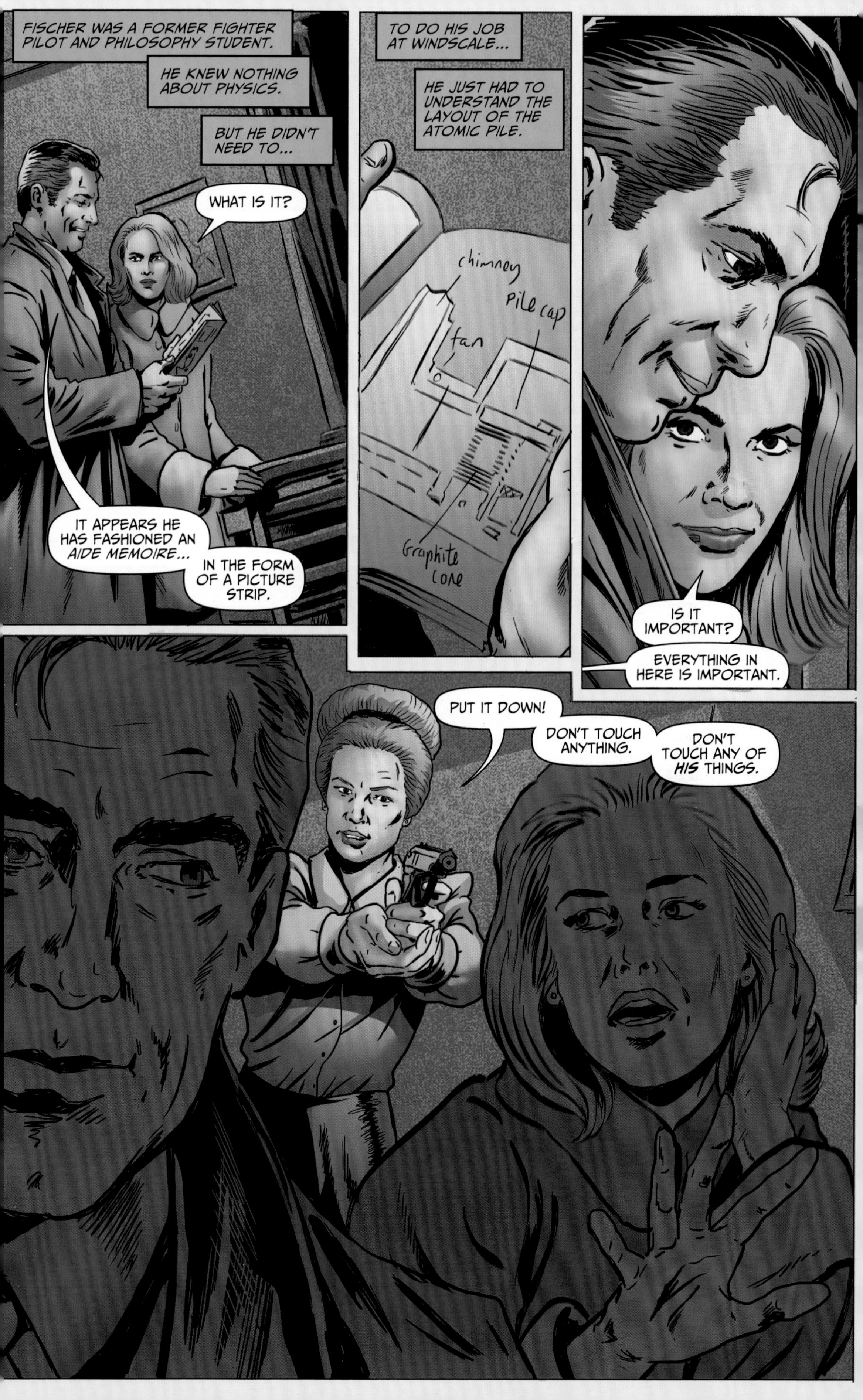
FISCHER WAS A FORMER FIGHTER PILOT AND PHILOSOPHY STUDENT.
HE KNEW NOTHING ABOUT PHYSICS.
BUT HE DIDN'T NEED TO...
WHAT IS IT?
IT APPEARS HE HAS FASHIONED AN *AIDE MEMOIRE*...
IN THE FORM OF A PICTURE STRIP.
TO DO HIS JOB AT WINDSCALE...
HE JUST HAD TO UNDERSTAND THE LAYOUT OF THE ATOMIC PILE.
chimney
Pile cap
fan
Graphite core
IS IT IMPORTANT?
EVERYTHING IN HERE IS IMPORTANT.
PUT IT DOWN!
DON'T TOUCH ANYTHING.
DON'T TOUCH ANY OF *HIS* THINGS.

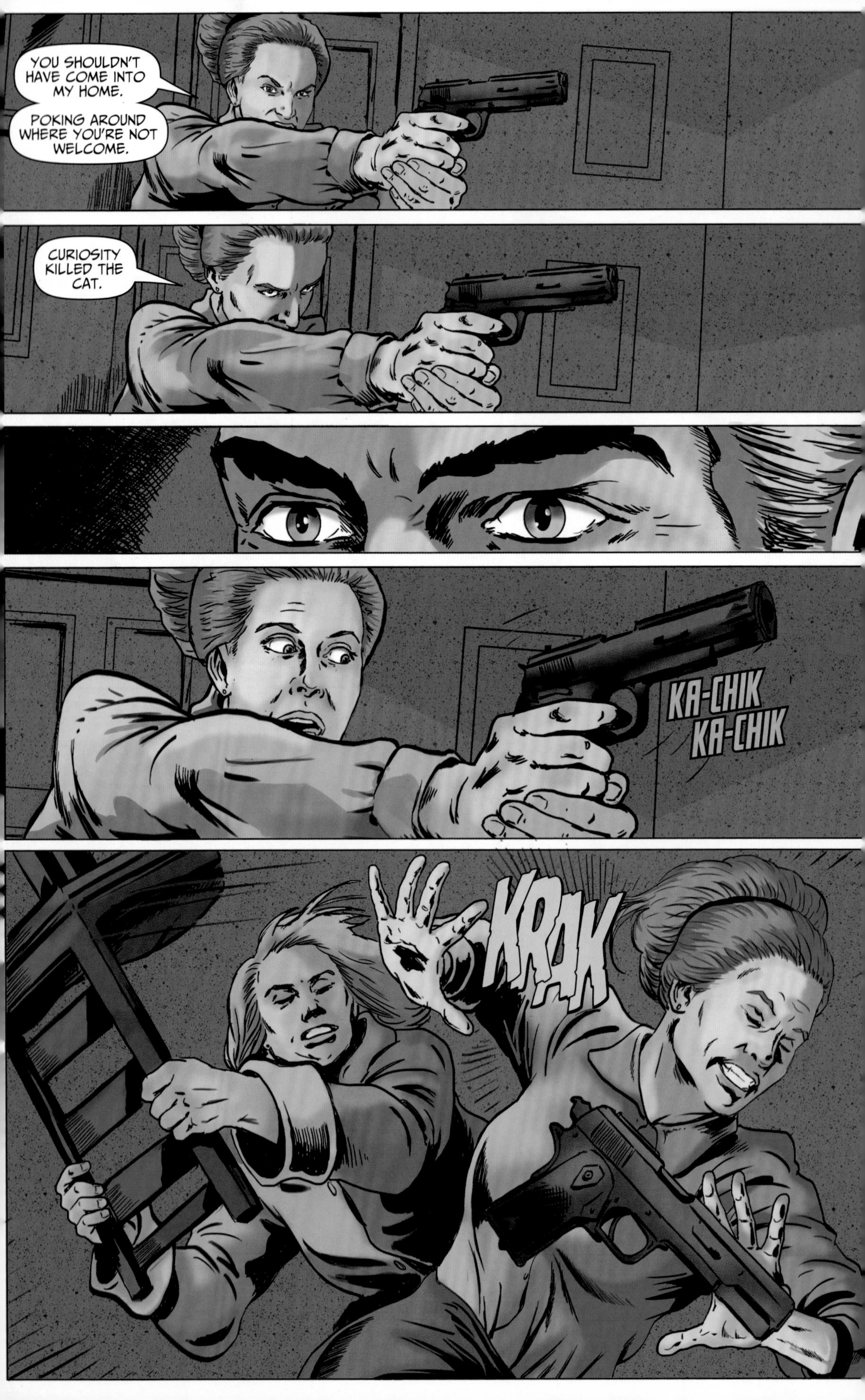
YOU SHOULDN'T HAVE COME INTO MY HOME.
POKING AROUND WHERE YOU'RE NOT WELCOME.
CURIOSITY KILLED THE CAT.
KA-CHIK
KA-CHIK
KRAK

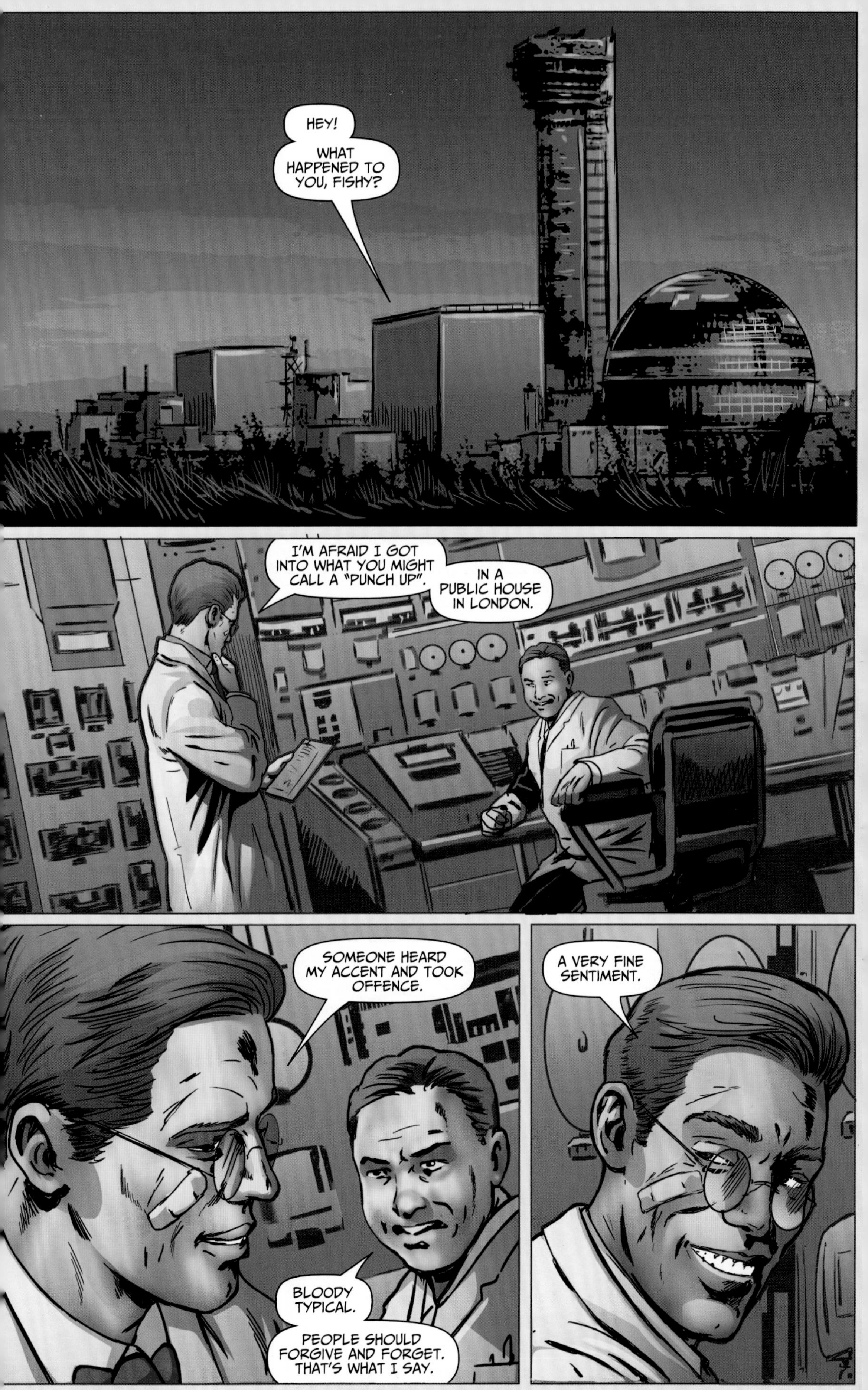
HEY!
WHAT HAPPENED TO YOU, FISHY?
I'M AFRAID I GOT INTO WHAT YOU MIGHT CALL A "PUNCH UP".
IN A PUBLIC HOUSE IN LONDON.
SOMEONE HEARD MY ACCENT AND TOOK OFFENCE.
BLOODY TYPICAL.
PEOPLE SHOULD FORGIVE AND FORGET. THAT'S WHAT I SAY.
A VERY FINE SENTIMENT.

AFTER THE SECOND WORLD WAR BRITAIN DECIDED IT HAD TO HAVE NUCLEAR WEAPONS, JUST LIKE THE COOL KIDS.

NUKES NEED PLUTONIUM. SO TO MAKE PLUTONIUM, WE BUILT WINDSCALE.

THE FIRST REACTOR, OR "PILE", WENT CRITICAL — WHICH MEANS IT STARTED UP —IN OCTOBER 1950.

IT WAS A BIG LUMP OF GRAPHITE WITH HOLES DRILLED THROUGH IT.

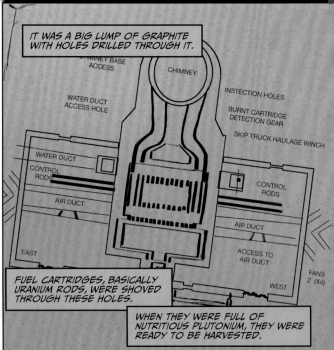

CHIMNEY BASE ACCESS

CHIMNEY

WATER DUCT ACCESS HOLE

INSTECTION HOLES

BURNT CARTRIDGE DETECTION GEAR

SKIP TRUCK HAULAGE WINCH

WATER DUCT

CONTROL RODS

CONTROL RODS

AIR DUCT

AIR DUCT

EAST

ACCESS TO AIR DUCT

WEST

FANS Z (X4)

FUEL CARTRIDGES, BASICALLY URANIUM RODS, WERE SHOVED THROUGH THESE HOLES.

WHEN THEY WERE FULL OF NUTRITIOUS PLUTONIUM, THEY WERE READY TO BE HARVESTED.

THIS WAS DONE BY THE SOPHISTICATED METHOD OF SHOVING NEW FUEL RODS IN AT THE FRONT...

CAUSING THE PLUTONIUM-RICH ONES TO FALL OUT OF THE BACK INTO A POOL OF WATER.

NO, SERIOUSLY.

OUR CHUM FISCHER WAS A PRICELESS ASSET.

HIS SPECIAL TALENTS ALLOWED HIM TO MOVE THINGS AT A DISTANCE WITHOUT PHYSICAL CONTACT.

USEFUL WHEN THERE'S DEADLY LEVELS OF RADIATION ABOUT THE PLACE...

HE WAS PARTICULARLY HELPFUL FIXING PROBLEMS CAUSED BY THE JAMMING OF THE BCDG* AND THE "CHRISTMAS TREE."**

*BURST CARTRIDGE DETECTION GEAR.
**A MOBILE SCANNING MACHINE.

WHAT COULD POSSIBLY GO WRONG?

WELL, THE PROBLEM WITH GRAPHITE IS THAT IT'S SUBJECT TO THE BUILD-UP OF WIGNER ENERGY...

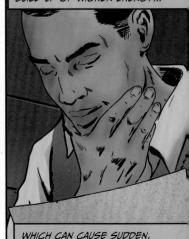

WHICH CAN CAUSE SUDDEN, UNPREDICTABLE AND DANGEROUS RELEASES OF INTENSE HEAT.

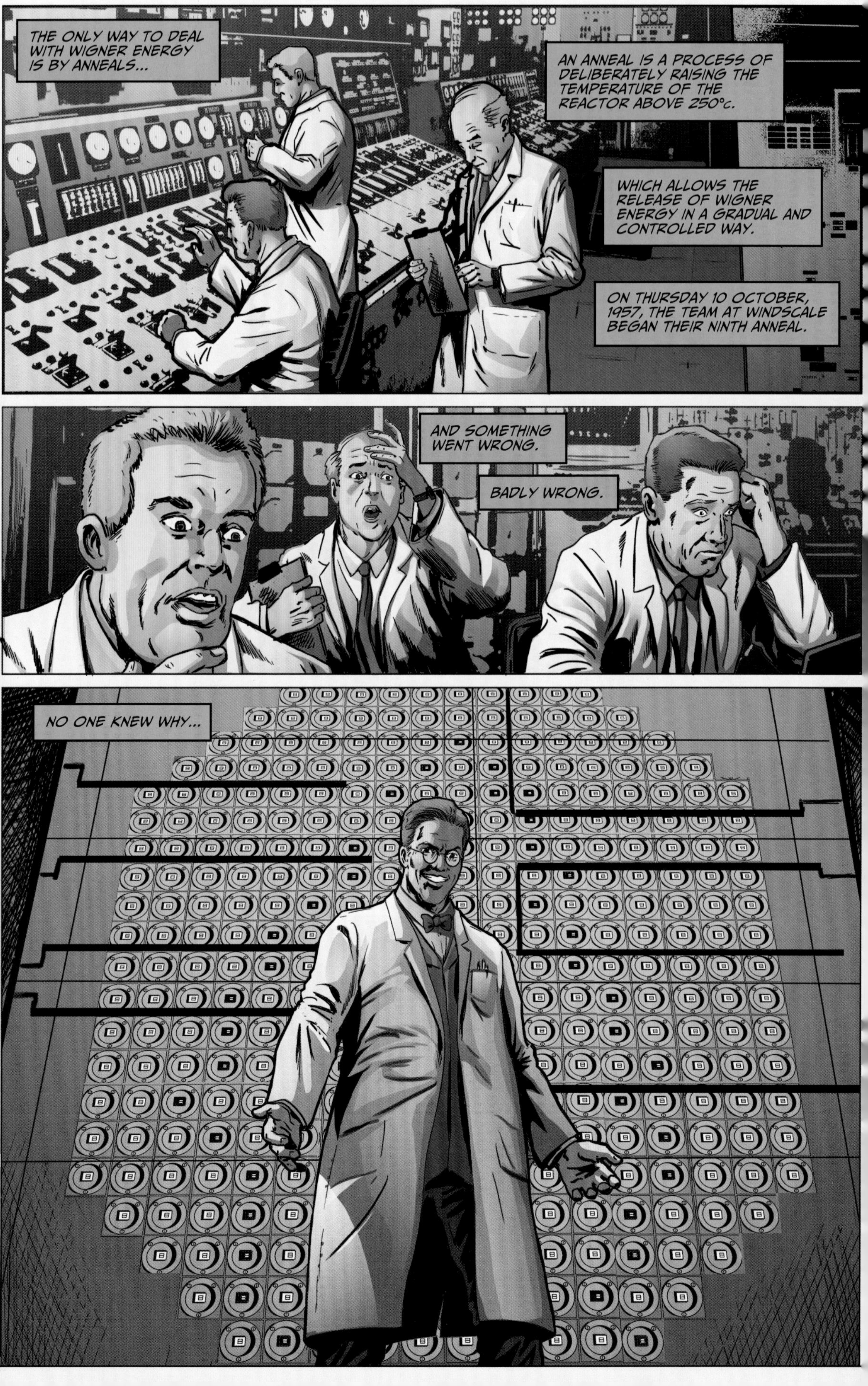
THE ONLY WAY TO DEAL WITH WIGNER ENERGY IS BY ANNEALS...
AN ANNEAL IS A PROCESS OF DELIBERATELY RAISING THE TEMPERATURE OF THE REACTOR ABOVE 250°c.
WHICH ALLOWS THE RELEASE OF WIGNER ENERGY IN A GRADUAL AND CONTROLLED WAY.
ON THURSDAY 10 OCTOBER, 1957, THE TEAM AT WINDSCALE BEGAN THEIR NINTH ANNEAL.
AND SOMETHING WENT WRONG.
BADLY WRONG.
NO ONE KNEW WHY...

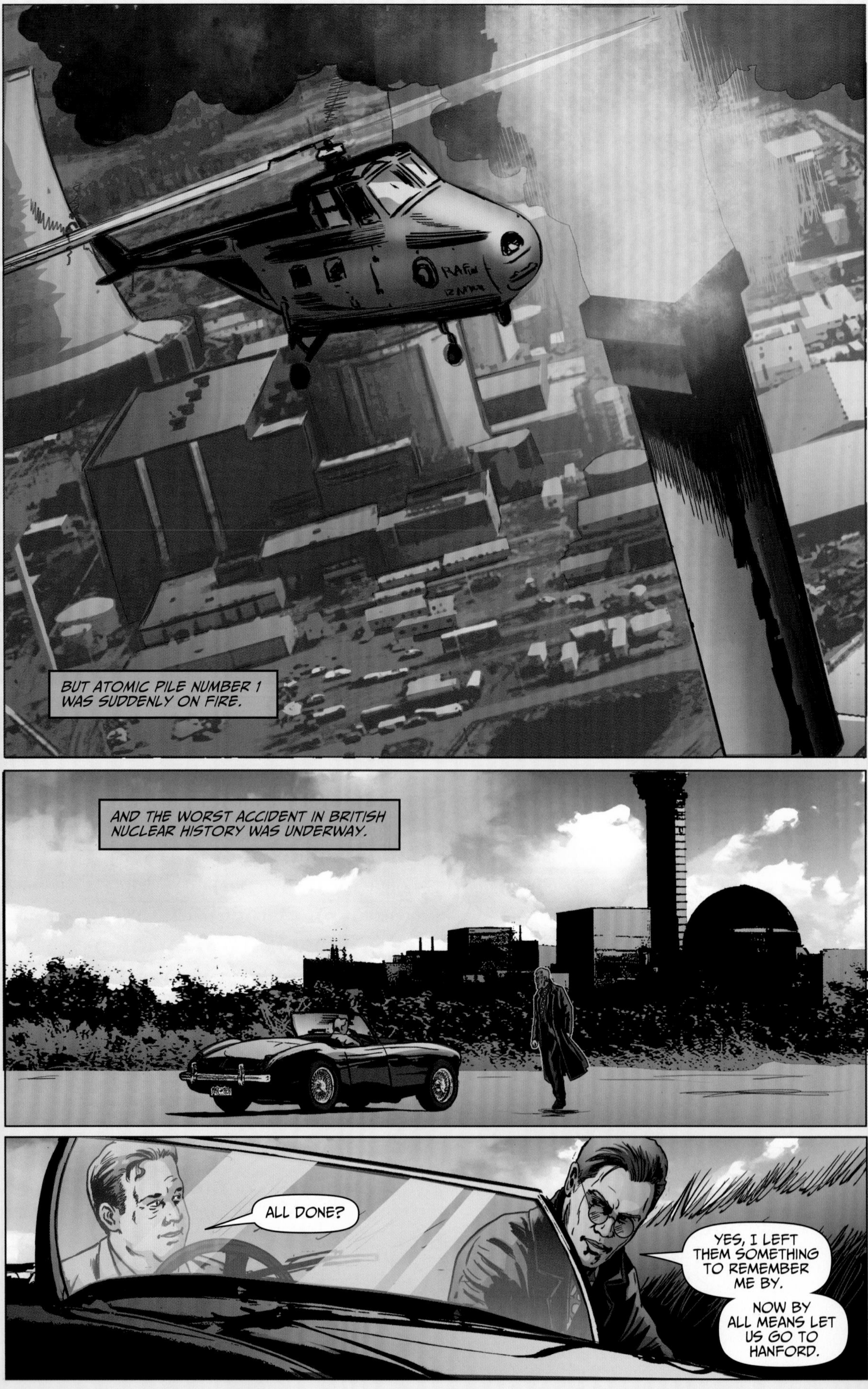
BUT ATOMIC PILE NUMBER 1
WAS SUDDENLY ON FIRE.
AND THE WORST ACCIDENT IN BRITISH
NUCLEAR HISTORY WAS UNDERWAY.
ALL DONE?
YES, I LEFT THEM SOMETHING TO REMEMBER ME BY.
NOW BY ALL MEANS LET US GO TO HANFORD.

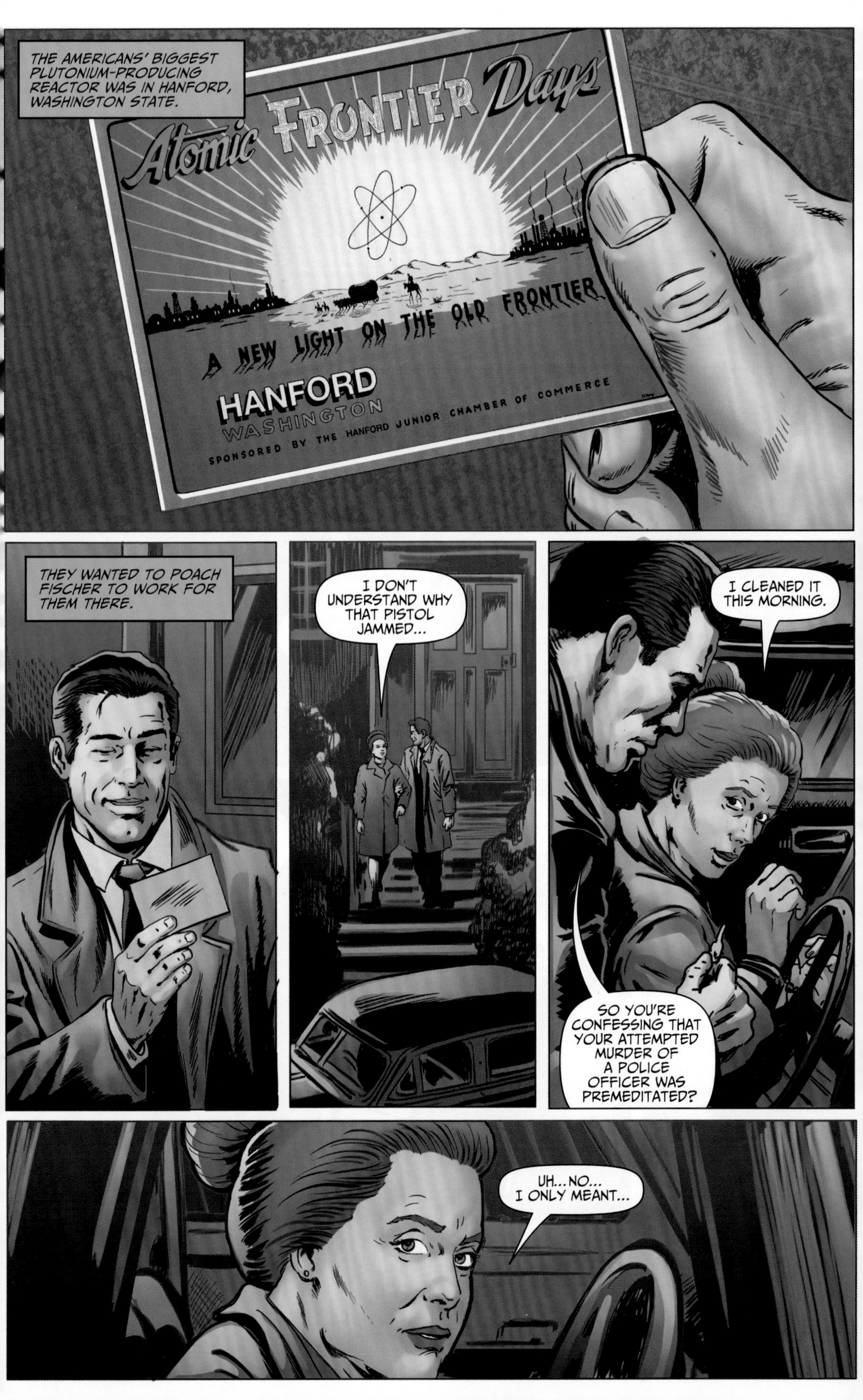
THE AMERICANS' BIGGEST PLUTONIUM-PRODUCING REACTOR WAS IN HANFORD, WASHINGTON STATE.
Atomic FRONTIER Days
A NEW LIGHT ON THE OLD FRONTIER
HANFORD WASHINGTON
SPONSORED BY THE HANFORD JUNIOR CHAMBER OF COMMERCE
THEY WANTED TO POACH FISCHER TO WORK FOR THEM THERE.
I DON'T UNDERSTAND WHY THAT PISTOL JAMMED...
I CLEANED IT THIS MORNING.
SO YOU'RE CONFESSING THAT YOUR ATTEMPTED MURDER OF A POLICE OFFICER WAS PREMEDITATED?
UH...NO... I ONLY MEANT...

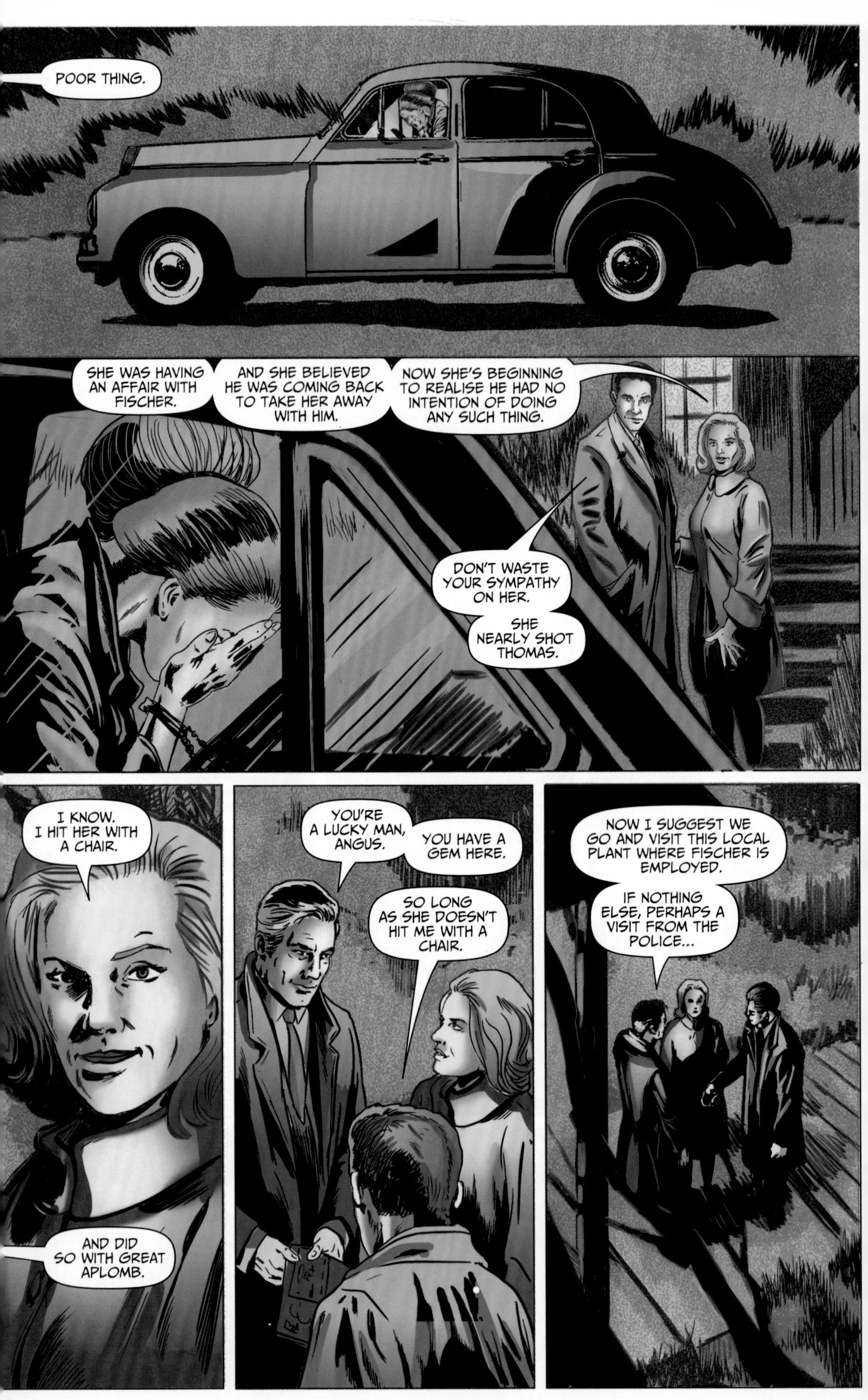
POOR THING.
SHE WAS HAVING AN AFFAIR WITH FISCHER.
AND SHE BELIEVED HE WAS COMING BACK TO TAKE HER AWAY WITH HIM.
NOW SHE'S BEGINNING TO REALISE HE HAD NO INTENTION OF DOING ANY SUCH THING.
DON'T WASTE YOUR SYMPATHY ON HER.
SHE NEARLY SHOT THOMAS.
I KNOW. I HIT HER WITH A CHAIR.
AND DID SO WITH GREAT APLOMB.
YOU'RE A LUCKY MAN, ANGUS.
YOU HAVE A GEM HERE.
SO LONG AS SHE DOESN'T HIT ME WITH A CHAIR.
NOW I SUGGEST WE GO AND VISIT THIS LOCAL PLANT WHERE FISCHER IS EMPLOYED.
IF NOTHING ELSE, PERHAPS A VISIT FROM THE POLICE...

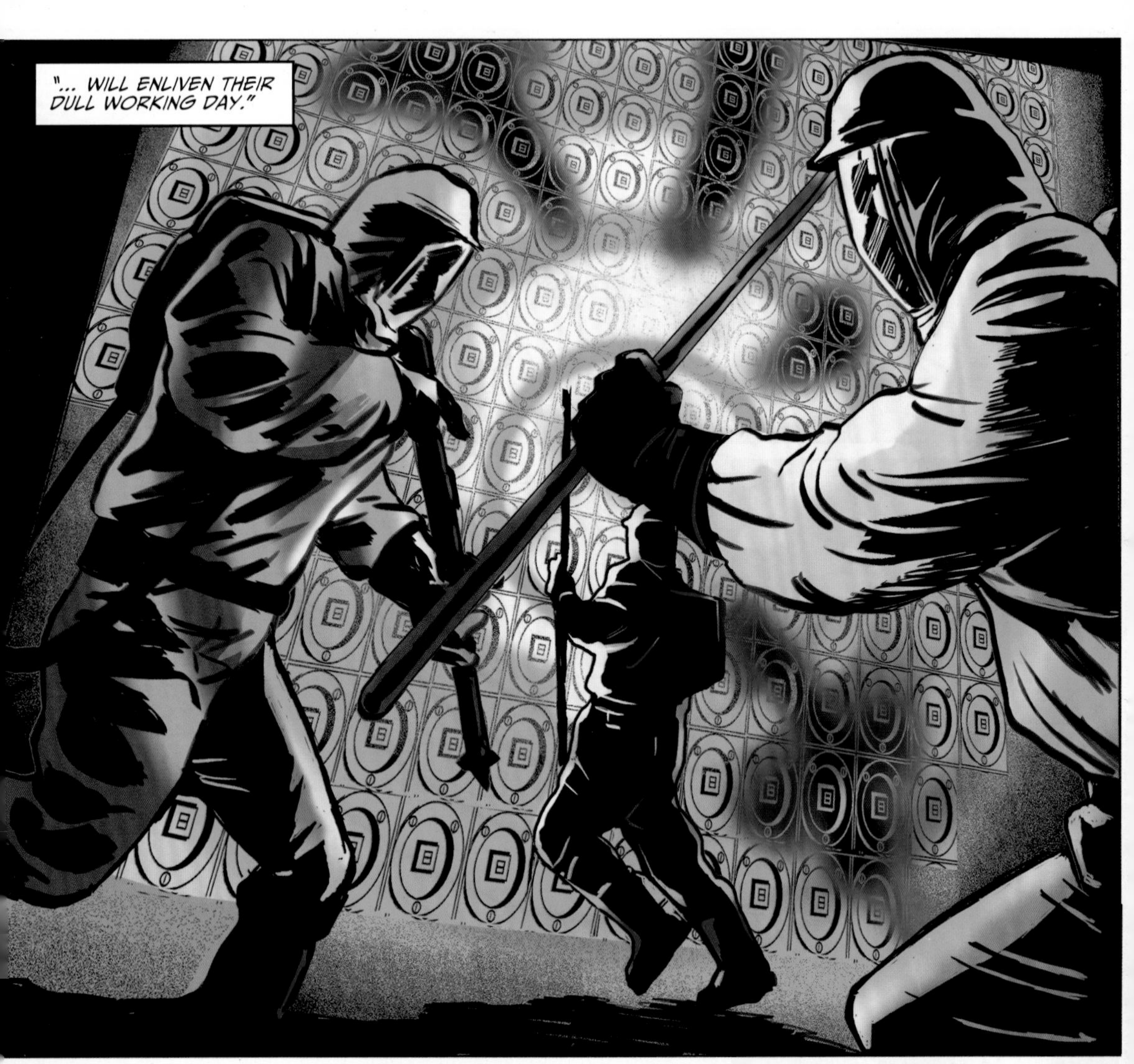
"... WILL ENLIVEN THEIR DULL WORKING DAY."

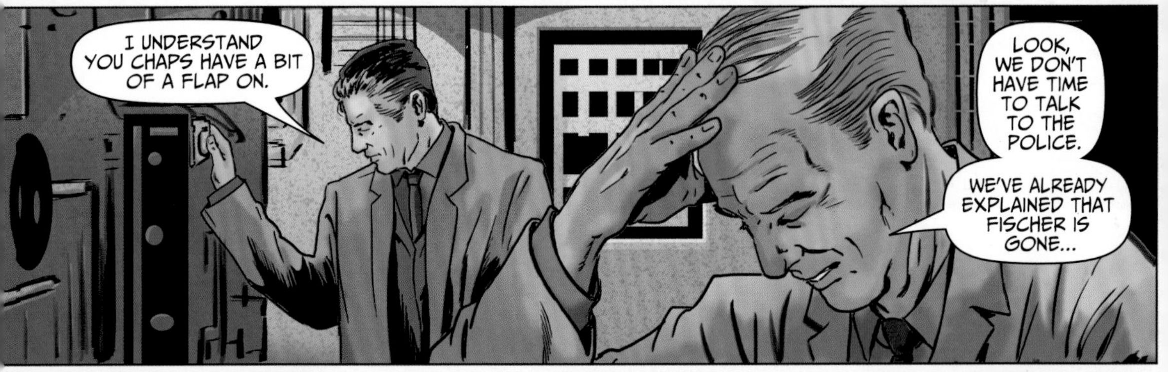
I UNDERSTAND YOU CHAPS HAVE A BIT OF A FLAP ON.
LOOK, WE DON'T HAVE TIME TO TALK TO THE POLICE.
WE'VE ALREADY EXPLAINED THAT FISCHER IS GONE...

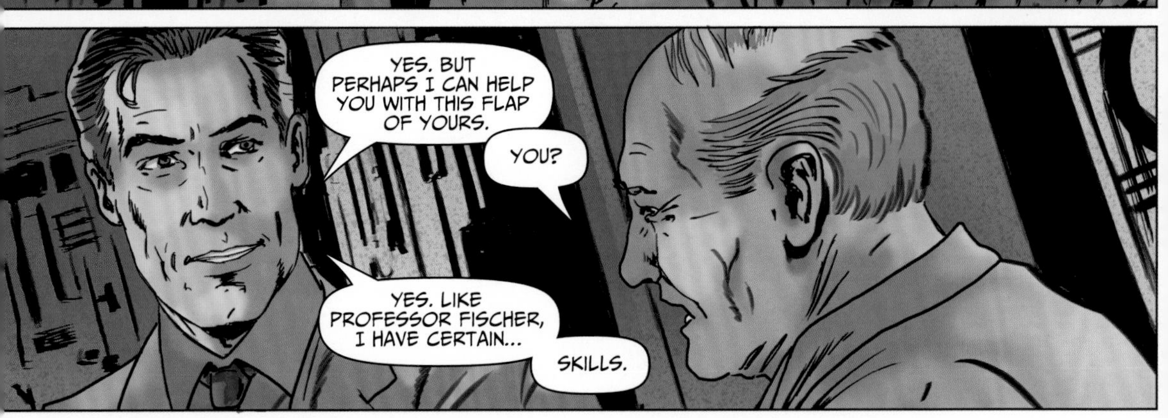
YES. BUT PERHAPS I CAN HELP YOU WITH THIS FLAP OF YOURS.
YOU?
YES. LIKE PROFESSOR FISCHER, I HAVE CERTAIN...
SKILLS.

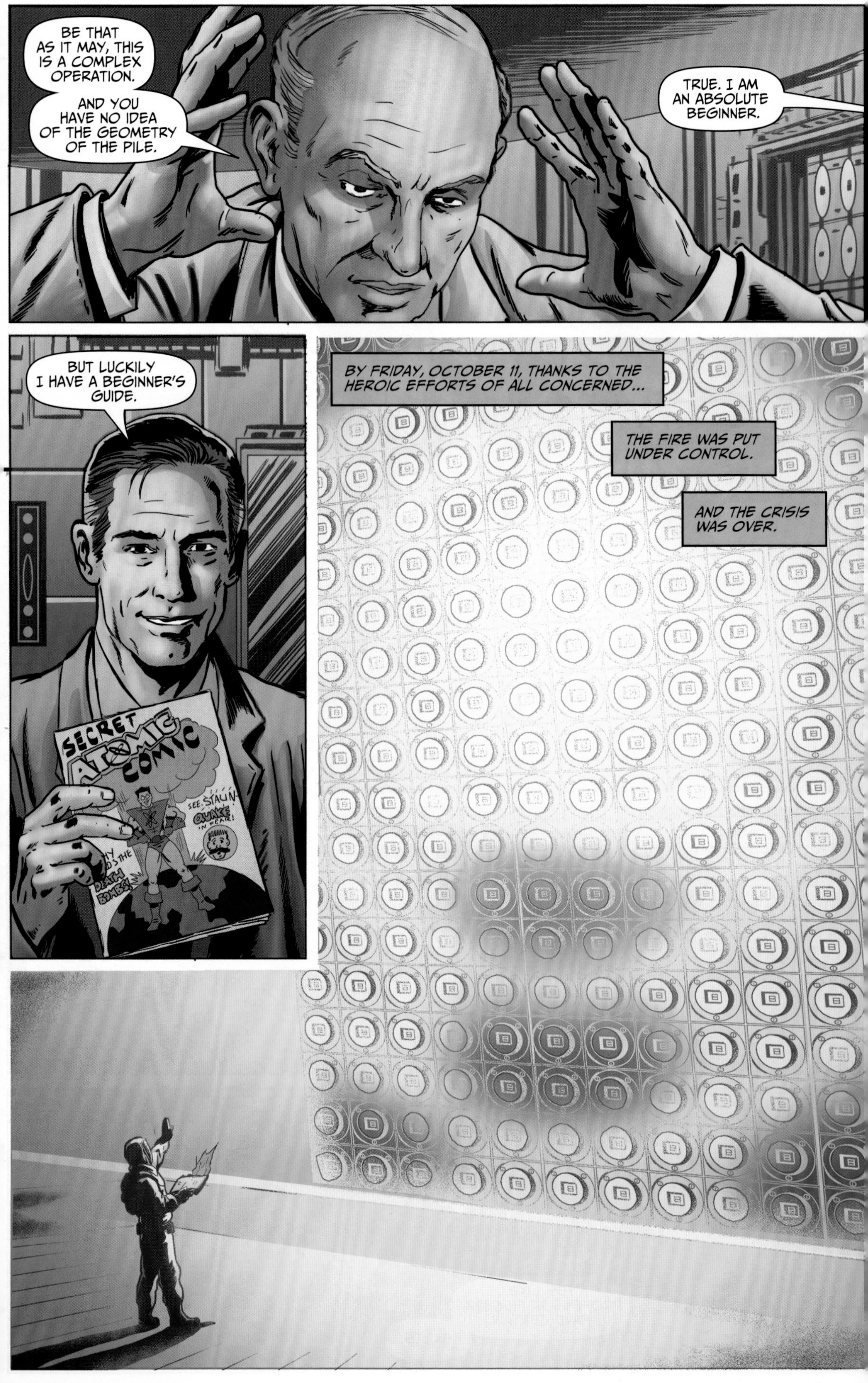
BE THAT AS IT MAY, THIS IS A COMPLEX OPERATION.
AND YOU HAVE NO IDEA OF THE GEOMETRY OF THE PILE.
TRUE. I AM AN ABSOLUTE BEGINNER.
BUT LUCKILY I HAVE A BEGINNER'S GUIDE.
SECRET ATOMIC COMIC
SEE, STALIN QUAKE IN FEAR!
BY FRIDAY, OCTOBER 11, THANKS TO THE HEROIC EFFORTS OF ALL CONCERNED...
THE FIRE WAS PUT UNDER CONTROL.
AND THE CRISIS WAS OVER.

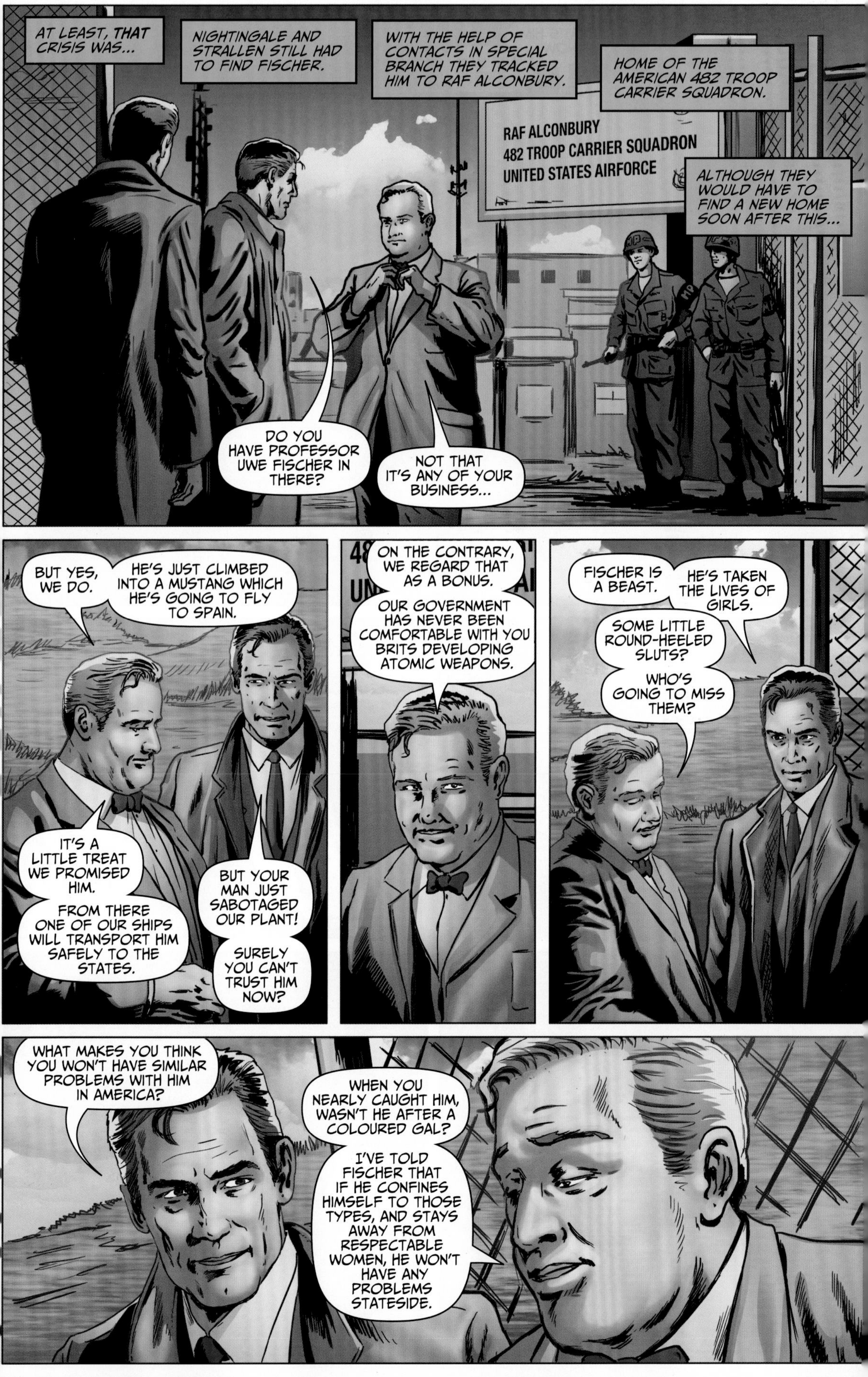
AT LEAST, THAT CRISIS WAS...
NIGHTINGALE AND STRALLEN STILL HAD TO FIND FISCHER.
WITH THE HELP OF CONTACTS IN SPECIAL BRANCH THEY TRACKED HIM TO RAF ALCONBURY.
HOME OF THE AMERICAN 482 TROOP CARRIER SQUADRON.
RAF ALCONBURY
482 TROOP CARRIER SQUADRON
UNITED STATES AIRFORCE
ALTHOUGH THEY WOULD HAVE TO FIND A NEW HOME SOON AFTER THIS...
DO YOU HAVE PROFESSOR UWE FISCHER IN THERE?
NOT THAT IT'S ANY OF YOUR BUSINESS...
BUT YES, WE DO.
HE'S JUST CLIMBED INTO A MUSTANG WHICH HE'S GOING TO FLY TO SPAIN.
IT'S A LITTLE TREAT WE PROMISED HIM.
FROM THERE ONE OF OUR SHIPS WILL TRANSPORT HIM SAFELY TO THE STATES.
BUT YOUR MAN JUST SABOTAGED OUR PLANT!
SURELY YOU CAN'T TRUST HIM NOW?
ON THE CONTRARY, WE REGARD THAT AS A BONUS.
OUR GOVERNMENT HAS NEVER BEEN COMFORTABLE WITH YOU BRITS DEVELOPING ATOMIC WEAPONS.
FISCHER IS A BEAST.
HE'S TAKEN THE LIVES OF GIRLS.
SOME LITTLE ROUND-HEELED SLUTS?
WHO'S GOING TO MISS THEM?
WHAT MAKES YOU THINK YOU WON'T HAVE SIMILAR PROBLEMS WITH HIM IN AMERICA?
WHEN YOU NEARLY CAUGHT HIM, WASN'T HE AFTER A COLOURED GAL?
I'VE TOLD FISCHER THAT IF HE CONFINES HIMSELF TO THOSE TYPES, AND STAYS AWAY FROM RESPECTABLE WOMEN, HE WON'T HAVE ANY PROBLEMS STATESIDE.

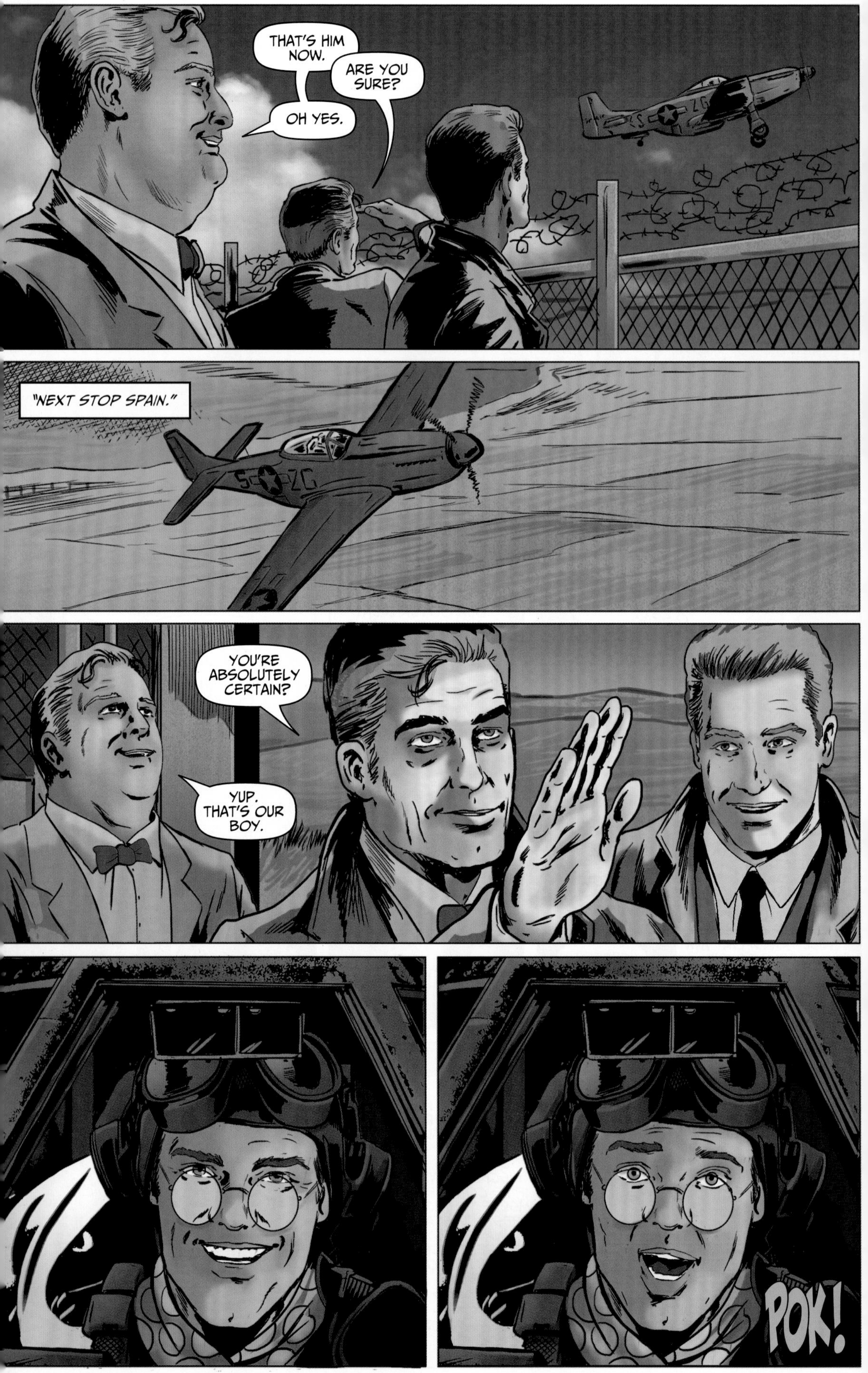
THAT'S HIM NOW.
ARE YOU SURE?
OH YES.
"NEXT STOP SPAIN."
YOU'RE ABSOLUTELY CERTAIN?
YUP. THAT'S OUR BOY.
POK!

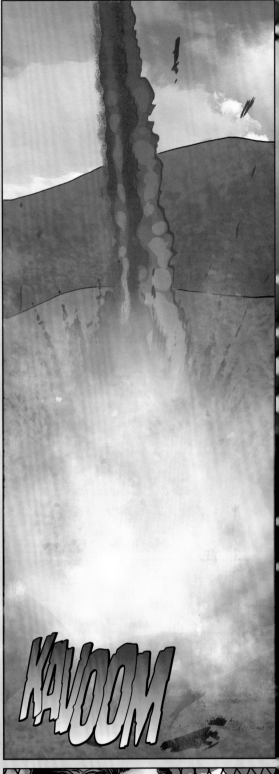

"OH DEAR."

HE SEEMS TO HAVE DEVELOPED ENGINE FAILURE.

KAVOOM

WHAT AN UNLUCKY COINCIDENCE.

"THOMAS?"

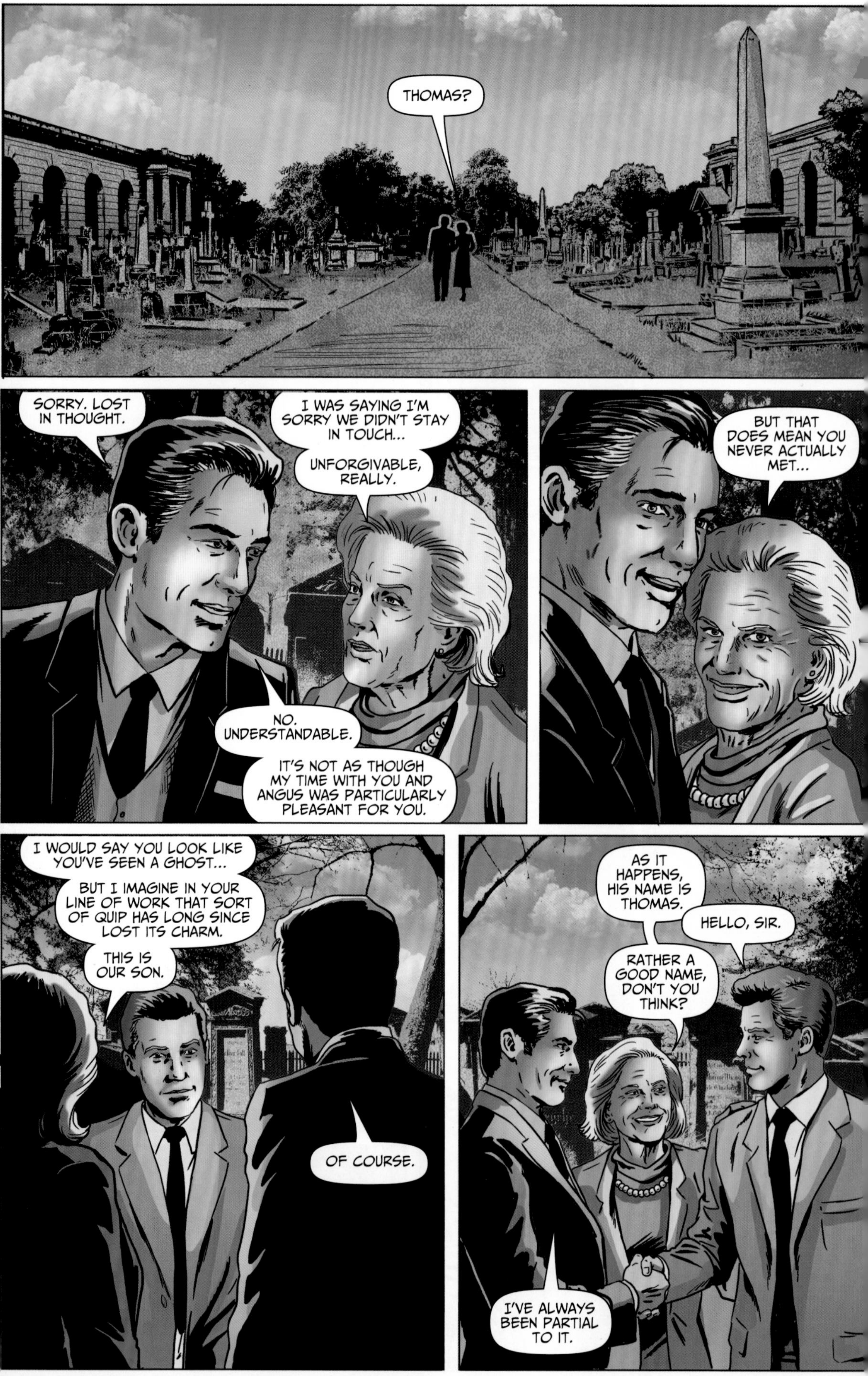
THOMAS?
SORRY. LOST IN THOUGHT.
I WAS SAYING I'M SORRY WE DIDN'T STAY IN TOUCH...
UNFORGIVABLE, REALLY.
NO. UNDERSTANDABLE.
IT'S NOT AS THOUGH MY TIME WITH YOU AND ANGUS WAS PARTICULARLY PLEASANT FOR YOU.
BUT THAT DOES MEAN YOU NEVER ACTUALLY MET...
I WOULD SAY YOU LOOK LIKE YOU'VE SEEN A GHOST...
BUT I IMAGINE IN YOUR LINE OF WORK THAT SORT OF QUIP HAS LONG SINCE LOST ITS CHARM.
THIS IS OUR SON.
OF COURSE.
AS IT HAPPENS, HIS NAME IS THOMAS.
HELLO, SIR.
RATHER A GOOD NAME, DON'T YOU THINK?
I'VE ALWAYS BEEN PARTIAL TO IT.

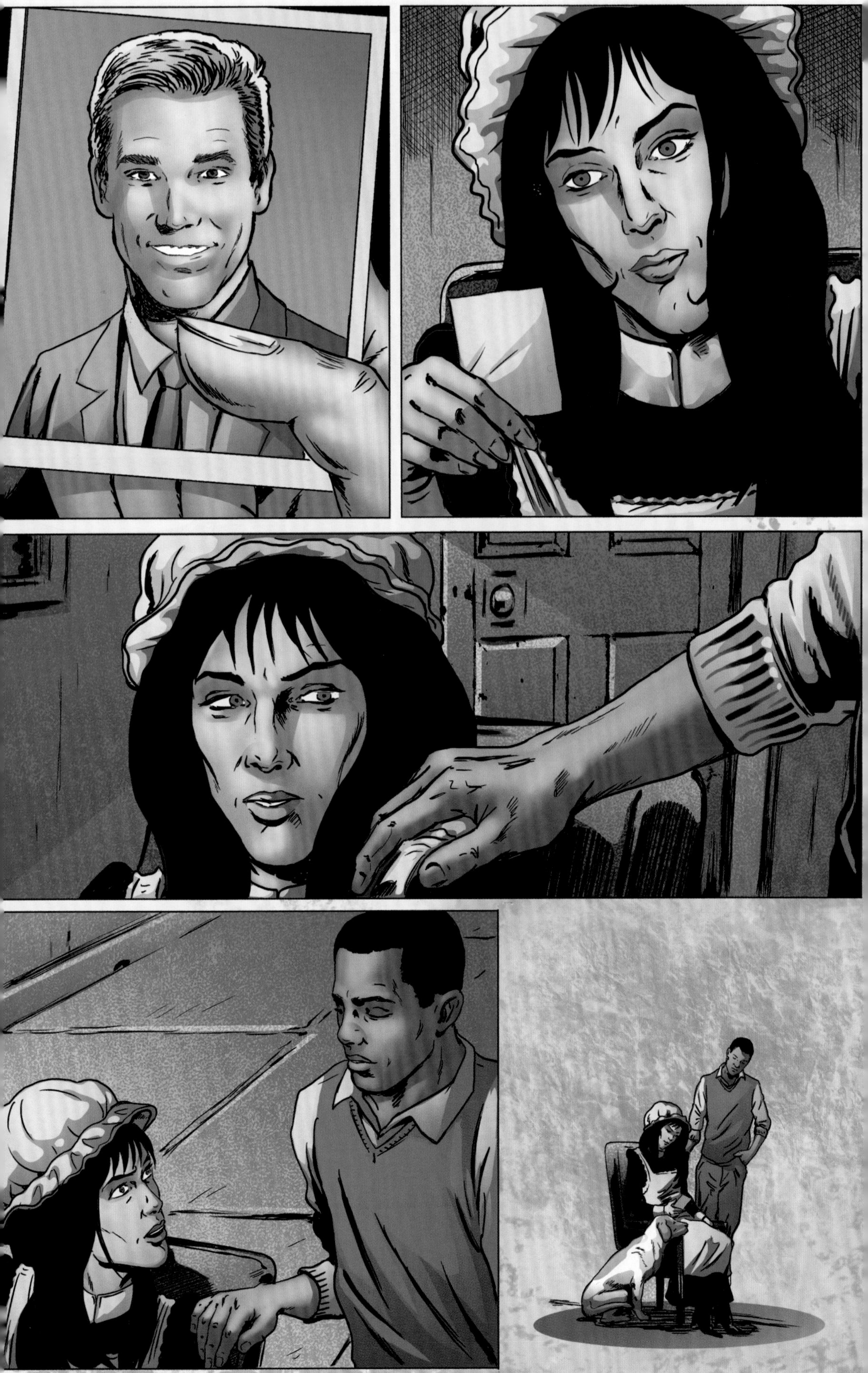

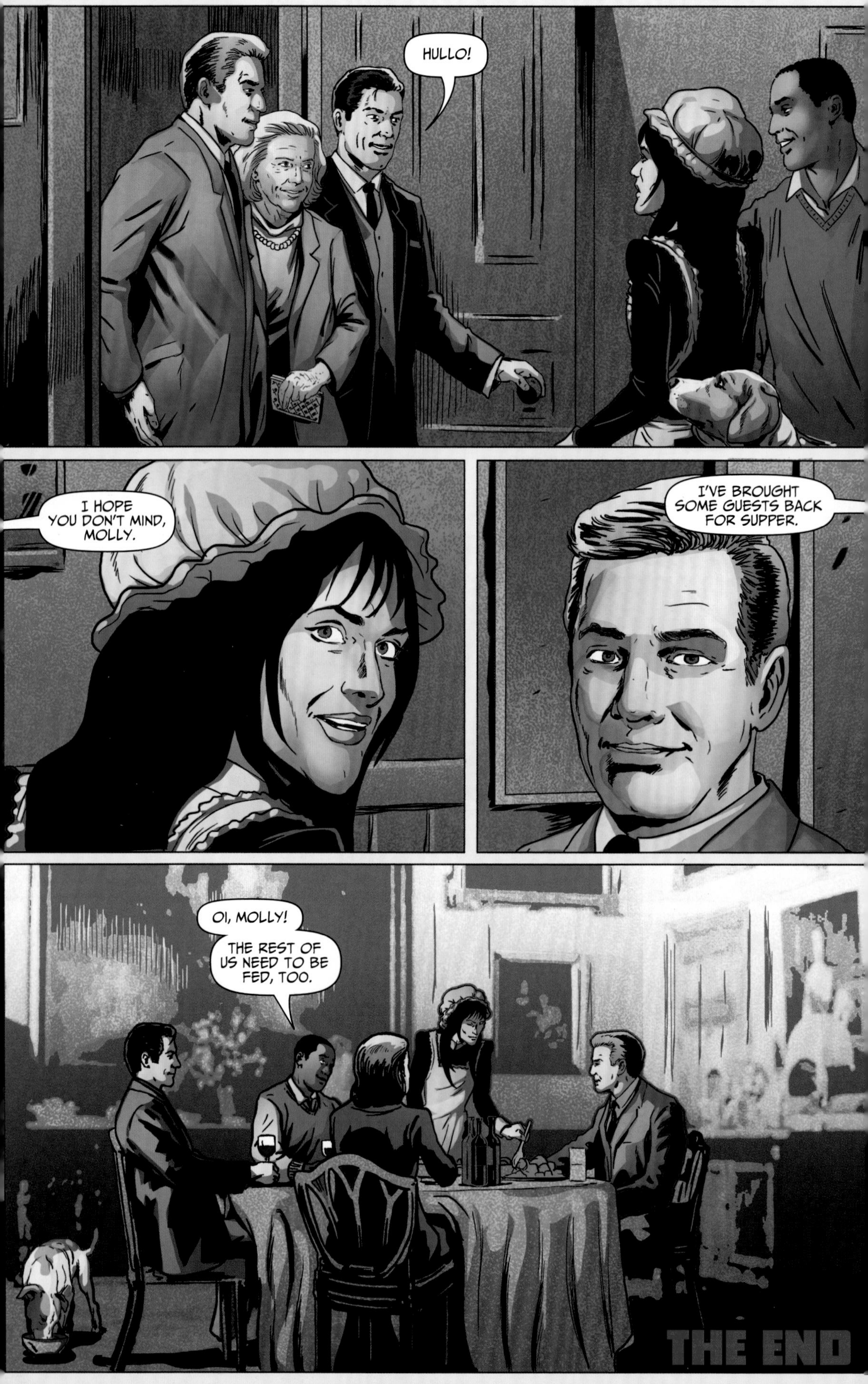
HULLO!
I HOPE YOU DON'T MIND, MOLLY.
I'VE BROUGHT SOME GUESTS BACK FOR SUPPER.
OI, MOLLY!
THE REST OF US NEED TO BE FED, TOO.
THE END

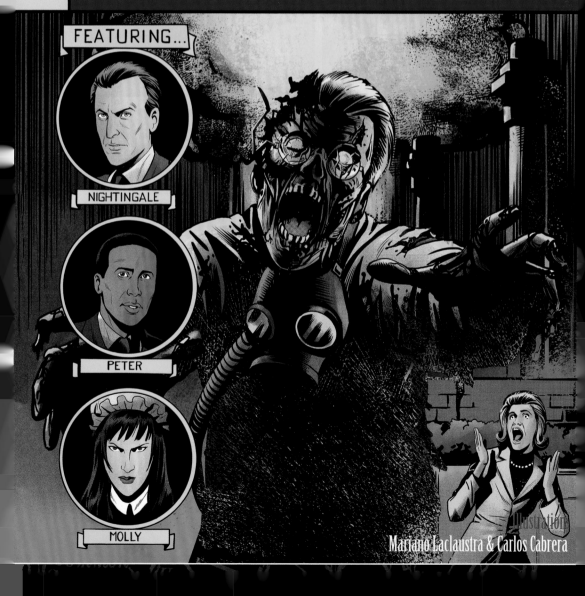

AARONOVITCH
CARTMEL
WILLIAMSON
RENNE

AN ATOMIC COMIC

HORROR

NO.4

RIVERS OF LONDON

FEATURING...

NIGHTINGALE

PETER

MOLLY

Mariano Laclaustra & Carlos Cabrera

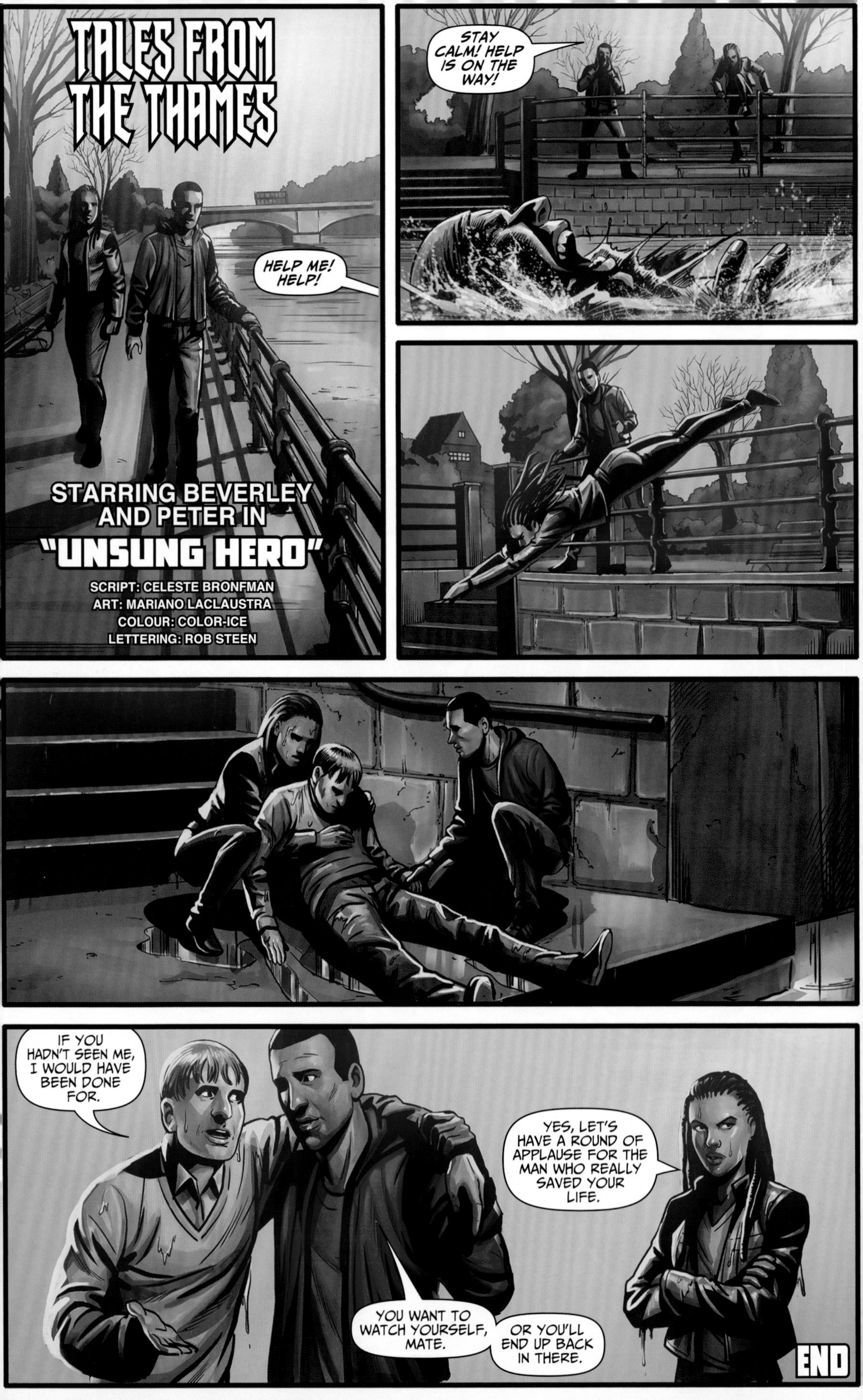
TALES FROM THE THAMES
HELP ME! HELP!
STARRING BEVERLEY AND PETER IN
"UNSUNG HERO"
SCRIPT: CELESTE BRONFMAN
ART: MARIANO LACLAUSTRA
COLOUR: COLOR-ICE
LETTERING: ROB STEEN
STAY CALM! HELP IS ON THE WAY!
IF YOU HADN'T SEEN ME, I WOULD HAVE BEEN DONE FOR.
YES, LET'S HAVE A ROUND OF APPLAUSE FOR THE MAN WHO REALLY SAVED YOUR LIFE.
YOU WANT TO WATCH YOURSELF, MATE.
OR YOU'LL END UP BACK IN THERE.
END

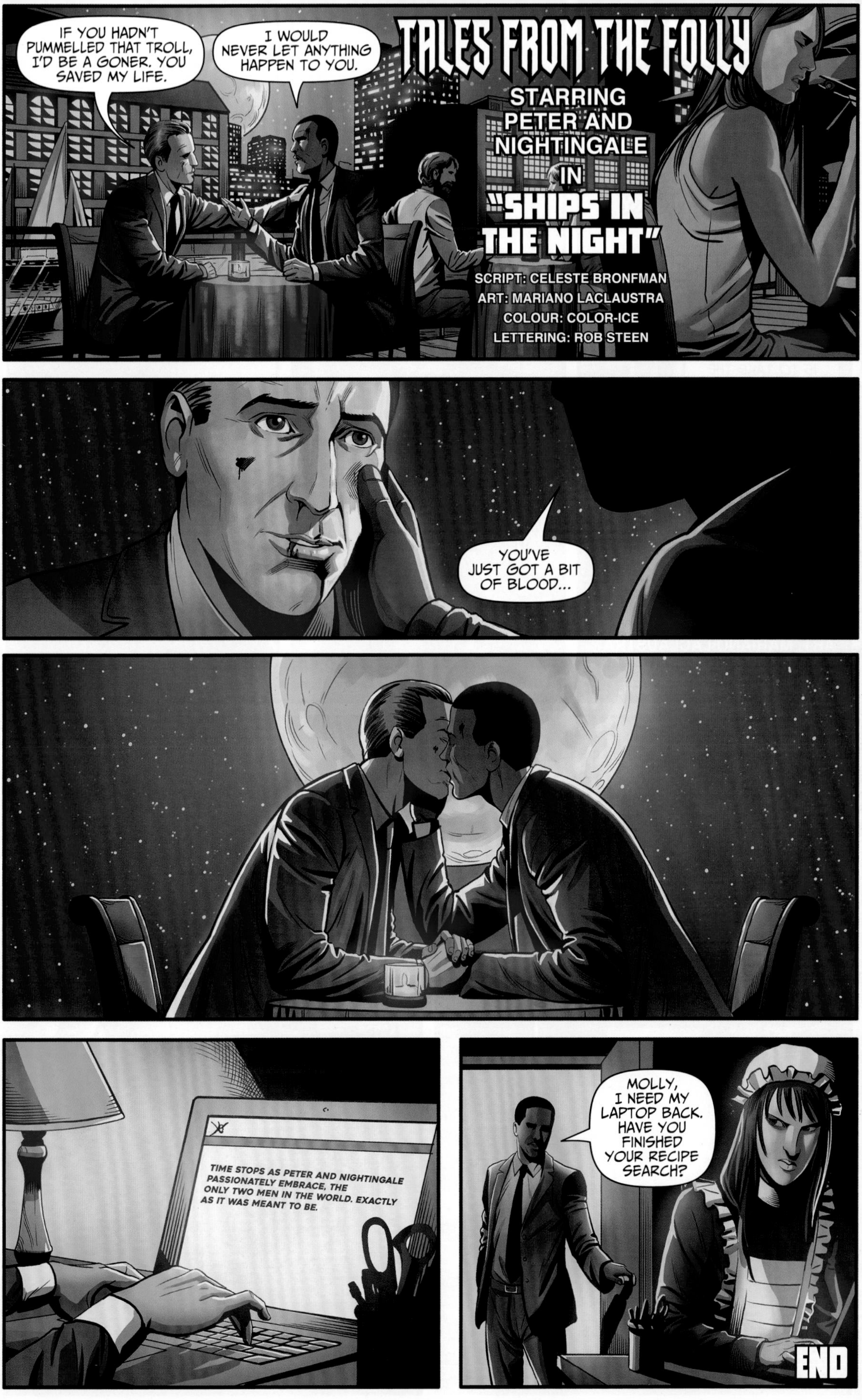
IF YOU HADN'T PUMMELLED THAT TROLL, I'D BE A GONER. YOU SAVED MY LIFE.
I WOULD NEVER LET ANYTHING HAPPEN TO YOU.
TALES FROM THE FOLLY
STARRING PETER AND NIGHTINGALE IN "SHIPS IN THE NIGHT"
SCRIPT: CELESTE BRONFMAN
ART: MARIANO LACLAUSTRA
COLOUR: COLOR-ICE
LETTERING: ROB STEEN
YOU'VE JUST GOT A BIT OF BLOOD...
TIME STOPS AS PETER AND NIGHTINGALE PASSIONATELY EMBRACE, THE ONLY TWO MEN IN THE WORLD. EXACTLY AS IT WAS MEANT TO BE.
MOLLY, I NEED MY LAPTOP BACK. HAVE YOU FINISHED YOUR RECIPE SEARCH?
END

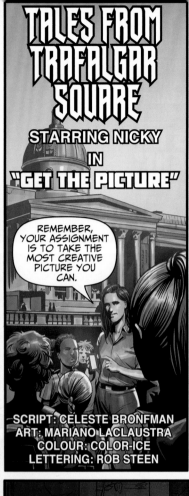

TALES FROM TRAFALGAR SQUARE
STARRING NICKY
IN
"GET THE PICTURE"
REMEMBER, YOUR ASSIGNMENT IS TO TAKE THE MOST CREATIVE PICTURE YOU CAN.
SCRIPT: CELESTE BRONFMAN
ART: MARIANO LACLAUSTRA
COLOUR: COLOR-ICE
LETTERING: ROB STEEN
NATIONAL GALLER
TOO KEWL TO SPELL COOL
ALL RIGHT, NICKY. LET'S SEE THE PICTURE YOU TOOK.
TOO KEWL TO SPELL COOL
IT REALLY IS ONE OF HIS MOST CREATIVE.
END

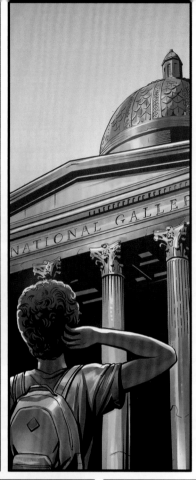

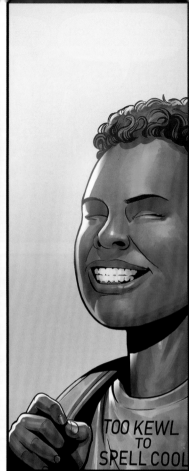

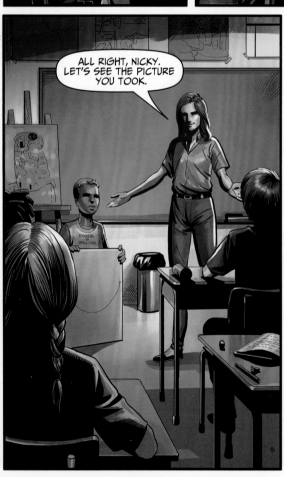

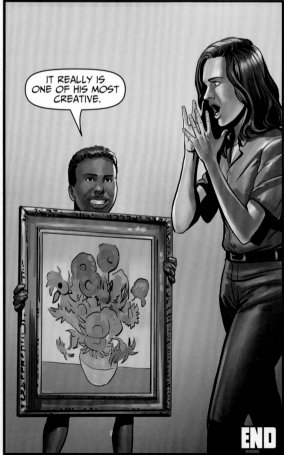

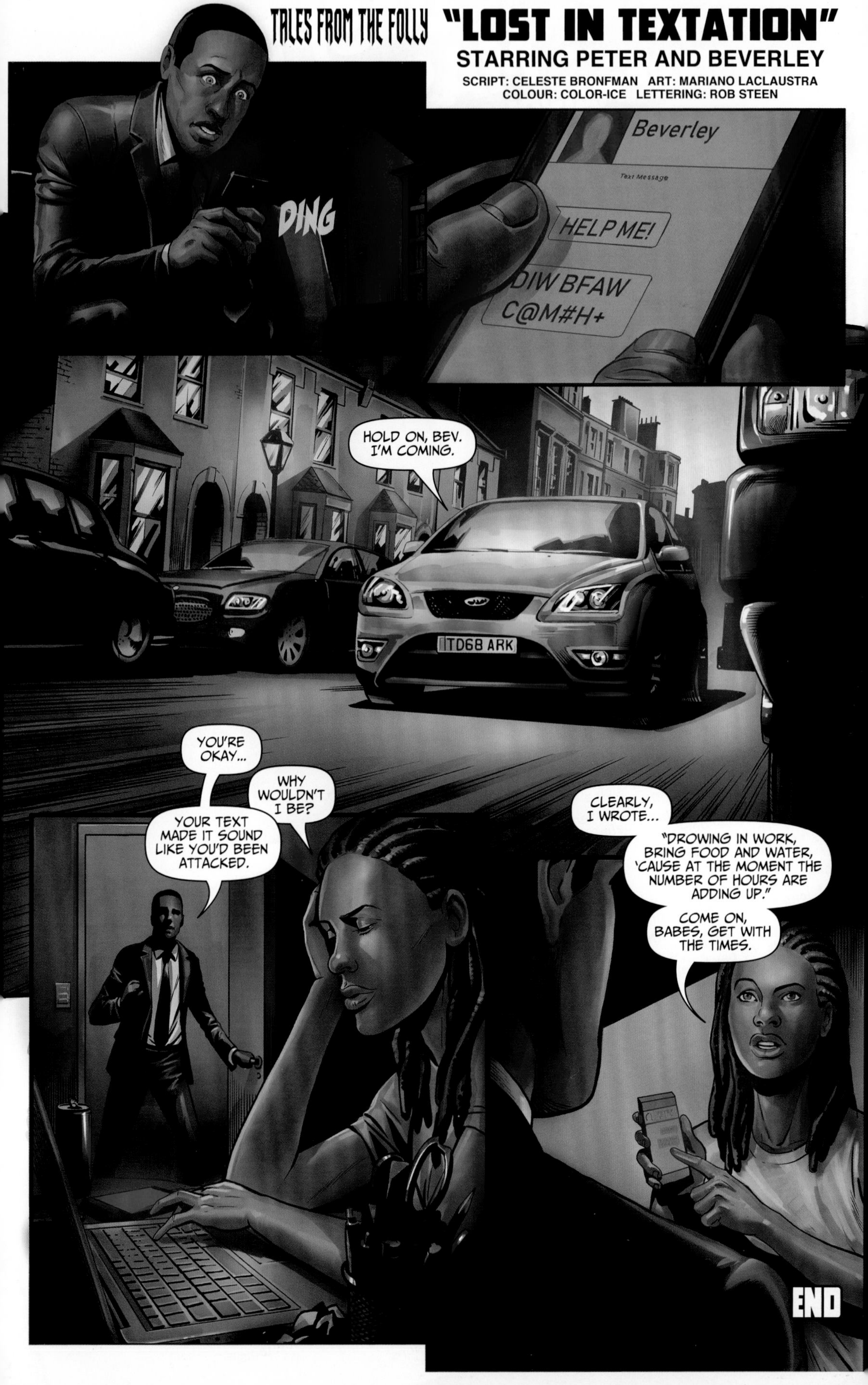
TALES FROM THE FOLLY
"LOST IN TEXTATION"
STARRING PETER AND BEVERLEY
SCRIPT: CELESTE BRONFMAN ART: MARIANO LACLAUSTRA
COLOUR: COLOR-ICE LETTERING: ROB STEEN
DING
Beverley
Text Message
HELP ME!
DIW BFAW C@M#H+
HOLD ON, BEV. I'M COMING.
TD68 ARK
YOU'RE OKAY...
YOUR TEXT MADE IT SOUND LIKE YOU'D BEEN ATTACKED.
WHY WOULDN'T I BE?
CLEARLY, I WROTE...
"DROWING IN WORK, BRING FOOD AND WATER, 'CAUSE AT THE MOMENT THE NUMBER OF HOURS ARE ADDING UP."
COME ON, BABES, GET WITH THE TIMES.
END

JASPER MASKELYNE
THE MAGICIAN WHO FOILED HITLER'S ARMY

The Second World War plummeted the world into chaos, so it's really no surprise that tales of paranormal activity, supernatural events, and unsolved mysteries continue to surface from a time of such trauma. Rumoured to be staunch believers in the occult, Hitler and the Nazi party have since been tied to stories of otherworldly pursuits. You'd be correct to think that the influence behind *Indiana Jones and The Last Crusade* isn't purely fiction. While they didn't confront a whip-wielding archaeologist, the Nazis did spend time searching for religious artefacts, including the Holy Grail. This search was deemed so important that Heinrich Himmler himself – leader of the SS – was tasked with finding the all-powerful cup. It has been documented that Himmler truly believed finding the Holy Grail would grant him supernatural power, allowing him to win the war for Germany. However, the furthest Himmler ever got to completing his quest was to arrive at Montserrat Abbey near Barcelona on the basis of an old Catalonian folk song, only to leave empty-handed.

The Allies were quick to act upon this notorious tendency to superstition, with military strategy often taking strange routes during World War Two. For instance, playing upon the Nazis' belief in astrology, the Brits employed an astrologer named Louis de Wohl to create false horoscopes in an effort to disrupt the Nazis' plans. Unsurprisingly, this didn't work – in fact, it's now believed Hitler's interest in astrology was purely propaganda – and MI5 later admitted their embarrassment at hiring such a "dangerous charlatan". If the Brits were to succeed in using the Nazis' belief in the paranormal to defeat them, they would perhaps have to use magic themselves.

Jasper Maskelyne was a third-generation magician, the grandson of John Nevil Maskelyne who invented the illusion of levitation, as well as the pay toilet which led to the creation of the euphemism "spend a penny". With such notorious lineage to live up to, Jasper was determined to add to his family legacy. When World War Two broke out, he volunteered to join the Royal Engineers. Finding his training frightfully dull, Jasper found himself spending more time acting as a troop entertainer than aiding in the war effort. In an attempt to convince his superiors that an illusionist might be of use to them on the battlefield, he used his skills to create a fake – but realistic – version of the Admiral Graf Spee floating on the Thames. This was no small task, as the German Panzerschiff was not only a 186-metre juggernaut, but had also been scuttled the year before. Jasper reportedly resurrected the battleship using balloons and mirrors. The illusion clearly impressed his superiors, as Jasper was promoted to Major and given his own unit made up of carefully selected electricians, magicians, artists, carpenters, and criminals called 'The Magic Gang.' With his new ragtag team in tow, Jasper was tasked with using magic to trick the Axis forces.

Shortly before The Magic Gang was assembled, the British military established MI9. This special unit of intelligence agents worked hard to provide aid for resistance fighters and to free captured prisoners of war. Many of their missions involved smuggling key equipment into hostile environments, including prison camps. This high level of trickery needed a keen eye and creative mind to oversee inventions. Enter Jasper Maskelyne.

As stated in the Geneva Convention, prisoners were allowed to receive care packages from humanitarian groups – a rule the Allies keenly exploited. The Magic Gang was tasked with creating clever contraptions that looked like everyday items to get past the guards but contained vital tools or information to help the prisoners survive and escape. Among some of these inventions

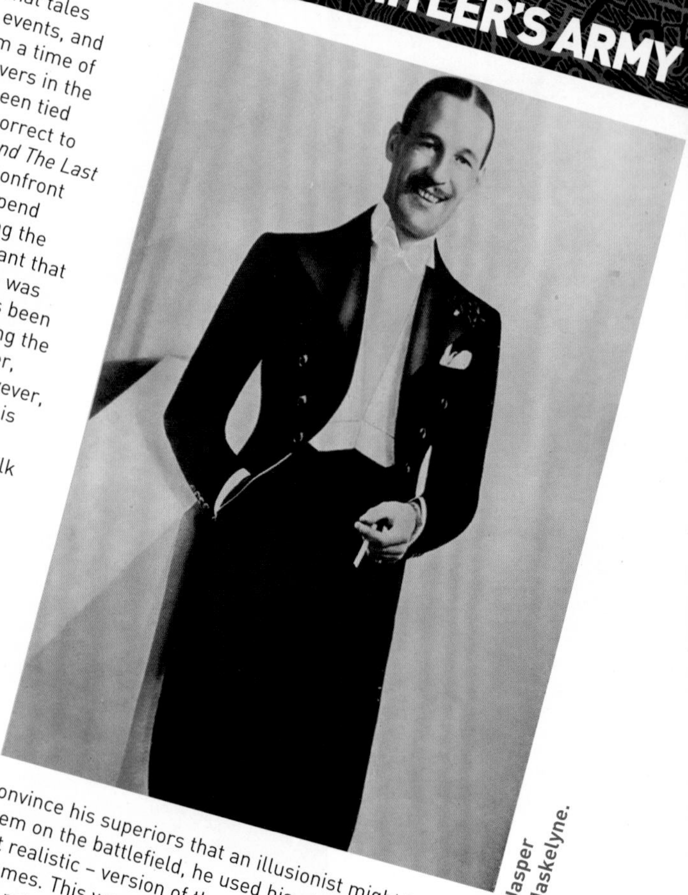

Jasper Maskelyne.

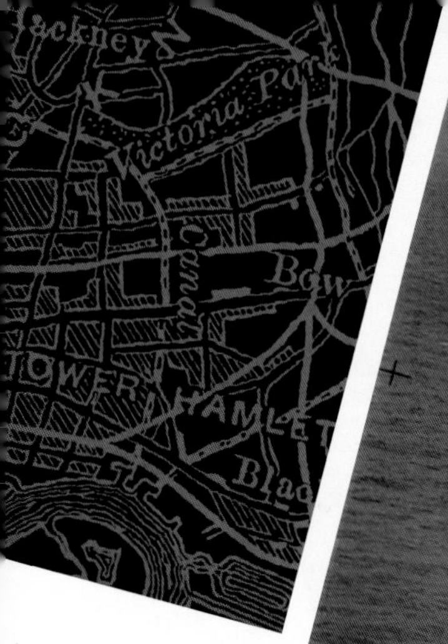
Victoria Park
Bow

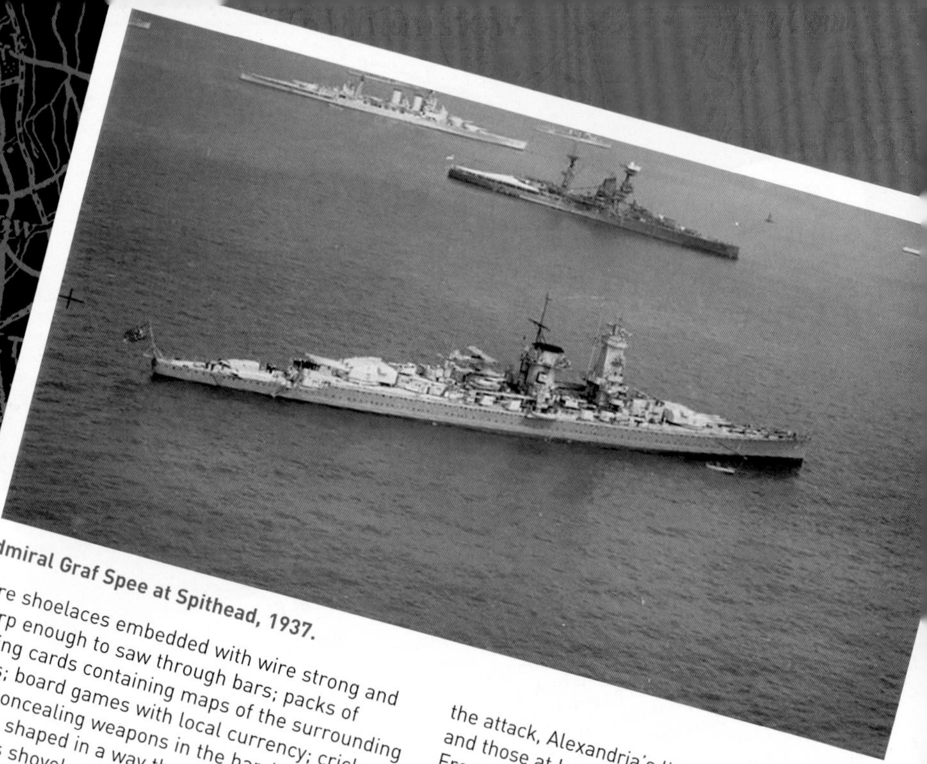

Admiral Graf Spee at Spithead, 1937.

were shoelaces embedded with wire strong and sharp enough to saw through bars; packs of playing cards containing maps of the surrounding areas; board games with local currency; cricket bats concealing weapons in the handle and blades shaped in a way that allowed them to be used as shovels. It has also been reported that a map was hidden inside a gramophone record, concealed so carefully that it's unlikely the prisoners ever would have found it if it hadn't accidentally been broken. Thanks to The Magic Gang's brilliant ideas that would have had James Bond watering at the mouth, MI9 managed to sneak over 1,600 undercover gadgets into Nazi POW camps.

But Jasper's most notorious cases of trickery lie within North Africa, where he was recruited by the head of the deception department, Brigadier Dudley Clarke. It was here that he helped devise the aforementioned gadgets, but Jasper knew his illusions could be bigger. With British troops setting up camp at various spots along the Suez Canal, it was a perfect target for enemy attacks. It was around this area that Jasper would create three mind-boggling tricks to deceive the Axis forces.

His first was at the Alexandria Harbour. Just a short boat ride away from the Suez Canal, this harbour was critical to the Allies. A primary Royal Navy base, it also acted as the main British port for deploying reinforcements. To protect the harbour, Jasper devised a plan which involved moving the entire base as well as staging a full-scale, fake war zone to convince reconnaissance pilots that their target had been destroyed and thereby prevent future attacks. A dummy harbour was set up at Lake Mariout, a body of water just one mile from Alexandria, separated only by a narrow strip of land. Using canvas ships and plywood buildings, Jasper and his team recreated Alexandria's light grid and lighthouse. On the night of the attack, Alexandria's lights were switched off, and those at Lake Mariout were switched on. From 8,000 feet above in the dark, the Luftwaffe were unable to tell the difference, and proceeded to attack the fake harbour. To give the illusion that they were engaged in battle, ground troops feigned fighting back with fake shells. Meanwhile, a team used truck-loads of papier-mache bricks and painted bomb craters to create the illusion of a devastated harbour at the real Alexandria in anticipation of reconnaissance aircraft the following morning. It has been rumoured that this deception worked a total of nine times!

Jasper's next and perhaps most notorious trick, was to hide the Suez Canal altogether. How does one hide a 20-mile-long, well-mapped

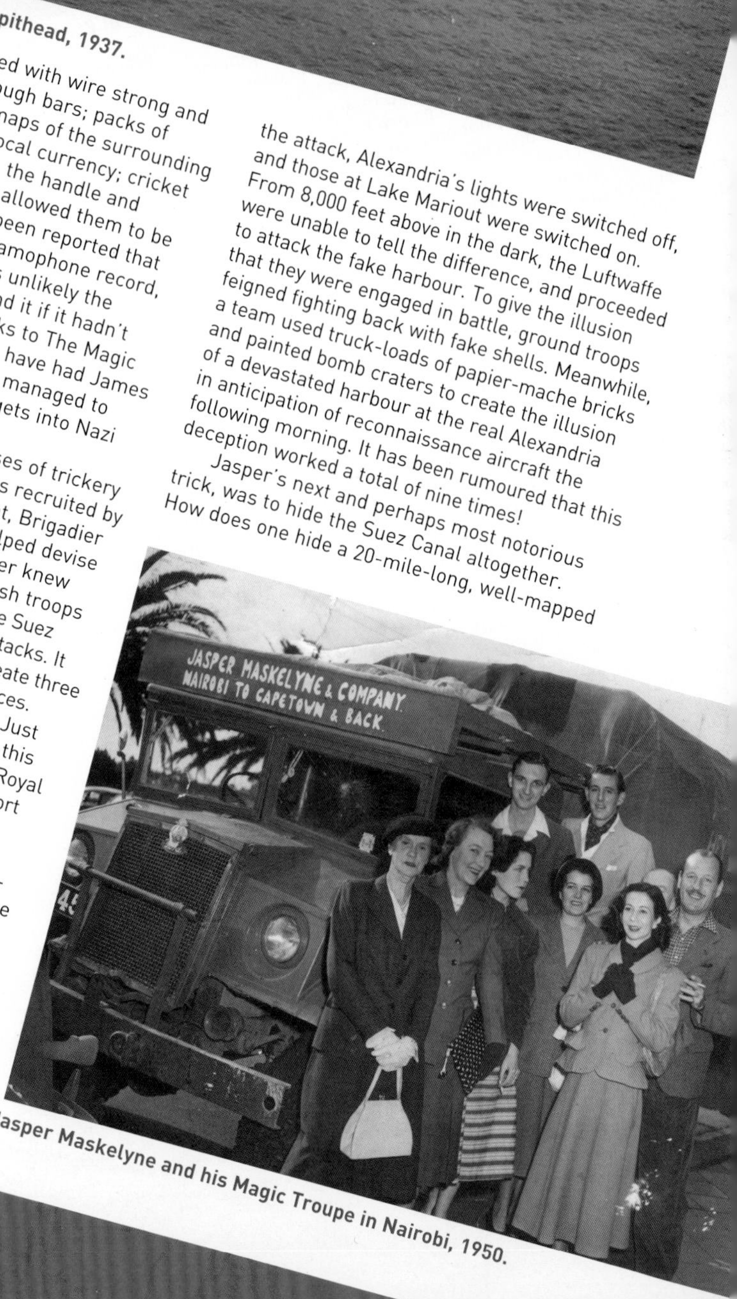
JASPER MASKELYNE & COMPANY
NAIROBI TO CAPETOWN & BACK

Jasper Maskelyne and his Magic Troupe in Nairobi, 1950.

body of water? His plan for this illusion was to give the Axis forces the ol' razzle dazzle – quite literally. Since the Luftwaffe conducted their raids at night, Jasper believed that using multiple huge, flashing lights would damage the Luftwaffe's chances of hitting their target. The Magic Gang reportedly built giant spotlights comprising of revolving tin mirrors with spinning searchlights which, when turned on, would shine cones of light that stretched for nine miles, the idea being that as German bombers flew into the light, they would be too blinded to spot the canal. If sources are to be believed, the impact was incredible, not only saving the canal from devastation, but disorienting enemy pilots and causing them to crash.

As with all great magicians, Jasper was saving his best trick until last. The Nazis were becoming desperate by October 1942, with their diminishing supplies and the British hot on their heels. The dream of conquering Egypt was slipping from their grasp. It was all leading to the Battle of El Alamein. The Magic Gang was once again employed in hope of deceiving the Axis forces just enough to tip the scales in the Allies' favour. They were set the task of tricking the Afrika Korps into believing an attack would be coming from the south, when it would actually be coming from the north. Once again, Jasper and his crew set out to create a large-scale illusion. In the north, the Magic Gang disguised 1,000 tanks by making them look like trucks, while in the south, they created an army of 2,000 inflatable dummy tanks. During this time, they also created a phantom war zone. Radio chatter played constantly with noise of construction echoing in the background, supply dumps were made, fake buildings and railway lines were manufactured. The true genius, however, lay in an ever-incomplete water pipeline, which convinced General Erwin Rommel that the Allies were not prepared for battle, and left completely flabbergasted when the Allies began their invasion on October 23rd. The battle was such a success that Churchill commended it in the House of Commons, praising the plan as a "marvellous system of camouflage."

The Magic Gang disbanded shortly after this mission, and Jasper Maskelyne eventually retired in Kenya. As a man who built his remarkable career on illusion and grandiose trickery, some are sceptical of his involvement in the Second World War. The real details of his work have been blurred by secrecy, lost documents, exaggerated stories, and lack of eyewitnesses, leading many to discredit Jasper's work. There is no photographic evidence of his battleship illusion; many believe the Alexandria harbour deception was someone else's idea for which Jasper took the credit, if it had been possible in the first place; hiding the Suez Canal is believed to be utter nonsense, with little evidence to suggest the lights existed or that Jasper was even there, with the canal instead protected by conventional defence methods; and despite the events at El Alamein being true, Jasper has been removed from almost all accounts, with camouflage expert Anthony Ayrton getting the credit. Reports about Jasper's final days are also contradictory. Some believe he was happily living in Kenya, a respected member of his community who taught driving and magic lessons, while others believe he died a bitter drunk. The real history of Britain's magician who aided in the war effort will never truly be known, but what is certain is that Jasper Maskelyne was a man who was every bit as elusive as his career.

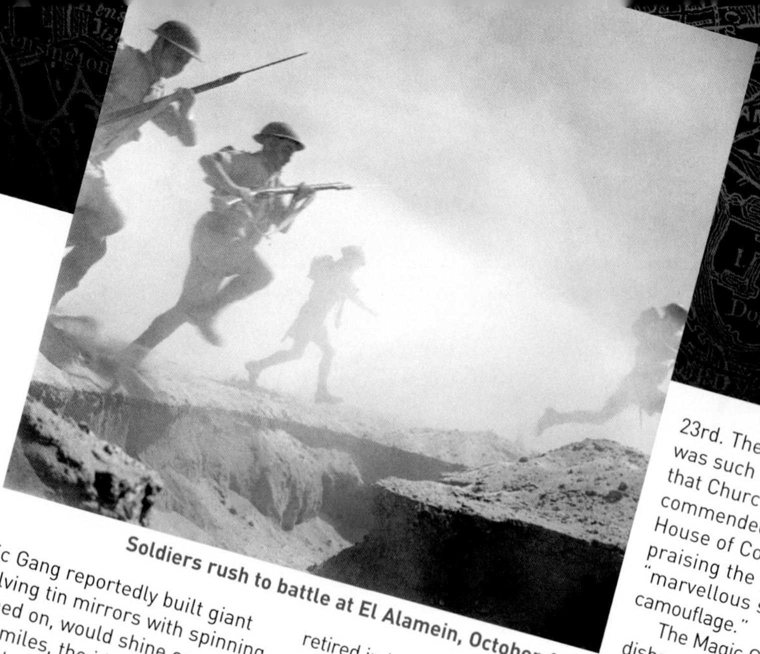

Soldiers rush to battle at El Alamein, October 1942.

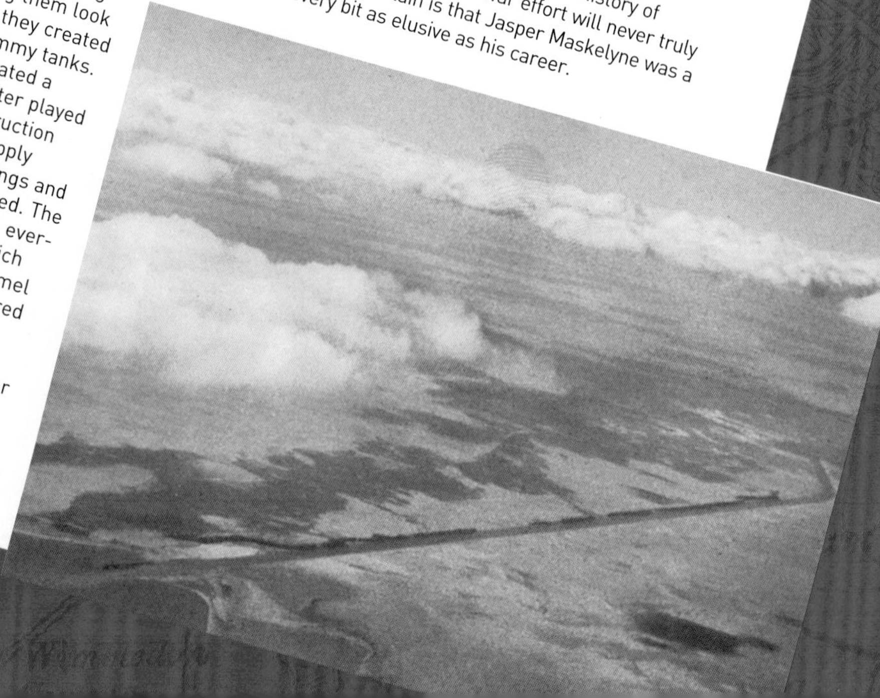

The Suez Canal, 1934.

BLOODHOUNDS: A DETECTIVE'S BEST FRIEND

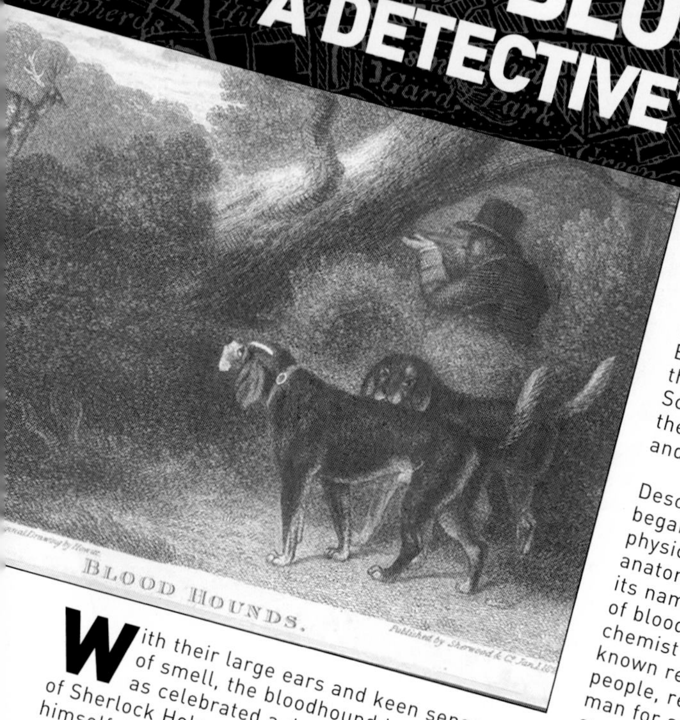
BLOOD HOUNDS.

Bloodhounds hunting deer, 1826.

With their large ears and keen sense of smell, the bloodhound has become as celebrated a detective as the likes of Sherlock Holmes or Thomas Nightingale himself. In fact, Sherlock Holmes employed the help of a "lop-eared creature, half spaniel and half lurcher, brown and white in colour" known as Toby in *The Sign of Four*, a dog who would later be portrayed by a bloodhound in the BBC's hit TV show, *Sherlock*. Holmes would have no other assistance, insisting he would "rather have Toby's help than that of the whole detective force in London." And it's no surprise that some of the world's greatest detectives have paired with these sensational sniffer dogs. With an olfactory bulb almost forty times larger than a human's, crammed with nearly 300 million receptors, bloodhounds have noses so strong, they can catch a whiff of the past! Their ability to pick up a scent in the air, combined with being absolutely tireless when tracking, makes them a detective's dream partner (and a crook's worst nightmare) when working a case.

The date of the breed's arrival to the UK is hotly debated, although it's considered that they are descendants of the hounds once kept at the Abbey of Saint-Hubert, Belgium. Used primarily for hunting deer and wild boar, there is evidence that bloodhounds have been employed to track humans from as early as the Middle Ages, particularly in the wilds of Scotland. Known in Medieval Scotland as "sleuth hounds", these dogs patrolled the Scottish borders from the 1300s to track Border Reivers – raiders of both Scottish and English descent who terrorised folks who lived near the border. So honored were these sleuth hounds in Scotland that poems were written about both Robert the Bruce and William Wallace trying to outsmart and outrun these tremendous hunters.

Descriptions of the bloodhound as we know it began to emerge in the 16th Century. John Caius, physician and pioneer in advancing the science of anatomy, wrote an account which gave the breed its name, describing how they would use the scent of blood to trace their quarry in game parks. Later, chemist Robert Boyle would write the earliest known report of the bloodhound's skill to track people, recounting one dog's capability in tracking a man for seven miles along a busy route, finding the suspect hiding in the upper floor of a building.

Bloodhounds have been excellent assets across the pond too, with some of the most famous noses in sleuthing history coming from the United States. Nick Carter, named after a famous detective from America's 'dime novel' pulp fiction, was born in 1900, owned and handled by Captain G V Mullikin of Lexington, Kentucky, and held the record for picking up a cold trail after a long period of time, catching the scent of a suspect in an arson case after 105 hours and leading authorities to the culprit. Nick Carter was responsible for successfully following over 650 trails, and ultimately became the inspiration for many fictional crime-solving bloodhounds. Nick Carter's record was smashed in 1954 when another keen-nosed, anonymous hound was capable of picking up a scent over 300 hours old to find a missing family in Oregon.

Perhaps the most famous bloodhounds from British history are associated with the first "official" experiment with police dogs – and the most notorious cold case from Victorian London. In 1888, Jack the Ripper was terrorising London's streets. With the Metropolitan Police still in its adolescence, the police found themselves under immense pressure to prove to the public that they were making headway with solving the case and catching the killer, which led to some unconventional methods of investigation. Police Commissioner Sir Charles Warren was under extreme scrutiny from the press who took every opportunity to ridicule his efforts (or lack thereof). When a letter to *The Times* was published following the murders of Elizabeth Stride and Catherine Eddowes in late September, suggesting that police allow bloodhounds the opportunity to try and trace the Ripper, Warren responded with cynicism, concerned that hounds would be unable to trace a suspect from a scene with no evidence to acquire a scent from, and the fear that the trail would be easily lost in the city's busy streets.

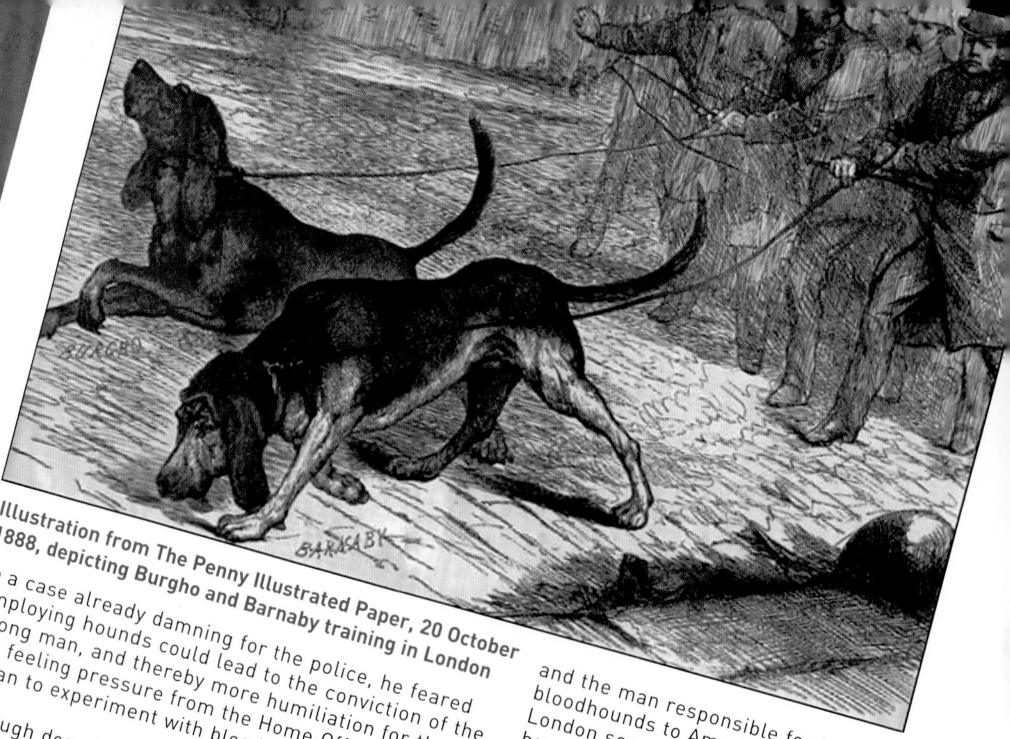

Illustration from The Penny Illustrated Paper, 20 October 1888, depicting Burgho and Barnaby training in London

In a case already damning for the police, he feared employing hounds could lead to the conviction of the wrong man, and thereby more humiliation for the Met. But feeling pressure from the Home Office, he quickly began to experiment with bloodhounds.

Although dogs have accompanied police officers since the 15th Century, they were not a fixed part of the force at the time of the Ripper murders. Instead, the police borrowed dogs from private owners when an extra snout was required for investigations. It was Sir Charles Warren's intention to buy dogs that could remain a part of the police department. It was with this in mind that he contacted Edwin Brough, a silk manufacturer from Scarborough, who was also a famous breeder of hounds – particularly well known for his successes in tracking competitions around the country – founder of the Bloodhound Association, and the man responsible for introducing bloodhounds to America. Brough arrived in London soon after with two of his finest hounds, Burgundy (known as Burgho) and Barnaby.

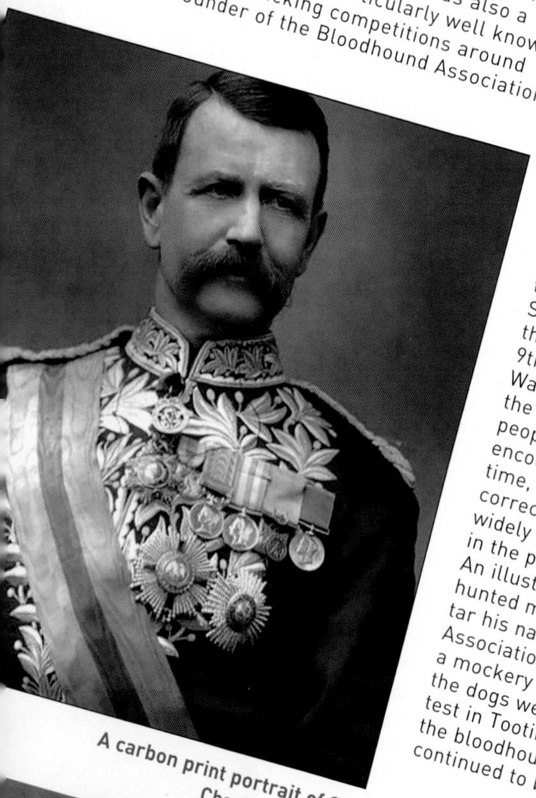

A carbon print portrait of Sir Charles Warren.

Two-year-old Burgho and four-year-old Barnaby were very used to working together, having both been through intensive training under Brough's watch. They were two of the breeder's fastest hounds and were capable of hunting "the clean shoe", that is, following a trail which wasn't strongly marked in any way. If there were two dogs who may have had the skills necessary to catch a cruel and clever murderer such as Jack the Ripper, it was unlikely to find them any more skilled than Burgho and Barnaby.

The hounds proved their incredible abilities during a period of trials. In the early morning of Monday 8th October, Brough took the dogs to Regent's Park where they successfully tracked a young man who had been granted a fifteen-minute running start for almost a mile, despite the thick hoar frost that coated the ground. That night, Burgho and Barnaby were taken to Hyde Park where they were tasked with tracking another man in the dead of night. Once again, they were successful. The final test would include Sir Charles Warren himself as a quarry to prove the bloodhounds' intelligence. At 7am on Tuesday 9th October, six test runs were made, with Warren twice acting as the hunted man. In all of the six tests, the hounds were required to track people they were unfamiliar with, occasionally encountering deliberately crossed paths. Each time, the hounds would successfully pick up the correct trail and find their suspect. Although widely praised, many used Warren's experiments in the park with the dogs as a source of ridicule. An illustrated image of Sir Charles acting as the hunted man proved irresistible to those keen to tar his name. On October 19th, the Press Association suggested the trials were making a mockery of the police force, claiming that the dogs were lost amidst the fog during a test in Tooting. Though completely untrue, the bloodhound experiments nevertheless continued to blemish Warren's reputation.

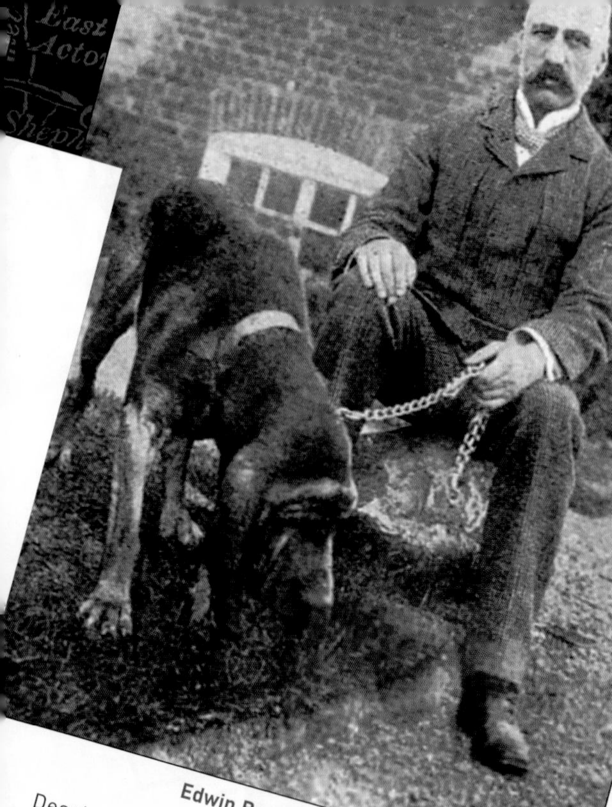

Edwin Brough with one of his bloodhounds.

Despite the trials being successful, the overall experience would prove to become another blunder for the Metropolitan Police and the Ripper case. Brough was required to return to Scarborough in late October, but left Burgho and Barnaby in London with his friend, W K Taunton. Brough called for Burgho to be sent to Brighton for a dog show soon after. As October neared its end, and still receiving no confirmation from the police as to whether or not they were keen to purchase or hire the dogs, he took Barnaby back from Taunton, and the three returned to their home in Scarborough. The news of the dogs' removal was slow to reach everyone in the police force, and the final embarrassment would coincide with the discovery of the Ripper's rumoured last victim, Mary Jane Kelly.

Overwhelmed with the embarrassment and slander the case garnered, Sir Charles Warren resigned on 8th November 1888, just hours before Mary Jane Kelly's murder. Authorities received news that Kelly's body had been spotted through the window of 13 Miller's Court at 11.30am on 9th November. Leading the investigation, Inspector Abberline recalled that no crime scenes were to be touched until Brough's bloodhounds arrived to pick up the Ripper's scent. The police waited outside Kelly's door for two hours before discovering the dogs were no longer in London.

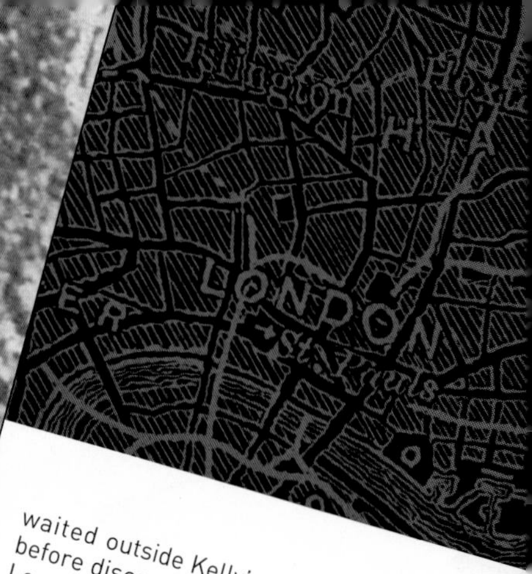
Islington
LONDON
St Pauls

Whilst Bungho and Barnaby may not have been able to catch the Ripper, never getting the chance to put their magnificent tracking skills to the test, it has been suggested that the dogs' presence in London deterred the Ripper from committing further murders, pausing his killing spree. In 1901, Brough told *Scarborough Magazine*, "[The hounds] were not put to the test so far as the Whitechapel Murders were concerned, for no murder was committed during the time the hounds were in London. This I consider some evidence of the deterrent effect which the employment of bloodhounds would have on crime, for another of the ghastly Jack the Ripper tragedies was committed shortly after it was known that the hounds had been sent back to Wyndyate." It's entirely possible that the vast media attention Burgho and Barnaby's presence in London received, combined with the notoriety of bloodhounds' tracking skills, deterred the Ripper from striking again to avoid the risk of being traced. Nevertheless, the experiment garnered negative press, with reporters creating a damning picture of comedic incompetency within the Metropolitan Police.

It wasn't until the 1930s that the UK police force finally recognised the potential of employing police dogs. However, their initial introduction leaned towards aggression rather than tailing, with attack dogs being introduced. Whilst bloodhounds are unquestionably the most skilled trackers in the dog world, their gentle nature means they're not much use at pinning down suspects once they've found them. Following the Second World War, the police began to favour German shepherds, replacing the role of the bloodhound on the police force. However, no dog has been able to capture the imagination – or replicate the astounding tracing ability – when it comes to crime such as the bloodhound; the ultimate sleuthing dog.

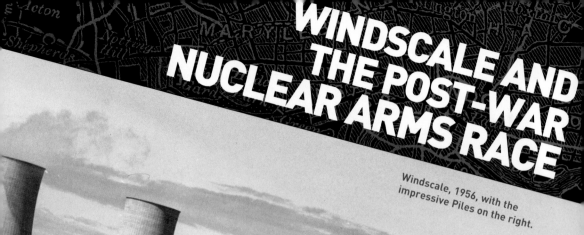

WINDSCALE AND THE POST-WAR NUCLEAR ARMS RACE

Windscale, 1956, with the impressive Piles on the right.

Seascale is a small, sleepy village in Cumbria on the north-western coast of England, looking out over the Irish Sea. The slow pace of family and farming life was interrupted in 1939 when Royal Ordnance Factories were built just three miles away to help with the war effort. Along with the influx of work came a flood of people, and the village consequently grew to accommodate the new workforce. Following the return to peace, Seascale found itself once again without major industry and its citizens became the consequential victims of post-war depression, so it was with open arms that the villagers welcomed the construction of the Windscale Piles, in the late 1940s. Britain's first nuclear complex, in the late 1940s. Little did these unsuspecting people know that one of these two new piles would create the worst nuclear accident in British history.

Britain was a prominent force in scientific research and the idea of an all-powerful super-weapon had been presented in British literature and political rhetoric since the early 1900s. Many recognised the potential influence of science, one notorious example being HG Wells, who carefully studied the work of William Ramsay, Frederick Soddy, and Ernest Rutherford – the first person to split the atom. Wells' understanding of the destructive power of nuclear science is perhaps best explored in his 1914 novel, *The World Set Free: A Story of Mankind*. Warnings in literature have rarely deterred scientists and politicians, however. So, with Otto Hahn and Fritz Strassmann's discovery of nuclear fission raising awareness of the possibility of the creation of a powerful weapon being closely followed by the outbreak of World War Two, Britain accelerated its experimentation with nuclear science in an effort to develop a real atomic bomb.

Long fascinated with science, one of Winston Churchill's priorities upon being elected Prime Minister in the spring of 1940 was to create a uranium subcommittee, titled MAUD, which would be responsible for advising his government on how to proceed and succeed. Throughout the war, British scientists worked with the United States and Canada to further develop nuclear technology. As this research continued, however, British scientists noted America's considerably advanced knowledge of this new science, with Michael Pernin remarking that the US would "completely outstrip us in ideas, research and application of nuclear energy and that then, quite rightly, they will see no reason for our butting in." This sparked Churchill's eagerness to remain a close ally with the United States, nurturing the 'special relationship', keen to maintain Britain's reputation as a worthy partner, equal in knowledge and power. Britain continued to work with America on the Manhattan Project, providing valuable resources such as British uranium and lending Britain's best scientists to the project, including James Chadwick, Klaus Fuchs, and William Penney. Chadwick became the key representative for Britain during the Manhattan Project, forging a close, strong partnership with the Americans to ensure that Britain would stay suitably involved. America, however, recognised their own powerful status in developing this new powerful technology and the British representatives found themselves increasingly pushed to the sidelines.

James Chadwick works with Major General Leslie Groves as part of the Manhattan Project.

The special relationship Churchill had so carefully cultivated began to fracture after the war ended. Considering the new technology and information uncovered during the Manhattan Project to be a joint discovery, Britain had expected that the sharing of advancements in the nuclear field would continue in peacetime. But the death of Roosevelt in 1945 would mark the end of wartime collaboration between the two countries, as President Truman brought to a conclusion the agreements previously reached with Britain and Canada, going so far as to introduce the Atomic Energy Act in 1946 which classified US atomic secrets. With this act, it became a federal offence to reveal such nuclear secrets, deeming it a matter of national security; a decision spurred on by the discovery that prominent scientist Klaus Fuchs, a man introduced to the project by the British, was a Soviet spy who had been feeding key information from the Manhattan Project back to the Soviet Union. Many considered the initiation of this act as marking America's return to isolationism, but the decision was a devastating snub for Britain's new Prime Minister, Clement Attlee, who saw in it a threat to Britain's status and influence as a Great Power. Attlee now felt under pressure to maintain the country's position, knowing that the British would need to develop an atomic bomb of their own to convince the US that Britain was a natural, powerful ally and hopefully reinstate their collaborative and special relationship.

And so, Attlee decided to independently pursue the research of nuclear science and creation of an atomic bomb. In 1945, he created the Gen 75 Committee, also known as the Atomic Bomb Committee, which established the government's nuclear policy. He knew he would need some of Britain's sharpest minds to successfully develop Britain's nuclear technology and brought some of the country's most prominent scientists on board, fresh from their time working on the Manhattan Project. Although these scientists had gained key experience in the States and returned home with valuable knowledge, none of them had a complete picture of how their research came together to create a nuclear weapon, having been limited in their roles. Therefore, British nuclear development was divided into three key areas: armaments, research, and engineering.

A pioneer of nuclear science, John Cockcroft was the immediate choice to lead the research team, establishing his station at Harwell. In charge of Armaments was William Penney, a brilliant mathematician from a modest background who had helped develop the Hiroshima bomb. No stranger to nuclear science, he had worked with the Americans at Los Alamos, witnessed the Nagasaki bombing, and gained experience working on Operation Crossroads.

Following his return to Britain, he faced the choice of resuming a quiet life in academia, with an offer to be principal of an Oxford college, or to help to develop Britain's first nuclear bomb. A little political persuasion convinced Penney to turn down Oxford and join Attlee's growing team of scientists. Penney's previous achievements had all been made in collaboration with American nuclear scientists, so this would present the challenge for him to develop something impressive on his own. Penney set up base at Aldermaston where the weapons would eventually be made.

But to make the bomb, the scientists would require plutonium and a factory to produce it in.

William Penney and John Cockcroft stand with key scientists Otto Frisch and Rudolf Peierls, having been awarded the Medal of Freedom by the US.

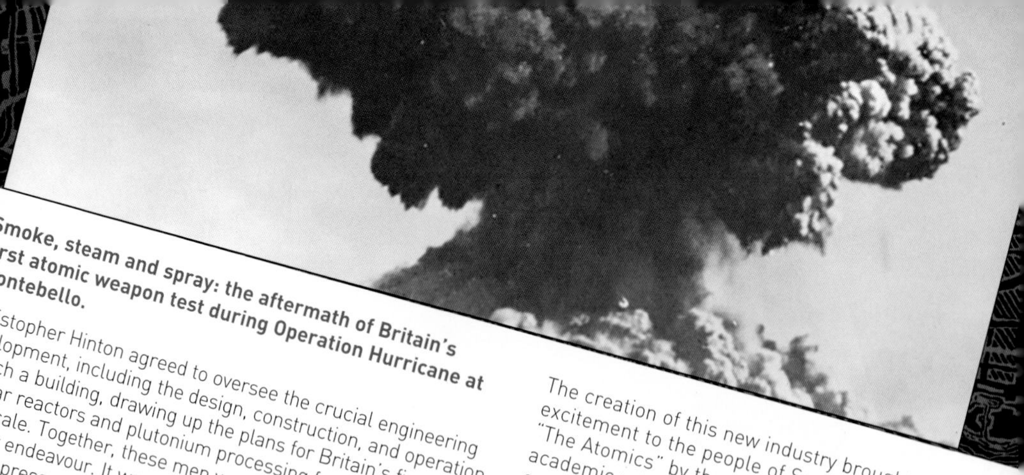

Smoke, steam and spray: the aftermath of Britain's first atomic weapon test during Operation Hurricane at Montebello.

Christopher Hinton agreed to oversee the crucial engineering development, including the design, construction, and operation of such a building, drawing up the plans for Britain's first nuclear reactors and plutonium processing facilities at Windscale. Together, these men would oversee Britain's first nuclear endeavour. It was a tough challenge under plenty of political pressure, but Attlee had faith in his scientists.

A staggering 4,000 tons of graphite were used to build Windscale's reactors, their walls seven feet thick, and chimneys towering 400 feet high. It was acknowledged that the core ran the risk of quickly losing control, and Hinton and his team were aware that Britain was far too small to have an unstable reactor built anywhere in the country. Instead, they would have to focus their efforts on developing cooling methods to keep the reactor under control, using air from the chimney instead of water, creating enough airflow to cool the reactor under normal operating conditions.

Hinton found himself under incredible pressure from Attlee and his committee, with strict, trying deadlines imposed upon him. Attlee believed Britain should be a nuclear power by 1952 – the same year it was anticipated that the Soviet Union would have completed their bomb. There was little time to do development work, which was terrible for such new and untried science, and construction was forced to begin before the site's research was even complete, forcing Hinton to take shortcuts during construction. The potential dangers of rushing ahead with nuclear science before concluding research reared its head one year into construction when Terence Price, a scientist at Harwell, made a startling discovery: if a cartridge containing a uranium rod was to burst, the uranium would burn and radioactive dust would be blown up the chimney and out into the open air. Price alerted the committee to this risk at a meeting, but it was dismissed, with no record of the warning being noted in the meeting's minutes. Fortunately, Cockcroft was concerned enough by this to order that filters be fitted, resulting in these additional elements being built on the ground while the chimneys were still under construction, finally being winched into position at the top once the chimneys' concrete had set. Nevertheless, the team pressed on, and Windscale was built just ten days behind schedule.

The creation of this new industry brought great excitement to the people of Seascale, being dubbed "The Atomics" by the press. Bringing in young academic minds from across the globe, the small seaside village was rejuvenated with a vibrant, intelligent population with a passion for science, eventually earning the town the nickname of "the brainiest town in Britain." It drew great media attention, with the new development being described as "science fiction intruding on our sober lives." The introduction of a thriving new industry and injection of life into Seascale gave people a sense of hope in the post-war environment. Little did the people know that this new factory was being constructed with the intention of building bombs.

Windscale's first pile was operational by October 1950, and the second by June 1952. By this time, Churchill had regained his position as Prime Minister. Once again, scientists were given a challenging deadline for experimenting with such new science, rushed on by the prospect of a test ban agreement heralded by the US and USSR which would take effect in 1958. Eager to impress the Prime Minister, Penney gathered his team in Montebello in October 1952, where Britain's first atomic device was tested. It was a great success for Windscale and for Penney, who returned to a hero's welcome and was awarded a knighthood. Churchill regained hope that the UK could re-establish its relationship with the US and reaffirm its position as a great power. He announced that a British atomic bomb would be deployed for military operational use in 1953.

But Churchill's confidence wouldn't last long.

Just weeks after Britain's triumph, he discovered the US had tested a new device in the Pacific – a hydrogen bomb. This new device ushered in the thermonuclear era, demonstrating that America was bounding ahead with nuclear technology. The hydrogen bomb could deliver a blast with the force of a megaton – ten times larger than the blast created at Montebello.

It started looking less likely that the UK would be able to stand alongside the US and Soviet Russia in the nuclear arms race. One American senator even went so far as to remark that a scientific partnership with Britain would be like trading a horse for a rabbit. Not to be deterred, Churchill ordered Penney to develop a hydrogen bomb: a decision that would lead Windscale to nuclear disaster.

THE WINDSCALE FIRE

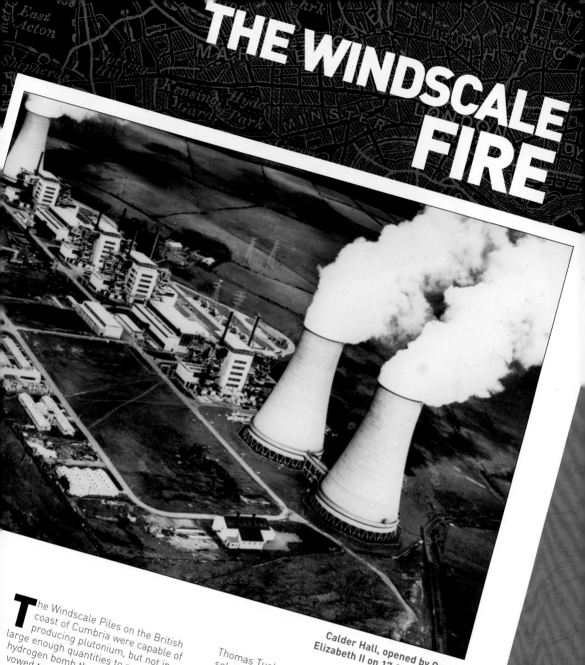

Calder Hall, opened by Queen Elizabeth II on 17 October 1956.

The Windscale Piles on the British coast of Cumbria were capable of producing plutonium, but not in large enough quantities to produce the hydrogen bomb that Churchill had vowed to construct. A new material was required, but there wasn't the time, money or resources to build another reactor to produce the necessary tritium – a material the reactor hadn't been designed to create. As a result, scientists had to develop a way to produce this powerful radioactive isotope by heating the uranium further. The only way to do this was to reduce the amount of aluminium casing that surrounded each rod. Windscale's deputy manager,

Thomas Tuohy, came up with an alternative solution: clipping the fins on the rods' casing. This would allow the rods to heat further, but it also removed one of Windscale's key safety features. Under pressure, the scientists had little choice, and the fins were clipped. This furthering of Britain's experimentation with nuclear weapons was considered to be in the national interest, but many workers were sceptical of the 'make do and mend' approach they were forced to take.

The experimentation with developing an H-bomb also raised public concerns, adding to the pressure already weighing on the scientists' shoulders. In an effort to garner public support and put minds at rest, Calder Hall opened beside Windscale in 1956, advertised as the world's first nuclear power station, built to generate electricity for the area. Receiving a royal unveiling, it was to become the

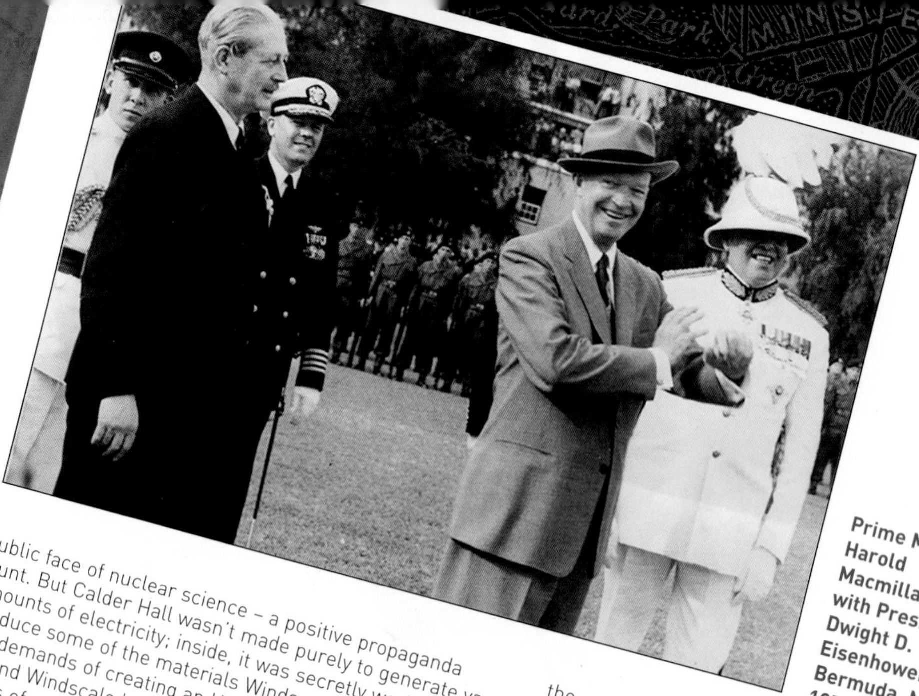

Prime Minister Harold Macmillan meets with President Dwight D. Eisenhower in Bermuda, March 1957.

public face of nuclear science – a positive propaganda stunt. But Calder Hall wasn't made purely to generate vast amounts of electricity; inside, it was secretly working to produce some of the materials Windscale needed to meet the demands of creating an H-bomb. Working conditions around Windscale became increasingly dangerous. High levels of radioactivity were recorded in the area, workers were required to walk into the reactors and push rogue cartridges into the cooling water system with brooms, and increasingly experimental methods to heat the cartridges caused concern as scientists advanced further into unknown territory. New cartridges were designed to hold enriched uranium and lithium magnesium which presented the risk of catching fire at high temperatures.

In 1957, as Maurice Harold Macmillan became Prime Minister, Britain tested its first hydrogen bomb, which proved to be a colossal failure. Macmillan was certain he could re-establish relationships with new US President Eisenhower, but the test H-bomb blast was barely bigger than that of the atom bomb Britain launched at Montebello. Leading British scientist William Penney had a back-up option up his sleeve, named Orange Herald. This project would require mass quantities of plutonium and tritium, and Windscale was consequently ordered to increase its tritium production by 500%. New cartridges were created, with even more of the aluminium being stripped away to make room for double the amount of lithium magnesium, and core temperatures were being increased. Once again, warnings of potential dangers were ignored, leading Christopher Hinton, the engineer responsible for the design and construction of Windscale, to resign in frustration. The suggested dangers were discounted following the first successful production of tritium, kicking full-scale production into high gear. But by raising the temperatures, undetected hot spots began to develop in the Piles.

On 10 October 1957, Macmillan wrote to Eisenhower in effort to convince him to consider the UK as a nuclear ally. As he put his pen to paper, Tom Tuohy was being urgently called into Windscale: Pile One had caught fire.

On 7 October, Vic Goodwin and his team working on the control panels noticed the reactor was overheating, and so activated a Wigner Release in an attempt to discharge any dangerous energy that might be stored in the core. This cooling method had been used eight times previously, but this time energy remained in part of the core, trapped inside channel 2053. Noticing that there was no change in temperature the next day, the team initiated a second Wigner Release, causing temperatures to rise in all channels once again, including 2053. On 9 October, scientists noticed that the reactor still wasn't acting properly, with areas of the core heating yet again and high levels of radiation escaping from the chimney. In response, the workers blew more air into the graphite core. Little did they know that a fire had broken out inside channel 2053. Introducing air to the mix allowed the fire to spread through hundreds of channels until it was out of control and radioactive material began billowing out of the chimney.

On 10 October, worker Eddie Davis arrived at Windscale to find signs of fire rising from the top of the reactor. No official emergency plan had been developed for such an event, leaving the workers to handle the situation on their own. Tuohy arrived from his nearby home and rushed to the top of the Pile to better judge what was going on inside the reactor, later describing the experience as if "[looking] down onto a blazing inferno." He quickly became aware that the thick concrete shield he was standing on, protecting himself and the world from intense radiation, could collapse if the temperature was to exceed 600°C.

Despite the blistering heat, workers entered the reactor in an effort to dislodge some of the burning fuel cartridges, desperately trying to push them loose with nearby scaffolding poles, but the heat proved too high and the workers couldn't last more than a couple of hours in the intense conditions. Discarding his personal radiation recording badge so he couldn't be dismissed from the scene, Tuohy continued to periodically climb 80 feet into the air to monitor the growing blaze inside the reactor. He led his team through the night, working to try and prevent the fire from growing. The next morning it was decided to add water to the Pile – a decision that carried serious risks in and of itself. Adding water to an already dangerous mix could create an explosive blend of water, gas and air, threatening to blow the Pile apart.

Hesitantly, the work proceeded and water began pouring in, while Tuohy watched anxiously to see if this would work. It was a disaster the world had never dealt with before, and he waited in a tense state of uncertainty. With the water failing to dampen the flames, Tuohy was left with one last option – to turn off the air coolers that had been left on to aid emergency workers. Tuohy ordered everyone out of the building, leaving just himself and the Fire Chief inside to continue introducing water to the fire. If this didn't work, Tuohy would be left with no further options to stop the fire. The last of the flames finally died, and five hours after turning on the water, Tuohy returned home to his family, the water flowing inside the reactor for a further 30 hours as a precaution, the villagers of Seascale never aware of how close to devastation they had come, or the dangers Tuohy and his men had faced to prevent radioactive release.

When word of the accident did finally reach the press, the Windscale men were initially hailed as heroes, but the public were awakened to the dangers such nuclear technology could present. Whilst it was confidently stated that any radioactivity released during the fire was blown out to sea, many scientists confessed that they feared it had actually blown inland, spreading across Britain. There was deep concern that babies in the surrounding area would breathe in isotopes that would be stored in the body, eventually leading to thyroid cancer, and farmers in the surrounding area were forced to dilute and discard the milk from their cattle for a month after the accident, fearing it may be contaminated. The workers at Windscale were praised for keeping their chimneys well swept, preventing an abundance of radioactive material being blown into the atmosphere. But the possible impact of nuclear devastation in the surrounding area was to be the least of the Windscale workers' concerns as the incident caught Macmillan's attention.

As Tuohy and his men fought the fire at Windscale, Macmillan met with Eisenhower in Washington, finally achieving the momentous prize of announcing the US and UK would be nuclear partners once again. The Windscale fire proved to

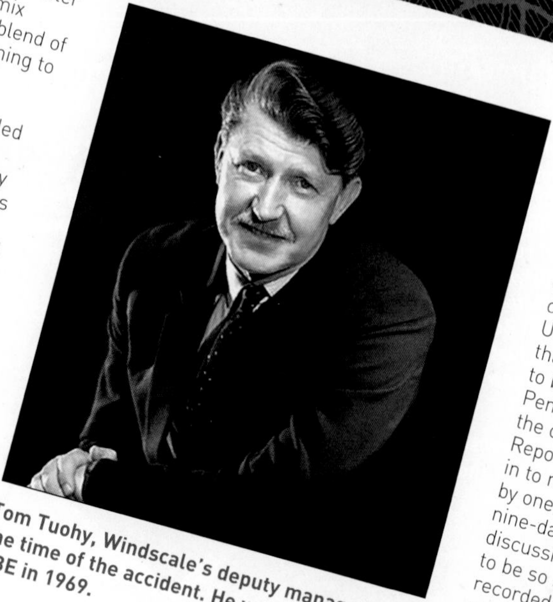

Tom Tuohy, Windscale's deputy manager at the time of the accident. He was appointed CBE in 1969.

threaten everything Macmillan had worked towards, and he couldn't bear the public embarrassment of the accident, deciding it was to be covered up to maintain US relations. He ordered that a closed inquiry was to be conducted under Penney's watch, leading to the creation of the Penney Report. Workers were called in to meet with Penney, one by one, over the course of a nine-day investigation. The discussions were deemed to be so sensitive that the recorded tapes were only released to the public in the early 2000s. Whilst Penney concluded that the thinning of the new cartridges to upscale production was a primary factor, he clearly noted that political pressure was a key catalyst in sparking the disaster. Upon reading Penney's findings, Macmillan recalled all copies of the report and in an effort to save face, instead issued a White Paper which withheld key information from the Penney Report. In an attempt to make it appear as nothing more than a minor accident, he leaned heavily on one crucial phrase: "error of judgement." Passing onus to the Windscale workers, junior staff members with no real means of defending themselves, Macmillan buried any account of political pressure. The press immediately began to target the workers, holding the operators accountable for the fire's outbreak. The sense of post-war trust between leaders, scientists, and the working man began to dissolve.

On the same day the White Paper was published, Britain detonated its first successful hydrogen megaton bomb, a triumph Penney described as taking "some of the sting out of Windscale" before returning to the US to lead collaborative nuclear discussions.

Windscale still looms tall, now known as Sellafield. The damaged reactor was sealed during the incident, and has remained closed since, with almost fifteen tons of uranium fuel still trapped inside. Whilst the surrounding buildings are still in use, acting as a nuclear fuel reprocessing site, the Piles are scheduled for final decommissioning in 2037. Fortunately, recent studies have shown initial fears of cancer and deaths caused by radioactive release from the incident did not come to pass. Nevertheless, the fire at Windscale was a crucial turning point for Britain's involvement in nuclear science. A nuclear health and safety executive was appointed in the aftermath, headed by a Chief Nuclear Inspector, in an effort to moderate health and safety rules in nuclear workspaces. It also opened the public's eyes to the true dangers that come with great atomic power, with the people of Britain narrowly escaping the threat of nuclear disaster.

CREATOR BIOGRAPHIES

ANDREW CARTMEL

began his career when he was hired as script editor on *Doctor Who*. He had a major (and very positive) impact on the final years of the original run of the TV show. He is currently writing the successful *Vinyl Detective* series of crime novels for Titan Books; the fourth, *Flip Back*, has just been published and a fifth, *Low Action*, will appear in May 2020.

He has also written a new stage play, Partner in the Firm and a book for children, K*itten on the Loose*.

BRIAN WILLIAMSON

is a London-based comic artist and illustrator who has worked on a number of Titan Comics projects including *Doctor Who* and *Torchwood*.

A graduate from Duncan of Jordanstone art school in Dundee, Scotland, he has brought a variety of characters to life for Marvel, DC Comics, Warner Brothers, DreamWorks, and Aardman.

STEFANI RENNE

Based in South America, Stefani has worked on a huge number of comics, colouring interiors for Titan Comics, DC Comics, and Zenescope.

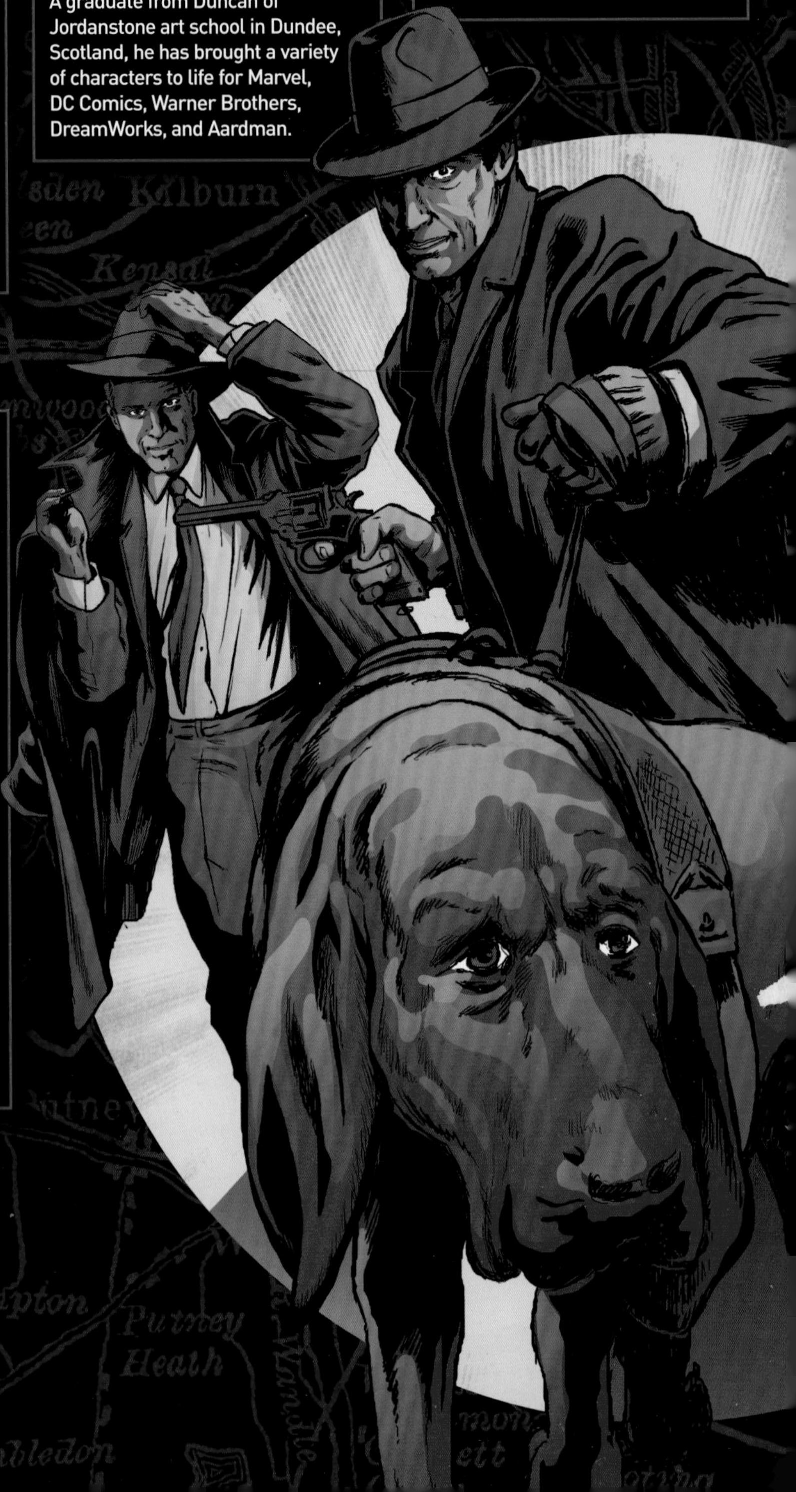

BEN AARONOVITCH

Ben is perhaps best known for his series of Peter Grant novels, which began with *Rivers of London*. Mixing police procedural with urban fantasy and London history, these novels have now sold over a million copies worldwide. The latest, *False Value*, is due in November 2019.

Ben is also known for his TV writing, penning fan-favourite episodes of *Doctor Who*; *Remembrance of the Daleks* and *Battlefield*. He wrote an episode of BBC hospital drama, *Casualty*, and contributed to cult SF show, *Jupiter Moon*.

Ben was born, raised and lives in London, and says he will leave the city when they prise it out of his cold, dead fingers.